WHEN SHADOW MEETS
THE BODHISATTVA

"Can one actually experience evolution? Or must it remain a scientific abstraction that can be mathematically modeled and genetically mapped but never really known as such? Moreover, and deeper still, do these Darwinian and genetic processes emerge from some deeper ground that is not in space and time at all? If so, how might these two levels of Becoming and Being be related, embraced, and practiced? Perhaps most importantly of all, are there moral pitfalls and problems awaiting us here? The present book is a most rare one—the story of the rise, fall, and re-emergence of a major modern guru *by the guru himself.* Andrew Cohen tells his story in these pages and explains both what went very, very right and very, very wrong. He takes responsibility for what happened and relates it to his own pride, authoritarianism, shaming techniques, and the traditional hierarchical role of the perfect mythical guru, but he also confesses those deeper evolutionary forces and absolute truths that have shone through his own Indian guru, himself as guru, and his gifted students all along. Here is an honest, open struggle through therapy, psychedelics, suffering, and further teaching—never perfect, never done, always frayed, and yet somehow also transcendent and true. We need this book. We need this Andrew Cohen. We need this evolution."

JEFFREY J. KRIPAL, AUTHOR OF *THE SUPERHUMANITIES:
HISTORICAL PRECEDENTS, MORAL OBJECTIONS, NEW REALITIES*

"This is an extremely important and highly recommended book. It's beautifully written and comes straight from the spiritual heart. Get it and read it—it will change your life."

KEN WILBER, AUTHOR OF *THE RELIGION OF TOMORROW*

"Andrew Cohen has boldly and courageously shared his deeply compelling journey into the core of the evolutionary impulse through emerging from the shadow of mythic absolutism into the realm of the Radical Spirit, where breakthrough revelations, extreme transformation, and the fire to catalyze collective transcendence for the benefit of the greater good reside."

DIANE MARIE WILLIAMS, FOUNDER OF
THE SOURCE OF SYNERGY FOUNDATION

"A brutally honest immersion into the creation and destruction of a spiritual group and the crucifixion of its leader. A primal pattern of hierarchical systems is at work—the hierarchical systems that dominate our lives and are even at work in spiritual movements that seem to preach the end of hierarchical leadership but embody the ecstasy of submission that only groups with leaders generate."

HOWARD BLOOM, AUTHOR OF *THE LUCIFER PRINCIPLE*

"Andrew Cohen's experiences are universal to all those who answer their transcendent calling in life: the rise to prominence, the wounding, and ultimately the reckoning that annihilates our former selves. It is in that place of surrender that we discover our authentic Self and begin our long journey to this new forbidden field. Andrew's searing honesty and rare bravery in the pages of this book, along with the conversations he shares with people on the leading edge of consciousness, are nothing short of a new guide on how to transcend the ego and the shadow and become a modern-day integral guru. It's a compelling read. I couldn't put it down."

SAID E. DAWLABANI, GRAVESIAN DEVELOPMENTALIST
AND AUTHOR OF *MEMEnomics* AND *THE LIGHT OF ISHTAR*

"Across the wide thematic context in Cohen's narrative, myriad paradoxical elements (each highly nuanced in themselves) are here: the nature of awakening and enlightenment; absolute and relative reality; epiphenomena and micro-phenomena; holons in dynamic systems; autonomy and communion; context dependency; freedom versus binary choices, causality, and co-arising; Advaita and Neo-Advaita; radical idealism; the pitfalls of the magic-mythic worldview and pursuit; mythic absolutism; guru function, mythical identity, and perfection; guru intervention and the mysteries of transmission and the numinous; the guru, dharma, and sangha; and finally, Cohen's predictions on the future of 'Triple Gem Integral' and 'Evolutionary Enlightenment.'"

KURT JOHNSON, PH.D., COAUTHOR OF *THE COMING INTERSPIRITUAL AGE, FINE LINES,* AND *NABOKOV'S BLUES*

"This is a book everyone who is sincerely on the spiritual journey should read. In every way, Andrew Cohen's rise, fall, atonement, and the fruits of his journey manifested in new understanding and vision—this is truly the drama of an archetypal hero's journey. Beyond the historical narrative of his passage, Cohen so often includes the larger significance of his experience and its relevance to the current evolutionary scene. He does this with the clarity and integrity so characteristic of his writings. Included in this book is a beautiful review of his teaching of Evolutionary Enlightenment, a stand-alone gem. This book is also enriched by the many dialogues the author includes with several leading integral thinkers as they consider various questions raised by his journey. Make no mistake: this is a book that challenges the reader on many fronts. The reader is asked to balance perceived rights and wrongs of how the guru position was carried out in the community setting and the consequences to his students, to forgive the teacher's human failings and to acknowledge the validity of his transformation. Finally, it is the reader's heart and soul that must answer whether the guru's gift—the realization of one's true nature—is worth it all."

RON FRIEDMAN, M.D., COFOUNDER OF VISTAR FOUNDATION

"A marvelous and enlightening book for any teacher or practitioner on the edge of cultural and spiritual evolution who wants to make the world a better place."

MARTIN UCIK, INTEGRAL RELATIONSHIP FACILITATOR AND AUTHOR

WHEN SHADOW MEETS THE BODHISATTVA

The Challenging Transformation of a Modern Guru

ANDREW COHEN

with HANS PLASQUI

Inner Traditions
Rochester, Vermont

Inner Traditions
One Park Street
Rochester, Vermont 05767
www.InnerTraditions.com

SUSTAINABLE FORESTRY INITIATIVE — Certified Sourcing — www.sfiprogram.org — SFI-00854

Text stock is SFI certified

Cataloging-in-Publication Data for this title is available from the Library of Congress

ISBN 978-1-64411-590-9 (print)
ISBN 978-1-64411-591-6 (ebook)

Printed and bound in the United States by Lake Book Manufacturing, LLC.
The text stock is SFI certified. The Sustainable Forestry Initiative® program
promotes sustainable forest management.

10 9 8 7 6 5 4 3 2 1

Text design and layout by Virginia Scott Bowman
This book was typeset in Garamond Premier Pro, Legacy Sans, and Gill Sans with
Garamond Std used as the display typeface

To send correspondence to the author of this book, mail a first-class letter to the
author c/o Inner Traditions • Bear & Company, One Park Street, Rochester, VT
05767, and we will forward the communication, or contact the author directly at
www.manifest-nirvana.com or **www.andrewcohen.com**.

Contents

Foreword

Allan Combs, Ph.D.

Before you is the story of a spiritual teacher becoming fully human. Like many young men of his generation, Andrew Cohen journeyed to India in search of spiritual inspiration. There he found it in spades when a remarkable guru triggered in him a powerful awakening of spiritual energies. The effect transformed his entire life. Others around him were touched by this new energy as well, and Andrew found himself, without choosing to be so, a modern guru. The story of his teaching, the creation of a large following, the foundation of an institute for his work, and even a globally published magazine exploring spirituality and enlightenment are well-known in the spiritual community and only partially reported in this book. Here, the story begins when it all fell apart.

This book is about his subsequent search for answers as to what went wrong. This search carried him deeply into his own nature as a human being. The Jungians say that to know yourself deeply you must go *down*. You must descend into the depths of your own being and confront the dark realities you will face there. Jung did this early in his life, and the result was the famous *Red Book*. In myth, Orpheus did it as well, but lost his concentration and let his beloved Eurydice slip away.

In the following pages, Andrew recounts his own descent, in part while working as a volunteer at Mother Teresa's Prem Dan house in Calcutta, a medical facility for the destitute, where he became one of her Missionaries of Charity, caring for some of the poorest and most diseased and dying people of India.

As a guru, Andrew has always been dedicated to evolutionary transformation—the evolution of consciousness to rich and profound states. Before the collapse of his teaching program and the dissolution of the institute he founded in Massachusetts, his students had begun to experience breakthroughs in which consciousness seemed to meld together within groups of participants, resulting in highly creative, if temporary, periods of collective experience. I will return to this topic momentarily, but first I want to address Andrew's journey, recounted in the following pages, to becoming a complete human being as well as a spiritual teacher and guide.

Andrew's journey, in fact, is emblematic of the story of civilization itself. His path led from an ordinary childhood and youth, to a young man's search for spiritual growth and transformation, to the realization of such growth and transformation, and, finally, to a deep exploration of the hazards and failures that can accompany such transformations.

Now, let us shift gears and compare this story to the big narrative of human consciousness itself. Skipping through the emergence of the earliest forms of symbolic thought, perhaps forty to fifty thousand years ago, and on through the origins of agriculture and the Neolithic revolution some ten to twelve thousand years ago, as well as the origins of civilization as we consider it today, perhaps three to four thousand years ago, we come to a worldwide period of interest sometimes termed the first Axial Age, extending from about the eighth to the third century BCE. During this period, for the first time, human consciousness turned toward transcendence on a large scale, giving birth to the great world religions.

Today we are entering a second Axial Age, this time shifting us toward a growing realization of our place within Gaia, the Earth, and at the same time our citizenship within the infinite community of the universe.

The first Axial Age gave birth to charismatic spiritual pioneers, and many gifted teachers followed—saints and philosophers, as well as women and men of wisdom including Christ, the Buddha, Lao Tzu, Hildegard of Bingen, and many others. Some embodied the very essence of transcendent consciousness.

Today human consciousness is again in motion, and with it, human nature. There is a pattern to human growth and transformation that, like history itself, moves forward to crest on some theme or variation, then slowly deteriorates and dies in the explosive birth of a new, higher level of consciousness that has never before been seen—at least if we make it that far.

Today we are living in a time of both rebirth and deterioration. This is not news. What *is* news is that we are in desperate need of people who can guide us through the disruptive social and spiritual surf and over the bar, toward higher consciousness and a new way of living as human beings.

All types of evolution move forward of their own momentum, and now human transformation is taking place with or without our guidance. In the midst of widespread social and ecological challenges, people are spontaneously awakening to wider and deeper realms of conscious experience. The growing frequency of such events, like wildflowers blooming in the spring, has been recorded in recent books, such as Jeffery Kripal's *The Flip* and Steve Taylor's *The Leap*. Such awakenings have been common among Andrew's students as well, but what is new is the appearance of collective experiences among groups of his students.

The idea that the future of human consciousness may involve a collective dimension is not new, but in the past has been rare. American Quakers report occasional but highly valued "gathered meetings," in which all participants have a sense of sharing a unified experience of togetherness. The idea of collective consciousness on a larger scale was anticipated in the writings of nineteenth-century French philosopher Pierre Teilhard de Chardin. Notably, the idea of collective consciousness was explored in some depth in the science fiction universe of British author Olaf Stapledon, especially in his celebrated novel *Star Maker*. The latter was the inspiration for Arthur C. Clark's *2001: A Space Odyssey* and Stanley Kubrick's film of that novel.

I believe it is clear that the future calls for—indeed, is desperate for—spiritual leaders who understand this territory and can act as guides for the increasing number of people who need guidance and perhaps a hand up in understanding this new continent of experience. Guiding people in a way that they learn to think for themselves while thinking collectively, all the while seeking a balance, is no small feat. What do we expect from our leaders? How do we learn from their successes and failures?

Enjoy this book. There are no others like it.

ALLAN COMBS, PH.D.

ALLAN COMBS is the author of *The Radiance of Being* and *Consciousness Explained Better*, professor of Consciousness Studies at the California Institute for Integral Studies, and the Founder of the Society for Consciousness Studies.

PROLOGUE

My Fall from Grace

A dark despair has enveloped my soul. I am in a state of shock. The grim forces of destruction have shattered my world. The devastation feels surreal. Everything is lost. The agony is unbearable . . .

For almost three decades I have been a teacher of enlightenment. I have taught thousands of people worldwide how to access their own true nature: the Buddha mind of pure silence, found in deep meditation. Now my own inner state has been reduced to turmoil. My gift was my ability to awaken others to the living, evolutionary current of creative unfolding that animates the kosmos* and drives it toward ever greater complexity. But all I see right now is a desolate universe, devoid of interiority, no longer lit up by the exhilarating spirit of creative emergence. I have inspired so many people to live a dedicated spiritual life, full of purpose, depth, and meaning. Yet now nothing makes sense any longer. I am staring straight into the gaping abyss of the darkest kind of nihilism . . .

It is midsummer 2013. I am wandering through the deserted grounds of our community center, Foxhollow, in Lenox, Massachusetts, the

---

*In this book, the term *kosmos* will be used to refer to not just the material cosmos of physics but to the kosmos as a whole—containing both exterior realities and interior realities, such as matter, body, mind, soul, and spirit. *Kosmic, kosmological,* and *kosmocentric* are terms that will also be used to refer to this concept.

1

headquarters of our worldwide organization EnlightenNext. What had been a thriving community of inspired spiritual practitioners not so long ago now looks like a ghost town. Everybody has left. As I am walking around here, alone and bewildered, reality hits me hard. I have lost my entire community! Our shared utopian experiment that took us all many years of unwavering commitment to build has violently collapsed in a mere few months. I was known for showing leadership and managing crises, but I have lost all my power to do so. However hard I've tried, I can no longer find my clarity or my strength. I am a mere shadow of my former self.

I have been a visionary for most of my life, always looking just over the horizon. I could constantly sense the imminence of exciting future potential right around the corner. My students were intelligent, sincere, well-educated people who had devoted their lives to the evolution of consciousness and culture. We were a close-knit group. We all cared passionately about what appeared to be humanity's next step at the leading edge. Over the years, we made great sacrifices and took many risks so that we could break new ground. And we did.

We had been known and loved for the depth we brought to critical questions about the emergence of a new consciousness and culture in the twenty-first century. We had brought together leading-edge minds to grapple with the greatest challenges of our time, and published their often innovative dialogues in the pages of our award-winning quarterly magazine *What Is Enlightenment?**

From this sustained in-depth inquiry as well as our intense commitment to actually live by our discoveries, our groundbreaking teachings, which we called "Evolutionary Enlightenment," emerged. These teachings were our attempt to integrate the modern-day understanding of evolution with the classical notion of enlightenment, that state of being immersed in the eternal rest of timeless, formless consciousness. Contrary to this ancient understanding, Evolutionary Enlightenment

*The quarterly magazine *What Is Enlightenment?*, founded in 1992, was renamed *EnlightenNext* in 2008.

not only calls us to awaken to the bliss of the timeless Ground of Being, as it is called in Buddhism, but also to the ecstatic urgency of Evolutionary Becoming, where that which is permanent is *Being* and that which is changing is *Becoming.* As such, enlightenment is no longer merely the end of evolution, but rather it is itself evolving. And we had set up an actual culture of practice to live by this principle.

But perhaps our most valuable contribution was that we pioneered the phenomenon of collective enlightenment. We discovered that when committed people who have gone beyond ego come together, the enlightened mind emerges between them. Whenever this occurs, everybody present enters a field in which the very ground of human relationship is prior unity. Whatever is being expressed and shared, then, no longer comes from accumulated knowledge; it bubbles up from that ever-fresh source. As such, new creative capacities are unleashed, allowing original insights to emerge and new connections to come alive. We called this innovative practice *the art of enlightened communication,* a skill of great value in a complex, globalized world in crisis. And I had always insisted that if enlightenment is to have any real impact on the evolution of culture, cultivating this ability is essential.

Because of all these contributions, our work had been an inspiration to the wider spiritual world. But now, everything we worked so hard for has crashed and burned. I can't wrap my head around the enormity of what has happened, and with feverish intensity I keep asking myself, *Why did this terrible destruction have to happen? How could something so precious collapse so completely?* But try as I might, right now it doesn't get any clearer . . .

I knew all along that our work together was risky—I was calling for a real spiritual revolution! We strived to move beyond the old ways to create new structures in consciousness and culture. I believed that such new structures could only emerge in a focused environment and as a result of creative friction. So I pushed everybody relentlessly, again and again, always building the tension between people's enlightened intentions to change and their egoic resistance to actually do so. I set up a hard school for radical transformation, a spiritually charged environment for those who were courageous enough to tread new pathways and were ready and willing to go all the way. Everybody who had committed themselves to our work knew they could expect nothing less than a fierce and demanding ego-transcending ordeal. We lived on the edge of the possible—and the stakes were high.

I was always aware of the demanding nature of our bold experiment. I also knew that in my relentless passion to force evolutionary breakthroughs, I had made some serious errors of judgment as a teacher. Yet I genuinely believed that regardless of my mistakes, it was all going to work out in the end because we loved one another and had made the lifetime commitment to go all the way. I was wrong. Now I have to own up to the unbearable truth that despite my good intentions, *I* actually caused this mayhem to happen.

Throughout my teaching years I was known for critiquing fallen gurus. I had looked at every new scandal emerging from the spiritual world with deepening concern. I was keenly aware that with every new story, people's trust in the benefits of spiritual life eroded further, and I wanted to stay clear of it all. But now my worst nightmare has become a reality. I too have become another failed exemplar, adding to the trail of cynicism surrounding gurus. I had always prided myself that those things that so often caused scandals in other spiritual communities were entirely absent around me. There had never been any sexual transgressions with students and our community was clear of drugs and alcohol abuse. My mistakes were of a different nature, though, and they have caused a different kind of backlash, and to my lasting shame I didn't see it coming. So now the chickens have come home to roost. I once inspired so many people to live by higher principles, but now I myself have become a source of disillusionment in those very principles, and this has carved a bleeding wound deep within my soul.

As I wander through the deserted buildings at Foxhollow, my thoughts flash back to the blessed moment when it all began. When I was thirty years old I was bestowed a rare, extraordinary grace. I had been given the precious jewel of enlightenment by my guru, H. W. L. Poonja. Ever since that moment, all my suffering had been erased, and my personality thereafter remained rooted in the empty ground of timeless, formless being. From that point forward I enjoyed an easy, natural state of boundless freedom, oneness, clarity, profound joy, and a sense of light-heartedness, and I was blessed with the ability to directly transmit that state to others.

But everything is different now. The shockwaves of the painful collapse of my work and community have shaken me to my core, so much so that I don't even know who I am anymore. I have lost myself in the drama of the story. My suffering has returned, and this time it has come back with a vengeance. I am living in a state of raw survival. As I am trying to come to grips with the gravity of what has occurred, all sorts of hellish feelings keep flaring up in me. I move through prolonged states of bottomless grief, abject terror, and sheer agony, over and over again. The torment never seems to cease. This is the fiercest emotional ordeal of my life. I feel as though I am trapped in the seventh ring of hell.

To my shock and horror I realize that the inconceivable has happened: my connection to that which is infinite has been severed. I have lost access to enlightenment and have fallen back into my small self. The ecstasy and urgency of the evolutionary drive I was once so deeply awake to all the time has vanished. I am no longer in touch with the spirit of my own teachings. All of a sudden it gets through to me: I have dropped the jewel my guru gave me! I feel deeply mortified . . . I have fallen from grace!

In my darkest hour now I am consumed by a single, nagging concern: the need to atone for all the wrongs and make them right. I must find a way to honor all that was real and true at the heart of what we stood for. This is all I truly care about. There is nothing else for me to do in this world, and I am committing the rest of my life to it.

PART 1

$\bullet\ \bullet\ \bullet$

THE RISE AND FALL
OF OUR SPIRITUAL
COMMUNITY

1

Overnight Guru

When I was sixteen years old I had an extraordinary mystical experience that shook me to my core and left no doubt in my mind that there exists an absolute reality beyond time, prior to anything we know. Late one night, as I was talking with my mother, for no apparent reason the doors of perception opened. My consciousness expanded in all directions simultaneously, all the way to infinity. This infinite spaciousness was conscious, and it became immediately obvious to me that this was the ultimate nature of everything. I was completely overwhelmed by an all-consuming, absolute love, so intense that I felt that if this sensation didn't stop I would simply die. I saw that there is no such thing as a separate self, subject to birth and death, and that life is without beginning or end. There is only one reality; it is limitless, timeless, formless, beginningless, and endless conscious being. This realization was so overwhelming that tears poured profusely out of my eyes. I was intoxicated with an unspeakable sense of awe and wonder at the mystery of existence. In the midst of this explosive widening into kosmic unity, a message emerged in my awareness: *If you surrender your life to me and me alone, you have nothing to fear.*

The impact of this experience was so profound that it took me several days to recover. It was so more infinitely real than anything I had ever experienced in my young life that it would become my true north for many years to come.

◀ ■ ▶

Throughout most of my youth my life had not been altogether happy. It was marked by a paradoxical psychological predicament that influenced my sense of well-being in significant ways. On the one hand, I was a confident, sensitive, articulate, and charming young man with a revolutionary spirit, strong opinions, and social graces. Yet on the other hand, I often found myself stuck in powerful emotional patterns of insufficiency and unworthiness that had been forming in me from as early as I can remember.

Except for brief moments, my childhood had been a troubled one. My parents didn't love each other. My mother was emotionally absent, and my father died from a brain tumor when I was just fifteen years old. Ever since I was a little kid, my older brother would beat me up violently. He resented me because I was the favorite child—smarter and better looking. He would scream at me over and over again, calling me stupid, an idiot. My parents hardly interfered with his aggressive behavior, and there was nothing I could do to stop the humiliation. By the time I was five years old it was clear that something was wrong. I displayed severe learning problems, even though it was obvious that I was bright. So my mother sent me to a child psychologist, someone I continued to see for the next ten years. Her treatment never worked, and throughout elementary school my learning disabilities persisted. I can still remember how the moment class began I would enter into an intense ADD state. I would become extremely self-conscious and would dissociate. I would look around in panic, acutely aware of how everybody else was absorbing information and getting it, whereas I consistently failed to grasp what was being said. It was horrible. Time and again I would get locked up in this agonizing, unbreakable cycle of *not getting it*. For whatever reason, I was basically proving my brother right: I was living out my ascribed identity as the stupid one. As much confidence as I had in myself as a human being, whenever I found myself in learning situations I was irrevocably blocked, and my confidence dissipated. Most things I wanted to learn or do or master were undermined by this self-destructive reflex of proving my own unworthiness. So as I grew into my teens, I developed a subpersonality as "the one with a problem," the loser who went to the shrink once a week. This was the context in which my shadow first took form.

Years of psychotherapy with different psychologists did not bring me the hoped-for result, and all throughout my teens my childhood trauma kept sabotaging my aspirations to succeed, both academically and in other areas of life where a certain level of performance was expected. By the time I was twenty-two I had grown sick of my emotional predicament, and along with that, of all the psychoanalysis. I wanted *real* freedom. I could feel the passionate calling of my earlier spiritual revelation, my true north, rising up from deep beneath my broken psychology. So one day, in a bold move, I looked my psychologist in the eye and said, "I don't want to do this anymore. I want to be free." He was stunned. But I was determined. I walked out and never looked back. That was the moment I began my search for enlightenment. Despite the fact that I never had much confidence in myself, when it came to achieving enlightenment, my certainty was atypical—I didn't have a shred of doubt that I would succeed! My spiritual experience at sixteen had instilled in me an unshakable confidence that I would surely make it, sooner or later.

I began to practice martial arts and Zen meditation, and I went to meet every spiritual teacher passing through town, absorbing everything they had to offer. I became deeply inspired, like countless others, by Paramahansa Yogananda's illustrious book, *Autobiography of a Yogi,* and soon after reading it I became a student of Swami Hariharananda, a direct disciple of Yogananda's guru, Sri Yukteswar. Being in his company, it was clear that he was not an ordinary man. His whole being radiated an infectious presence that seemed to emanate from a deeper source. I loved him dearly and diligently practiced the kriya yoga technique he taught.

Inspired by these yogic exemplars, I chose to practice strict celibacy with great discipline for almost three years during my midtwenties. Over time I realized that my mind was stronger than my body and its biological impulses.

I also began to do long, twenty-day Vipassana meditation retreats led by well-known American teachers, in which we would sit for eight to sixteen hours a day. I learned to witness my body and mind with clarity and objectivity. Still, I didn't feel moved to fully commit to a Buddhist path because I couldn't relate to the Buddhist notion of nirvana as emptiness, which I understood to mean nothingness, total absence. This seemed to contrast with the overwhelming love and joy I had experienced when I was sixteen. I also noticed that with most of the American teachers I didn't feel the inner radiance of living enlightenment that was so obvious in my Indian guru, Hariharananda, even as most of the American teachers had no doubt meditated for thousands of hours. One of the Buddhist teachers who did attract me at the time was Christopher Titmuss, an Englishman who had once been a Buddhist monk. He exuded a spiritual confidence that felt like it was rooted in a deeper dimension, and he possessed a humorous lightness that at times felt like an expression of spontaneous liberation. I attended several of his meditation retreats and considered him to be my teacher for a while. Every year he led retreats in Bodhgaya, India, the holy place where the Buddha achieved enlightenment under the bodhi tree, and one day I decided to join him there. And so it was that my inner journey brought me to incredible India, the motherland of spiritual wisdom. I was twenty-seven.

Being in India was a great relief after having lived in New York City, where so few seemed to care about higher consciousness. Becoming enlightened was my first priority, and here, unlike anywhere else on Earth, this was recognized as being a culturally acceptable, noble aspiration. So I continued to live, travel, attend retreats, and deepen my meditation practice in this vibrant, colorful country that was so deeply alive spiritually. In the midst of all my travels, I fell in love with Alka, a young Indian woman from Bombay who would later become my wife. It was an intense, challenging, and enriching time, and before I knew it, two and a half years had passed.

By then I had arrived at a point where I had decided not to involve myself with teachers or gurus anymore. I was certain I could make it on my own. I had a rock-solid meditation practice and could sit for long stretches of time. My meditative state had beautifully deepened, and I could sense how some mysterious current was at work in me. Sometimes I could see that the mind was just a filter, and that enlightenment was nearer than near. I was confident that if I submitted to strict discipline for a long period of time, the veil of the mind would dissolve and enlightenment would eventually reveal itself. But because India was so chaotic and noisy, I decided to go to South Korea in search of a more focused practice environment. My plan was to stay there for five years, no matter what. I would live by myself, practice celibacy, do intensive Zen meditation retreats every month, and practice martial arts. Little did I know that the universe had different plans for me . . .

Earlier, a friend had told me about the master H. W. L. Poonja, who lived in Lucknow, in northern India. He was a direct disciple of the illustrious Ramana Maharshi, the most revered realizer of the twentieth century. My friend, a seasoned spiritual practitioner, spoke about Poonjaji with great wonder, amazement, and enormous enthusiasm. It was clear from his stories that this master had a rare spiritual attainment. So I decided to delay my trip to Korea and visit with him for three days.

I arrived in Lucknow on March 25, 1986. I can still remember that first fateful meeting with the master as if it were yesterday. I entered his small room, where he was sitting on his bed. He was a large, imposing man with a beautiful face and incredibly luminous, big eyes. I said "Hello!" and sat down on the floor. With confidence I continued, "I don't have any expectations," thus boldly declaring my independence. "That's good!" he exclaimed with even greater confidence. His words made me feel at ease at once because he let me know that he didn't want anything from me.

Then I asked him, "How much effort do you have to make to be free?" With a slightly singsong tone in his voice, he almost whispered, "You don't have to make *any* effort to be free." The moment I heard those words, a vision appeared in my mind's eye. I saw water flowing down the side of a mountain. I realized that this water was like my own true nature, ever unobstructed and always free-flowing. With a shock of recognition, I saw that I had *always* been free, and that *un*enlightenment was just a thought. It wasn't real. Suddenly he shouted loudly, "That's it!" and burst out laughing. I was stunned, and somewhat puzzled, I asked, "How did you know?" He replied, "When a man sees his own face, he recognizes it." That very instant I realized that I was in the presence of an extraordinary being.

I was thrilled, yet couldn't quite grasp what had just happened. So I went back to my hotel and, as was my habit, sat on my bed and crossed my legs to meditate. The minute I closed my eyes I got a terrible headache. Then the thought dawned on me, *Oh my God, he just told me that you don't have to make any effort to be free, and look what I'm doing!* I burst into laughter, realizing that I was defying him and his teachings. Master Poonjaji taught the direct, nondualistic path of Advaita Vedanta. His position was very radical: you are always already free, therefore there is nothing to be done except to recognize your own true nature as that freedom. He didn't teach any spiritual practices and even made jokes about people who meditated. By that time I had given up everything in my life to be free except the practice of meditation, and the thought of having to give that up as well was intimidating. But I trusted him. So I got off my bed, stopped meditating, and surrendered.

The next three weeks spent in the presence of this remarkable being would be the most mysterious and wonderful of my life. Most of the time I was alone with him. We would talk or drink tea together. Sometimes we would just sit quietly or go for a walk in the park. He was gracious, kind, generous, compassionate, and enormously patient with me. He answered all my questions and told me the most amazing stories about his life, his experiences with Ramana Maharshi, and profound events and mysterious encounters with extraordinary beings. His inner experience was alive to deeper dimensions of consciousness that were unknown to me. And soon a deep bond of divine love and sacred intimacy came alive between us. I suddenly found myself living in a fairy tale with a perfect master. We shared many magical, transcendental moments together that I will never forget. There were experiences of love and deep mystical union, and powerful Zen-like breakthroughs in which new insights suddenly announced themselves with thundering clarity.

One day we spoke about an existential conundrum I had been wrestling with for a long time. In Buddhism, ultimate reality is said to be *sunyata,* or emptiness. But my own deepest experience of ultimate reality had always been one of intense fullness, of love and bliss. I shared with him my first experience of kosmic consciousness when I was sixteen. His eyes got very big and he said, "You already know everything!" He spoke with such authority that I literally felt something unlock deep within my being, as if his affirmation allowed me to once again embrace the extraordinary truth my initial experience had revealed to me—as if that truth was now set free to come to full fruition. He pointed out that my experience had arisen spontaneously, without effort or practice, and that afterward I had tried to recapture it with effort. He instructed me that instead of *me* trying to grab *it,* I should simply surrender and let *it* grab *me!*

Then we dove deeply into my existential quandary about the nature of ultimate reality and the paradox of emptiness versus fullness. He explained how emptiness and fullness are two sides of the same coin, and how the manifest universe is only the outward creative expression of the uncreated. But he added that there is something unknowable that is beyond emptiness and fullness that witnesses both. It is the Self—the beginningless, endless being that can never be grasped with the conceptual mind, but can only know itself. When I heard him explain this, I was suddenly struck by the inescapable obviousness of his clarification, and a huge burden lifted off my shoulders.

On another occasion, we were sitting quietly in his room together when out of nowhere I heard myself say, "I am ready to die but I don't know how." I was startled, because my words did not come from my mind. His eyes opened wide and welled up with tears. He looked at me with great intensity but remained silent. The deepest part of me had just expressed itself, a part I later came to call my *authentic self.*

At some point during my stay, I made a remark that indicated that I was second-guessing my own intuition. He promptly rose up from his bed and screamed right in my face, "Never, ever doubt yourself!" His ferocity was scary, as if God was shouting a divine ordinance in my ear. It was immensely impactful and awakened a deep self-confidence in me.

Many such powerful transformational moments unfolded while I stayed with Poonjaji, and as a result the mist of my ego, ever-concealing the immediacy of enlightened awareness, was slowly dissipating. Little by little I was dying to everything I had ever known.

When I came to the end of my stay, the master said, "Andrew, after you leave, something very big is going to happen to you." I had no idea what he could possibly mean, and my inner skeptic thought, *How does he know?* I expressed my gratitude for our precious time together and then said goodbye. As I was walking down the street, I turned around to look at him one more time. He burst out laughing. He was wildly mysterious, and his laughter was both annoying and compelling. I boarded the train to Delhi and sat down quietly in a carriage by myself.

All of a sudden I could feel a powerful current of spiritual energy pulsing through me. My consciousness widened. I could see myself sitting in the train from some other dimension, an infinite distance away. I was overwhelmed by waves of extraordinary love and bliss, the ecstasy of freedom without limit. I was consumed by the living, conscious presence of the infinite, vibrating powerfully, pulling me into itself. I hadn't meditated for weeks, yet all of a sudden I was being meditated by reality itself, by a seamless oneness, unborn and never dying. It was so compelling that I had no choice but to let go. It felt like boundless love, and I realized that this was who the master truly is.

This state kept washing over me in waves, waxing and then receding like the tides. The profound exhilaration and ecstasy I experienced was interspersed with deep terror because I realized that "I" was dying. But I knew that this was exactly what I had signed up for. My dream was coming true, and it was infinitely more profound than I could ever have imagined. This mystical process, this metaphysical alchemy, would continue unabated for three weeks.

The next morning when I woke up in my hotel room in Delhi, I sat up in my bed and heard myself say, *I surrender my life to you, do with me what you will.* My authentic self revealed itself again, affirming my surrender to this beginningless, endless presence that was consuming me. As these words arose in my mind, I saw a whirlpool of water going down a drain. I realized that the water was my life, my karma, my destiny, and my will, and that all of it was being swallowed by the infinite. That was the moment when something deep within my being completely shifted. I stepped out of the ordinary world and entered a different dimension.

I wrote to Poonjaji:

Dear Master,
I love you . . . The process has continued since I left you . . . You have entered me . . . I am dying, and soon there will be nothing left . . . There is only joy and love . . . I am somewhere beyond time and yet at the same time fully here . . . I feel the cells in my body are changing . . . Other people can feel it . . . You and I are One . . .

The nightmare of samsara had come to an end, and with that, all the unresolved anguish and pain of my early life was completely obliterated by the transcendental brightness of enlightened awareness.

From Delhi I traveled north to Rishikesh, the famous holy pilgrimage town on the banks of the river Ganges, to reunite with my friends and share with them what had happened to me during these most extraordinary three weeks with Poonjaji. As soon as we gathered and I began to speak, an amazing phenomenon occurred: the whole room filled up with spiritual energy and my friends were miraculously drawn into the same state that I was in. I had never heard of anything like this. As far as I knew, enlightenment was a purely internal state of the individual. At the time, I hadn't been fully aware that it could actually be transmitted and shared with other people. But that was exactly what was happening. We began to spend all of our time together, lit up by the wonder of this mystery. My friends would ask me questions, and somehow the answers would flow out of me spontaneously. For no apparent reason, I suddenly had access to depths of wisdom about enlightenment, about life and death and the mysteries of the universe, knowledge that I hadn't earned or worked for. I could speak with clarity about the subtleties of the human condition and about the way to attain liberation from it. I somehow had gained the ability to look deeply into a human being and tell them exactly what they needed to hear. Day after day, we came together in a room overlooking the Ganges, constantly inquiring into the nature of consciousness, often until deep into the night. And so it was that I began to teach.

I was only thirty-one and was thrust into the role of a guru overnight. For some inexplicable reason, I was able to serve that time-honored function effortlessly, and people responded in the most profound way by becoming my disciples. Soon word got out, and more people began to gather around me. That was the beginning of our remarkable spiritual community, or sangha, as Buddhism would call it. The love we were feeling for one another was spellbinding and there was a sense of innocence and sweetness in the air. It was like being on a honeymoon together in a magical wonderland. Whenever we came together, enlightened awareness would fill up the room, creating an intersubjective field of bliss and ecstasy between us that felt so beautifully pure and deeply intimate that we were all enthralled by it. Some of us began to wonder what it would mean to live together in this powerful field we all shared. In it, we could sense the bright promise of Heaven on Earth, and that nascent intuition was the beginning of our utopian vision.

After a few of these grace-filled weeks, I went back to Lucknow to be with the master once again and express my immense gratitude for the infinite grace he had bestowed on me. The moment we met, I fell at his feet and burst into tears. Again he laughed out loud and teasingly alluded to what he had foretold on the day I had left him in Lucknow.

The next day, while sitting with him on his bed, he told me that our work together was over. Then he looked into my eyes with a seriousness that was unusually intense, and with gravitas in his voice, he said, "I want you to accept responsibility for the work. I have taught you everything I have to teach. From now on I want you to stand on your own two feet. Don't rely on me for anything." I didn't fully understand what he meant. But I remained silent, willing to accept whatever would be my destiny.

Soon after that meeting with my master, I began to teach in England, and the same phenomenon would happen there as well. The moment I sat down, the atmosphere in the room became spiritually charged; wisdom started flowing through me, and people experienced powerful breakthroughs into nonduality. It was as if a force of nature had been unleashed, one that couldn't be stopped. Month by month, our sangha expanded. We all felt inspired by the thrilling sense that something new, meaningful, and noble was emerging, and we were all part of it. We felt like spiritual revolutionaries shaking up the fossilized spiritual world, and we were all energized by the vision of creating Heaven on Earth—the mythic land of Shambhala—together.

During that early period I received hundreds of letters from my students expressing their gratitude for unlocking the hidden treasures in their hearts. Some excerpts read like classical mystical poetry, others like testimonials of extraordinary breakthroughs:

Beloved Master,
I am like a dying star, collapsing upon itself in a giant cosmic implosion, every bit of its separate existence transformed into something inseparable from the Absolute. As the force of that implosion leads inexorably to my total destruction, the light of your blessing is radiating back out. The Enlightenment is no longer my own. I am experiencing this in a very real way. My perspective is continually opening up to encompass the totality of existence, and I am lost in that totality, no longer to be found.

◆ ◆ ◆

Beloved Master,

The wind blows free, scattering the pieces of my personality like leaves on a fall day. The leaves twirl, float, shimmer, and come to rest in an endless mosaic of dancing light. I see that who I thought I was is no more than a reflection, an endless ever-changing configuration of light and form.

Where to be in this far-flung freedom? Enough to know you are the wind blowing me free, and I rejoice in this flight. I surrender to let love blow me where it will, for everywhere I alight I find You.

My life is in your hands and I kiss your feet, beloved Andrew.

◆ ◆ ◆

Dear Andrew,

The simplicity and undeniability of the fact *of Enlightenment—of the Divinity and Holiness of* everything*—shatters the mind and explodes in the Heart like fire. Over and over again I smile and shake my head at this secret, and I almost burst out laughing at the simplicity of It and how I never saw it until you revealed it to me.* This is it! *In each and every moment there is only Truth, only God, and there is* nothing *more or less than This, for it is Everything. The only delusion is the delusion of un-Enlightenment, bondage comes from this, and you have* destroyed *this delusion in the fire of your love. I am on my knees before you, my true and Holy Master, you have taken my burden from me and given me everything. A ceaseless current of Love and wonder runs through me, and I am yours.*

◆ ◆ ◆

Dear Andrew,

Something has exploded inside my chest and there has been a shift. Each breath comes to me, each breath seems to come from my heart—it's even a physical sensation in my chest, like I can't control my breathing anymore. I can't control anything, or rather, there is no need to control, there is no fear. I see it manifesting in my relationships with people, somehow I don't feel the separation anymore. It feels like one and so natural and warm and quiet—so love-full! Within my chest is often a gurgling joy which just rolls out. It is not me—it rolls between me and other people and it is something that could never be held, or controlled, or reproduced, it feels like the other side, just completely something beyond what I could ever create. Andrew, it is just beautiful, being is just beautiful, and there is just love in this.

Oh Andrew, how can I ever thank you? I saw in a flash that this is how it has always been—it was a very fast flash in light, as if for a second the earth had opened up and the inside was revealed. There is a big warmth, a burning in my chest—my chest has cracked and opened. For this, for you, I have always longed, all my life. Thank you thank you, I have always known somewhere, but been blind, you have given me sight. It really feels like this.

I love you Andrew.

◆ ◆ ◆

Master,
I am exploding! My mind is frazzled!

Who am I, in the face of this unbelievable power, the power of Truth boiling in my veins, shining through my eyes, forcing itself into every cell of my being! I am alive! Who was I in the past? It was all a lie—every idea I ever had about myself was a lie! I see them, those ideas, hovering here and there, and they are just ghosts—illusions pretending to be real. The Truth will have none of it—the Truth is constantly awake, brandishing its sword, mercilessly cutting the head off of any fear or doubt that dares tempt me.

Master, I am discovering more and more and more clarity every day— sheerly by submitting totally to your Grace and Wisdom. I see the ego every- where, trying to defend itself at any cost. It is so obvious! So obvious! The pride, the arrogance, the aggression, all the ugliness that lies underneath even the sweetest looking face of pretended humility. It is all a refusal of Enlightenment, a denial of the reality of Enlightenment now. But your sword is blazing in me, showing me real humility, real integrity. It is nothing like I ever imagined. And it is completely your Grace. Such sweet submission! Submission to the fire that is my death, the fire of your Life-commitment to turning my life over to you, Master!

Humility, humility is the key. The realization that I am nothing, that You are everything!

What an incredible life! What a miraculous happening in the midst of the endless confusion in this world! I am at your feet forever, Master!
My heart is Yours.

◆ ◆ ◆

Unbeknownst to me back then, amid the vibrancy of this extraordinary new territory that was emerging between us, the contours of some of my future problems as a teacher began to take shape—hardly visible at first, but present nevertheless.

Thereafter, my reputation as a powerfully enlightened new teacher continued to spread. More people joined our sangha, and many of them responded to me in deeply appreciative ways. The generous amount of positive feedback I was receiving was as encouraging as it was overwhelming.

Seasoned spiritual practitioners came to attend my *satsangs,* as such spiritual gatherings oriented to developing a relationship with truth are called in India. Many attendees had given their lives to the practice of meditation, yet sitting in my presence, they suddenly experienced a breakthrough into enlightened awareness that couldn't compare to anything they had ever experienced before. The consequences were often life-changing, and some of them were so deeply moved that they left their teachers and came to sit at my feet. Even disciples of gurus far more famous than I, such as the American spiritual teacher Adi Da and the Tibetan Buddhist master Chögyam Trungpa Rinpoche, were leaving their teachers to become my students.

Established spiritual leaders came to meet with me and acknowledged my status as a powerful teacher, often in the most outrageous terms, saying things like, "Now I know what it's like to sit with the Buddha."

These wild affirmations and all the positive feedback that kept coming my way seemed perfectly congruent with the extraordinary predictions my guru, in his generous love for me, had made. He had said that I was God's gift to humanity, that I had the same look in my eyes as Ramana Maharshi, and that he had seen this look only three times in his life—in his guru's eyes, in his own, and in mine. And he had said that what had happened to me occurs only once every several hundred years. Coming from such a powerfully enlightened sage, it was hard for me to resist a sense of specialness.

He had also prophesied that I would start a revolution among the young. His prediction supported my own strong sense that we were really breaking new ground together. And sure enough, little by little, I began to be known as a spiritual reformer, a radical revolutionary. The message I received from life was that I had been blessed with unusually powerful gifts and that what was happening around me was of a different order. That message was repeatedly confirmed because powerful breakthroughs kept occurring and more and more people continued to gather around me. And thus day by day, my confidence as a spiritual teacher grew.

All of this was happening during a time when the wider spiritual world was being shaken up again and again by countless scandals about Indian gurus, Zen masters, Tibetan rinpoches, and spiritual teachers of all varieties sleeping with their students. I watched all these developments closely and could never understand why spiritual authorities who had achieved an extraordinary depth of spiritual liberation couldn't control their sexual impulses and would risk their mission and break people's hearts because of their sexual escapades. Because of my own success with abstinence several years earlier, I had known without any doubt from the minute I started teaching that I would never cross that line. This knowing was a source of great strength for me as a teacher. Yet at the same time I slowly came to believe that I possessed a level of purity and moral development that many didn't seem to have, and I developed ego around it. I was the pure one, the one without stain. I even began to assume the impossible: that I was entirely free from shadow. My mastery over my sexual impulses inflated my sense of moral superiority, a flaw that would unfavorably influence me as a guru, as I would later come to learn.

And thus, without being aware of it at the time, the success I had achieved so quickly began to inflate my ego and bolster my arrogance and pride. Because of my unresolved childhood issues of unworthiness, I needed to overcompensate, to be the best. It felt psychologically healing to me to take refuge in my image of greatness, and I began to believe that I was somewhat of a Second Coming. My early history had created a receptivity in me for an unwholesome measure of narcissism to gradually take hold. Had I been more mature or more experienced, or had I had deeper self-knowledge, my ego's investment in what I saw emerging around me would have been different, and all the positive feedback I received probably wouldn't have affected me as much as it did. But I was young, inexperienced, and thrust into guruship literally overnight.

That my presence kept generating profound transformational results in so many people made it extremely challenging for me to notice the subtle and covert impact my unresolved psychological issues were beginning to exert on our sangha. I was convinced that as long as I remained aligned with the brightness of enlightened awareness, none of my petty psychological nonsense would matter in the slightest. And thus living in this grace-filled awareness would become the central aspiration of our lives together.

2

A Radical Heart

After several years of teaching like a wandering savant, traveling from place to place, giving satsang and allowing the guru force to work its awakening wonders through me, I began to notice a pattern in the way people responded to my presence. Many continued to have mind-blowing breakthrough experiences into nonduality and enjoyed the overwhelming sense of ecstasy, love, and bliss that often comes with that, but didn't seem to be able to hold on to that state for very long.

Initially I had assumed that such experiences would be so impactful and compelling that they would liberate a person conclusively, as had happened in my case with my own teacher. But even though we were sharing the very same state of enlightened awareness, my students kept falling back into their original condition of separateness, the unenlightened state, where the mind with its confining habitual patterns is the governing principle of the self. Despite the obvious profundity of their experiences, their basic self-structure hadn't substantially changed. The one fundamental difference was that they now knew beyond any doubt that there exists an ultimate reality of timeless, formless being that they felt to be their own most intimate nature, and that knowing had lit a fire under them to realize that truth and live their lives in alignment with it.

As I kept observing this pattern of breakthrough and regress, I began to wonder why in a few cases a single glimpse of enlightenment produces radical and permanent transformation, whereas in most cases it does not. After plenty of further observation and deep inquiry into this phenomenon, I came to better understand the nature of the many powerful forces that determine a person's capacity for awakening, such as their developmental level, their degree of egoic investment in their present condition, the intensity of their desire to want to be free, and their capacity to radically surrender to Source.

It dawned on me that to bring people to a state where they could actually accommodate the ever-present nature of Spirit in a lasting way, their body-mind needed to be made susceptible to this radical reality. They needed to be free of the grasping tendencies and narrowness of the ego in order to build up the inner structures that could hold and express the vast expanse of enlightened awareness in every single moment. For most, some sort of gradual process seemed to be a prerequisite to achieving such a degree of spiritual maturity. It occurred to me that in my own case as well, enlightenment, even though it had appeared quite suddenly, actually only happened after nine years of serious, one-pointed practice. And thus it became apparent that we all had to do the work. There was no magic bullet.

So from 1991 onward, I introduced a daily practice regime consisting of traditional, time-honored spiritual techniques like meditation, chanting, and self-inquiry to strengthen people's capacity to access the wholeness of their true nature and achieve greater clarity about the obstacles blocking their further growth.

During those early years it also became apparent to me that most of my students remained ambivalent in their commitment to unconditional freedom. On the one hand, their higher-consciousness experiences revealed to them the extraordinary potentials of their own consciousness and awakened their desire to truly transcend the small self as a fundamental identity. But on the other hand, their excessive investment in egoic concerns kept undermining that noble aspiration. They lived in the tension between the authentic self's unbridled passion to be free and the ego's fierce resistance and inertia that kept sabotaging radical transformation.

It became clear that the ego is a formidable obstacle on the path of real change, an insidious, tenacious force that won't just move out of the way willingly or gracefully, making room for the higher Self. Quite the contrary, time and again I observed that the higher Self simply disappears the moment the ego is allowed in the driver's seat. I wanted my students to deal with their ego and take ownership and responsibility for their experience of enlightened awareness. Many of them, I felt, were riding on my energy. They wanted to bask in the light of the guru but didn't want to stand *with* the guru *in* that light. It was as if everybody wanted to be enlightened, but nobody really wanted to change. Observations like these began to convince me that my teaching approach needed to be improved.

So rather than simply continuing to inspire those around me to lead a spiritual life and awaken to their true nature, like I had done up until now, I began to become more actively involved in my students' growth process. I started to push against their egoic resistance to change and the possibilities of higher consciousness offered by the authentic self, and began to wrestle with their conditioning, hoping to catalyze a more lasting, liberating breakthrough.

When Poonjaji heard that I was putting pressure on people's egos and introducing certain spiritual practices, such as meditation, he was deeply dismayed. Both such measures were antithetical to his own approach, and so he began to signal to other people that he felt that I was ruining his teaching.

For him, the ego was but mere illusion, so why bother putting pressure on it? When it came to practice, Poonjaji never gave an inch, unlike his own guru, Ramana Maharshi, who still appreciated the usefulness of certain practices, such as self-inquiry and satsang, and in some cases mantra recitation and various other yogic techniques. For Poonjaji, engaging in spiritual practice to seek enlightenment only strengthens the false presumption that enlightenment is not already your actual condition right now. It perpetuates the spiritual search, rather than ending it, for it projects enlightenment off into the future. His gift was his powerful capacity to directly transmit the Absolute to people, and his skillful insistence on no practice helped many cut through the veil of the mind and revealed to them their true nature. But he kept insisting that one such glimpse of ultimate reality was permanent and final, and he all too often considered people to be enlightened after that. Consequently, the moment they had crossed that bridge, his work with them was over. So he effectively only taught the end of the path.

Yet for me, such an initial glimpse, in most cases, only marks the beginning of the real work, which is to practice it to the point of stability. I felt that both the gradual path of practice and the path of direct awakening to the transcendental Ground of Being had an important role to play and needed to be part of an overall approach to liberation. It was clear that our teachings, or Dharmas, as Buddhism would say, had begun to diverge.

As time passed, our dharmic differences began to generate emotional complications as well, and soon these began to overshadow the blessed nature of my relationship with my beloved master. A number of my disaffected students had visited Poonjaji, telling him stories about how they had been wounded by the pressure I was putting on them to transcend their egos. I noticed that after their encounter with him, invariably something about them was different. They often approached me with a strange sense of empowerment, and sometimes even seemed to have lost their respect for me as a teacher. Some of them told me that Poonjaji was upset with me and disagreed with my teachings. He apparently began to contradict the instructions I had given to my own students. This both shocked and surprised me. Poonjaji had overtly and unambiguously acknowledged my independence as a teacher and had blessed me on my path, and thus I felt that changing my approach came out of my evolving insights as Poonjaji's Dharma heir, and was as such authentic and entirely legitimate. What made the hearsay all the more puzzling was that whenever I raised my concerns with my teacher directly, he would be as loving and supportive as he had always been. His tone would become soothing, reassuring, and reconciling, and he would say things like, "Don't listen to the comments you hear from other people. They are just barking dogs. Everything is fine."

My devotion for this man was unspeakably profound, my love for him out of this world. But ever since he had declared that our work together was over, an undefined and uncomfortable sense of separation clouded the air between us. I still wrote him ecstatic love letters in which I liberally shared all the new insights that were emerging in my teaching and enthusiastically reported on the eruption of enlightened awareness that continued to grace our sangha. And he consistently responded in affirming and encouraging ways. Yet whenever we actually spent time together, he remained strangely aloof to it all, only minimally interested in the details of the revolution that was exploding around me—the revolution that he himself had predicted.

Soon, more uncertainties began to overshadow our relationship, as Poonjaji now began to tell some of his other devotees to teach. Some of these new teachers treated me with a sense of antagonism and disrespect, and I was disturbed by that. I didn't know how to organize my relationships with them in the context of our lineage. So in an attempt to clear up the confusion, I visited Poonjaji to discuss the situation. When we sat down face-to-face in the familiar intimacy of his room, I poured my heart out to him, candidly sharing my concerns about the rising tensions within our lineage. He told me that he too was disturbed by all the friction and asked me in a slightly helpless tone of voice, "What should I do? Tell me what I should do?" I said, "Master, you have to make things clear." In a fatherly way he put his hand on my leg and said, "Andrew, you mustn't have this pain—it's *my* responsibility. I'll take care of it. We don't have to talk anymore about this, okay?" Despite the genuine affinity and profound intimacy I felt during our encounter, I left Poonjaji still feeling unclear about the future. It was obvious that he wasn't being straight with me. A sobering truth began to dawn on me: perhaps I was still enacting my fairy-tale relationship with the perfect master when in reality it had already turned sour.

In time, Poonjaji's duplicity created a cloud of suspicion and doubt around me and my work, and a schism that caused me deep pain on a soul level began to form between us. Up to this point my students had been visiting him regularly to pay their respects and express their gratitude, as he was the source of their own teacher's awakening. But as our dharmic divide appeared unbridgeable, my students stopped seeing him. He was displeased about that, and his behavior toward me began to show signs of competitiveness, pettiness, and jealousy.

At one point, when I was teaching a large retreat for about three hundred people in Bodhgaya, he went so far as to give instructions to his devotees to set up a tent across the street and have the American-born spiritual teacher Gangaji, one of his appointed teachers who had attended my satsangs for a while, teach there in an attempt to attract people away from me. He had apparently instructed her to clean up after Andrew, heal the wounded egos, and restore the integrity of the Advaita teachings. I was outraged by his intervention and deeply hurt.

The gap between the obvious profundity of Poonjaji's enlightenment and the idiosyncrasies of his personality was utterly perplexing to me. His ability to transmit the boundless freedom of nondual bliss with a mere glance was unparalleled. Still, he could also be shockingly small-minded and mean-spirited. I had observed similar contradictions in other enlightened beings as well, and soon this paradoxical conundrum began to haunt me. What could enlightenment possibly mean if it did not translate into enlightened behavior? What was the actual relationship between one's conduct and enlightenment? If the Buddha nature is forever clear and pure, like a perfect mirror, then how is it even possible that in the case of obviously enlightened beings the mirror still appears to be covered with dust, and the light isn't reflected in all its brightness? Questions like these had catalyzed my inquiry into the nature of enlightenment, which culminated in 1992 with the birth of our magazine, *What Is Enlightenment?*

As the contradictions in Poonjaji's character became more and more apparent, the strange sense of separation between us grew, and I began to find it almost unbearable to be in his physical presence. I even began to feel averse to his spiritual transmission. Eventually we parted ways, and even though it was the most heart-wrenching breakup I had ever experienced, I was unwilling to compromise my integrity as a teacher. I knew I had to stand alone in the truth and forge my own path.

Slowly but surely, a new approach to the teachings began to emerge, nourished by what I had come to understand as the insufficiencies in Poonjaji's radical Advaita Vedanta teaching. His unwavering, dogmatic insistence that every legitimate breakthrough was final made him oblivious to the obvious influence of unwholesome egoic residue that continued to affect the lives and behavior of those lucky enough to have been blessed with such a grace. It also allowed him to sanction as teachers many of his students who were mostly, from my perspective, only halfway up the mountain. This large influx of new teachers had a profound impact on contemporary spiritual culture. It initiated the Neo-Advaita movement* which had by now become popular in the West. Despite its obvious positive effect of opening the doors to spiritual life for many people, I was deeply concerned about its core philosophical beliefs.

I felt that Neo-Advaita's unyielding insistence that there is only one single reality—the Self Absolute—and its uncompromising emphasis on the unreality of temporal existence leaves too many important questions unanswered, questions like: "How do we live in the world?" and "What is the right relationship to life?" One of its most prominent tenets, its denial of the faculty of volition and its insistence that deeds are done but there is no "doer," can be severely paralyzing, for it invalidates our laudable efforts to assume any real responsibility for our behavior and

---

*Advaita Vedanta was founded by the eighth-century master Shankara and originally consisted of three stages: *sravana,* or "listening" to the word of the realizer; *manana,* or "hearing" (intuitive understanding); and *nididhyasana,* or contemplative practice. Some of the modern-day proponents of Advaita, like Ramana Maharshi and Nisargadatta Maharaj, still employed this model to a degree. The generation of teachers after them (i.e., H. W. L. Poonja, Ramesh Balsekar, and others) largely abolished it and brought forth many teachers who started offering nondual wisdom through a postmodern lens that denies hierarchy, and thus the stages on the path. These teachers focused exclusively on sravana. The thinking went that merely listening to the word of the realizer was sufficient to attain enlightenment. Spiritual practice, or nididhyasana, was no longer required. They cut out the preliminaries and emphasized the direct recognition of the Absolute. And thus we ended up with what now goes by the name of Neo-Advaita, which sometimes is somewhat derogatorily called "talking school Vedanta."[1]

actions. As such, it presents some very serious conundrums relative to the ethical dimension of life. If everything is but the dance of the Self Absolute, then so is my less-than-enlightened behavior. From the vantage point of the Absolute, any kind of conduct is perfectly acceptable exactly as it is, for it is nothing but the signature of the one and only ultimate reality. Any inconvenient questions can therefore be silenced by responding, "Who is the doer?" or "Who misbehaved?" or "Who is responsible?" or "Isn't it all just the play of that same One without a second?"

Proclaiming everything to be unreal or nothing but the play of the Absolute, and thereby evading responsibility for your actions, is a move I came to call the "Advaita shuffle." This mental tactic, which is abundantly used by modern-day proponents of the Neo-Advaita movement, distracts us from the hard questions and real challenges that come with living in the relative world. It fails to fully come to grips with the fact that even if the world of form appears to be illusory from the vantage point of the Absolute, it still is arising. And thus, just like formless emptiness, form carries a legitimacy of its own, an integrity that needs to be honored.

From my perspective, the teachings of Neo-Advaita failed to present a true nondual unity of the manifest reality and the Absolute. They appeared stuck in the Absolute view and remained strangely defective in their validation of the relative world. And thus I began to teach a more human, more world-embracing nonduality, a nonduality that not only recognizes the legitimacy of the Absolute but fully includes the form aspect of material existence as well. I began to emphasize that there is indeed a choosing faculty in a real world, subject to real cause and effect and bound to create good and bad karma.

Even an enlightened one still exists as a human being in this world. His or her actions are a testimony to the degree to which enlightened awareness has saturated the many dimensions of that person's being. Thus, for me, the real question was: how can we transform *as human beings* in such a way that we become convincing expressions of the perfection of the Absolute? I began to see more and more clearly that striving for a worthy ideal like that requires a rigorous process of liberating one-self from the stranglehold of egoic attachments and impure motives.

As I kept seeing examples of those who had realized their true nature to an extraordinary degree but still expressed questionable behavior, it became easier to understand that those who had merely a taste of it—which were most of my students—could so easily fall back into their old egoic ways. And thus I began to develop a much deeper, more comprehensive and sophisticated teaching in which one needs to be willing to shine the light of truth into every hidden corner of one's life and relentlessly address even the slightest trace of self-deception.

This change in my teaching approach marked both the completion of the first phase of our work, the phase I later came to call "personal enlightenment," roughly covering the first five years after my awakening, and the birth of the second phase, "impersonal enlightenment." During this new phase I began to inspire my students to no longer pursue enlightenment merely for their own personal sake, but for the sake of the whole. I taught them to look at themselves from the perspective of enlightened awareness, a vantage point that unequivocally exposes the radically impersonal nature of the human experience. I urged them to grow beyond their exclusive identification with their personal world, and realize the universal nature of our human condition, with its wide range of emotions and impulses that we all share with our fellow human beings. Joy is joy; it's not *my* joy. Fear is fear; it's not *my* fear. Lust is lust; it's not *my* lust. Yet the ego contracts around these emotions and impulses and creates the illusion of a "me" that is special, unique, and deeply personal. And so, I taught my students to keep their attention grounded in our impersonal shared nature instead. Few means are more powerful to dislodge our attention away from the firm grip of narrow-minded personal concerns and the self-absorbed quality of one's egoic motivations. I could sense that if people could take responsibility for their egos in this way, the pure and open space of consciousness would open up between us, allowing enlightenment to flow through all of us. I knew that if such a collective breakthrough were to occur, our utopian ideal of intersubjective nonduality, the shared higher state of enlightened awareness, would be nearer than near. So I expected those who had really committed to our work to firmly root themselves in this ego-transcending perspective. I wanted them to fully align themselves with the highest aspirations of their authentic self and face their egos head-on.

When I refer to the ego I am not talking about the healthy and all-important self-organizing principle, our command center, if you will, responsible for coordinating the different aspects of the self and enabling us to function smoothly in the world. I am talking about all our conscious and unconscious identifications with and attachments to aspects of the individual self that inhibit our higher evolution. The ego's expressions are manifold, but they show most prominently as pride, arrogance, self-importance, superiority, a sense of specialness, and self-infatuation—all aspects of experience and behavior that directly oppose everything that is truly wholesome in the human experience and that sabotage the emergence of higher and nobler qualities such as compassion, generosity, freedom, innocence, and love.

I wanted my students to remain connected to their spiritual heart all the time, without being deterred by the voice of the narcissistic ego. And so we set out to ruthlessly confront our excessive investment in egoic concerns. This battle with the ego was at the heart of the impersonal enlightenment phase. It catalyzed a period of extreme transformational intensity that would later become known as the hardest and most trying time of our work.

I began to subject my students to a raw, intense, and rigorous training. I wanted those who had tasted the primordial freedom of their awakened nature to live up to the extraordinary potential their experience had revealed to them. Their hearts had been set on fire with the passion of their authentic self. They had sensed the imminence of higher possibilities, and they had often confessed that they wanted to serve the emergence of new structures in consciousness and culture more than anything else in their lives. But even those in whom this sacred passion had awakened to such a powerful degree kept being pulled out of it by the ego's irrational resistance to change.

So I deliberately set up crises for my students to help them see through their ambiguity and deal with their unconscious drives, which were preventing them from truly living in accordance with their highest calling. My teaching approach was confrontational. At times I used unconventional and politically incorrect shock tactics to shake people out of their egoic complacency and wake them up. I wanted those who had fully committed to our work to give it everything they had. We saw ourselves as the Navy Seals of the spiritual world, and we all worked intensely to become strong players, able to hold the work independently. I set up a hard school for radical transformation, a laboratory for evolution to be approached only if you felt ready for the fiercest kind of self-transcending ordeal.

From the very beginning I was transparent about what was required, and everybody knew exactly what they had signed up for. My students knew that what they would get from me was more demanding than sweet smiles, loving hugs, and soothing consolations. I was a revolutionary, ready to do whatever it would take to catalyze a liberating breakthrough—and sometimes it was too much.

I have a radical heart. A force that knows no compromise burns deeply in my veins. It is the pristine clarity of liberation itself, untouched by the anxious concerns and strategic calculations of this world. It is the direct awakening power of enlightenment that only serves to catalyze the freedom of all. It sets my heart on fire with a passion for truth. Like the spirit of the samurai, it is fierce and fearless. Whenever it is met with egoic resistance it draws its sword and ruthlessly cuts through whatever obstacle is blocking Spirit's next emergence. It is not considerate. It only works to expose the false and shallow. It doesn't bow to the status quo. It cares about nothing but effecting change in the world. It is none other than the force of evolution itself, the telos and directionality that animates every particle in the universe. It forces me to speak the truth to those around me about what I see as their condition. It is the guru function itself, the raw and naked intensity of absolute Spirit without any mask. It calls us to respond to our heart's deepest desire: to wake up, relinquish the ego in the fire of truth, and be free. Like the Hindu deities in their wrathful forms, it can be frightening to those who are still entangled in the web of ego and intimidating to those still lost in the mists of self-concern. Such a person will feel threatened, and so will recoil. But those who see through truth's wrathful appearance and notice the radiant light of unconditional love shining brightly behind that fearful mask will be moved to surrender to this fierce grace—and with a shock of recognition, a new world will open up for them.

During the course of my work, many such transformational breakthroughs did indeed occur, often after a painful ordeal involving a prolonged struggle with powerful primal emotions. Yet in the end, the person's resistance broke, their self-perceived limitations dropped away, and their own higher potential was released. Then a changed person expressed profound gratitude for what they now saw as their guru's perseverance and care for their own liberation. To this day, many still attest to the powerful effects of having their egos lastingly transformed in the heat of that alchemical process. They emerged as spiritually mature, independent, self-confident, joyful, and open-hearted people, with a rare kind of inner strength.

So in order to thrive in this hard school my students needed to stand in their own radical heart just as much as I did.

But for all too many, the pressure became too much and, as I now can say, did not fulfill its objective. It ended up creating fear and withdrawal, and evoked primal survival responses instead. Because I was so on fire with my love for consciousness evolution, I was oblivious to the subtleties of all the emotional complexities at play. And because of that, I at times failed to skillfully apply the right measure of pressure. I lost sight of the vulnerable nature of people's humanity, and in my single-minded passion for truth I would keep pushing, all too often resulting in a breakdown rather than a breakthrough.

Living the teachings meant everything to me. When students consistently failed to do so, I often gave them an unambiguous choice: "Either you push through your stuff, or you leave." I didn't want what I saw as their stubborn refusal to determine the outcome of our work together. And thus many were asked to leave until and unless they were ready to play ball.

Being exiled from the tribe was much more destabilizing for most than I was aware of at the time. Many of my students had literally given up everything to join our sangha—careers, families, homes, and all the comforts of worldly life—in order to respond to my vision of creating a revolution in consciousness and culture. Our community was a close-knit group in which deep and rich friendships had blossomed. For some it was like their new family. So having to build up a new life from scratch, outside of our community after being exiled, was almost always a deeply traumatizing, emotionally painful, and intensely disorienting ordeal.

Understandably, many of those who were asked to leave or who left of their own accord became angry and resentful about being pushed too hard. Most of them began to reinterpret their experience with me and our community, seeing it now mainly through a purely psychological lens, devoid of the radical spiritual depth and urgency that had inspired them before. My passionate call for higher evolution turned into an unrealistic infatuation with naïve idealism. The depth of awakening that these students had experienced was now seen as delusional, based merely on transference and countertransference, and their surrender to me as their guru as having been inspired by nothing more than an immature need for a father figure. I was reduced to the cultural stereotype of the corrupt, manipulative guru, able to use his unusual charisma to seduce weak-minded and innocent seekers, get them in line with the program, and make them serve my every wish and whim.

And thus a one-sided public narrative was born that reduced my radical heart and spiritual fire to narcissism, arrogance, and an inflated ego. But the magnificent mystery of the transmission force that continues to flow through me can't be reduced to psychological shadow motivations by any stretch of the imagination. Its source is the Absolute, even as it moves through this particular vehicle, with all its imperfections.

As much as this reductionist narrative damaged my public image, inside the subculture of our sangha these dissenting voices were largely ignored. People who left were seen as weak-minded failures, lacking the inner strength to be on a heroic revolutionary path, out of touch with their own authentic selves, and firmly in the grips of their ferocious pride and insidious egos. Their departure was seen through a binary lens: you were either in or out, with us or against us. Leaving was seen as betraying your own highest purpose and as such, hardly ever a dignified choice.

By now I had been teaching for a decade, and those who had stayed around and had faced their egos began to grow into a certain maturity. I had centers in Holland, Denmark, Germany, France, England, California, Boston, Australia, India, and Israel, and was traveling from place to place, offering my teachings. But as our community matured, the need arose to have our own place, a sanctuary for spiritual evolution where we could all live together and dedicate some focused attention to our lofty pursuit. So in 1996, Foxhollow was purchased. This beautiful estate amid the forests and lakes of the Berkshire Mountains in Lenox, Massachusetts, became our international headquarters. To everybody's great joy, our culture of practice was now centralized and began to blossom, and a surge of fresh energy swept through the community.

Living in Foxhollow allowed us to further intensify our practice of co-creating a shared, intersubjective, egoless field between us. We would hold group meetings and practice what we called "enlightened communication," a form of in-depth group conversation in which we aspired to speak to one another with sincerity, transparency, dignity, vulnerability, and clarity about any topic relative to the human condition. We wanted to learn to be together beyond ego and relate to one another from the deepest possible basis: the indivisible oneness of our true nature. And thus each participant was expected to move beyond his or her tendencies of self-absorption and self-concern and make room for the emergence of a collective interpersonal intelligence, a presence in itself, wiser than any single individual in the group. Whenever such an awakened We-field came alive among us, we would experience states of deep intimacy, communion, and oneness, out of which an often refreshing wisdom would arise and express itself through the group. When these meetings were most successful they would bring forth fresh and sometimes surprisingly innovative insights or generate new answers to old conundrums.

This group practice was the capstone of our work together. All the spiritual practice we so diligently engaged in—the meditation, the chanting, the self-inquiry—all served to prepare us to go beyond the automatic habitual patterns of *me* and surrender to the greater collective intelligence of *we*.

As we would gather more and more experience through what we called our Higher We work, we found that this rarified intersubjective intelligence would only emerge among us if everybody in the group was able to rise above their ego. Whenever the forces of ego would enter our group field through one or more of us, it would be experienced as a toxic force, a pollutant, a destroyer of love, and an inhibitor of the emergence of the greater potentials we were all aspiring to give rise to together. And thus to create optimal conditions for higher emergence, students were joined together in groups based on their ability for ego-transcendence and spiritual maturity. This marked the emergence of a natural form of hierarchy within our sangha.

Within these groups, people would hold one another accountable and call others to task whenever somebody demonstrated a lack of responsibility for the forces of ego. Since ego transcendence is a learning edge for everybody, many experienced these group meetings as a truly challenging ordeal.

But whenever this mysterious shared field of awakened awareness opened up among us, we would remember why all the hardship had been worth it. We would light up with a sense of awe and metaphysical exhilaration, with a purity of being beyond ego that was just exquisite, and with an ecstasy most people can't even begin to imagine. We could feel in every fiber of our being that we were birthing something new and noble in the world, and that our shared utopian vision of creating an enlightened society beyond personal and cultural differences was moving one step closer to reality.

During sacred moments like these, we knew that all the hours of practice, all the drama of doing battle with the ego, all the discomfort and the pressure—all of it had led to this.

3

The Ecstatic Urgency
of Evolution

As our work together deepened, a fresh breeze began blowing through our community. We became increasingly curious about the intriguing intersection between science, philosophy, and Spirit and began to familiarize ourselves with the ideas of Brian Swimme, Sri Aurobindo, Pierre Teilhard de Chardin, Ken Wilber, Elisabet Sahtouris, Don Beck, Georg Wilhelm Friedrich Hegel, Jean Gebser, and Alfred North Whitehead. Many of their central insights into our part in the grand evolutionary process humanity is involved in confirmed my own intuitions. I believed that the groundbreaking scientific discovery of the reality of evolution harbored profound implications for our understanding of spiritual life, implications that had yet to be articulated clearly. What exactly does it mean for our spiritual lives that we are all part and parcel of an evolving kosmic process that moves from lesser to greater complexity and depth? What does it mean that every aspect of the kosmos—the world of matter (physiosphere), the world of life (biosphere), and the world of mind (noosphere)—is in perpetual evolution, driven by a mysterious evolutionary impulse that is alive in every fiber of the kosmos? The answers to these questions have yet to be fully integrated into our classical conceptions of spirituality. So we took a deep dive into the works of these distinguished philosophers, exploring their essential contributions in the pages of *What Is Enlightenment?* As a result, I introduced some powerful new distinctions in my teaching, such as the difference between Being and Becoming and traditional enlightenment versus the new enlightenment. This recontextualized and supercharged every aspect of our work and lives together, so much so that it ushered in an exciting third phase in our work, now well known as Evolutionary Enlightenment.

The philosophical richness of all these big, evolutionary ideas—especially our exposure to Ken Wilber's Integral Theory and the series of innovative and widely appreciated public dialogues I had with Wilber, a visionary genius—had considerable impact on clarifying the distinctions that marked this new phase of my teachings. In his work, Wilber points out that in the course of history, our understanding of the nature of enlightenment underwent a series of evolutionary shifts, with often far-reaching consequences for the way people enact their spiritual lives.[1]

He explains that throughout the ancient world, the basic spiritual orientation, in East and West alike, was to flee this world of the many in search of the One. Spirit was seen as being divorced from the body, and thus spiritual practice was about life-, body-, and world-denying asceticism, and about ascending upward, to Heaven. In Theravada Buddhism, the school closest to the original teachings of the Buddha, the ultimate goal was to get off the wheel of birth and death, escape this hellish world of suffering called *samsara,* and attain the enlightened state of eternal peace, emptiness, and bliss in the heavenly realm of nirvana. Nirvana was thus seen as being separate from samsara, just as the world of form was believed to be divorced from formlessness. This remained the leading-edge view for almost eight hundred years. This orientation, however, is deeply dualistic.

Then, in the second century, the philosopher-sage Nagarjuna caused nothing short of a revolution in Buddhism when he began to object to the strange duality between samsara and nirvana. He pointed out that emptiness and form are not two, and that reality is actually nondual—a breakthrough perhaps most strikingly summarized by the famous verse from the Heart Sutra: "That which is form is not other than emptiness, that which is emptiness is not other than form." This new insight ushered in the Mahayana revolution in Buddhism and later inspired the Tantric revolution as well. The world of form was now no longer seen as a dreadful illusion, a prison cell one needs to escape from. It was understood to be illusory only when seen as being separate from Spirit. But the moment it is recognized as being one with Spirit, it reveals itself as the direct expression—the radiant gesture—of Spirit's exuberance. This radically new orientation swept the ancient world and dramatically changed the way people conducted their spiritual lives. Spirituality was no longer about fleeing one half of reality and hiding in the other, but about uniting both halves. And enlightenment came to mean the nondual union of emptiness and form.

This view of spirituality lived into the modern era, when around one hundred fifty years ago the discovery of evolution, particularly in biology and physics, opened our eyes to the fact that the manifest aspect of reality is not an already fully formed whole. Form keeps evolving, and thus the nondual union of emptiness and form is always moving. This evolutionary view refined our insights into the nature of reality and enlightenment yet again. Unpacking these insights led us into a profound philosophical contemplation, one that requires us to view our existence from the cosmological vantage point of deep time and big history.

So consider, if you will, the awe-inspiring majesty of the evolutionary journey that has led to you and me.

Modern cosmology tells us that before the universe was born there was only nothingness—a timeless, formless, primordial singularity. Then, in a massive explosion, the universe burst into existence about 13.7 billion years ago. With this big bang, the world of form was born and an immense evolutionary process began to unfold. The early universe was made up of nothing but a vast expanse of energy and inanimate matter. This primordial substance slowly organized itself over unimaginable stretches of time into the celestial bodies of our solar systems, including somewhere among them our beautiful Earth, which was formed around 4.5 billion years ago from the remains of extinct stars. A billion years later on Earth, in an astounding new emergence, inanimate matter brought forth life. As the first living, single-cell organisms began to grow in complexity, a dramatic chain of biological evolution was initiated, out of which, around two hundred thousand years ago, we humans emerged. With this remarkable new creative advance, life brought forth mind and, in turn, the capacity for self-reflective awareness.

If we stand back for a moment and contemplate the marvel of our deep-time journey, what else could we feel but awe and wonder? How could something come from nothing? How could inanimate matter transform into life? And how could life generate something so stunning as our consciousness? This is a mystery that not even our brightest minds can adequately explain. How could any of these leaps into novelty actually occur if there wasn't a creative principle built into the kosmos from day one? Ever since that initial act of creation, that mysterious "first cause," the universe has demonstrated an equally mysterious capacity for self-organization and a vibrant, ongoing creativity that tirelessly drives the evolutionary process forward, organizing its creations into ever-greater levels of complexity and structural order. Even now, more keeps emerging from less. The big history of the kosmos is indeed an extraordinary evolutionary tale of creative advance into novelty, and thus the presence of a built-in creative principle that keeps driving kosmic evolution is one of the foundational insights that comes to light in an evolutionary view of spirituality.

If we then pick up the thread of our majestic evolutionary journey, we discover that the emergence of human consciousness ushered in a whole new revolution in the further unfolding of the world of form.

When early hominids walked the African savannah, taking their first hesitant bipedal steps, their consciousness was still in a state of undifferentiated fusion with the natural world. Today, we humans have walked the surface of the moon, and humanity has brought forth powerfully enlightened sages like Ramana Maharshi. Between these iconic achievements lies the long journey of the flowering of consciousness, an intriguing inner process that we, by now, have researched in great detail.

Wilber points out that human beings, in their individual psychology from infancy to adulthood, as well as humanity at large, in its culturally shared values and worldviews, have moved through a series of concrete, observable stages of development. His Integral Theory model points to the evolutionary trajectory of consciousness *and* culture. Each higher level we grow into transcends but also includes its predecessor, which is why, as we advance through these stages of development, our consciousness expands and we become capable of greater complexity, care, inclusivity and embrace. The figures on the following pages, figure 3.1 and figure 3.2, depict these successive levels.[2]

Today, the center of gravity of most people's inner development situates itself somewhere around the amber-traditional, the orange-rational, or the green-postmodern level or "altitude." The teal and turquoise Integral stages, as defined by Wilber, are the leading edge of consciousness and culture in our times. These newly emerging levels of consciousness are forming right now, as more and more people begin to grow into these stages. We are actually creating them as we evolve. In other words, the interior of the kosmos is evolving through us, and there is no reason to believe that there is an upper limit to its evolution.

This modern-day understanding is profoundly liberating. It radically breaks open the closed worldview in which enlightenment was traditionally embedded. Throughout the ancient world it was believed that all the levels of evolution were already preexisting somehow, as the real ontological structures of the universe—as if they were present since the beginning of time, like Platonic forms* simply waiting for us to step into them on our path of the great return to God. Evolution was a pregiven, fixed route. But in the new worldview, the further stages of our evolution are no longer simply waiting for us to discover them; they are literally being created by brave consciousness pioneers pushing the leading edge and venturing into new, uncharted territory. This means that the future is radically open, and we can co-create it together in an almost infinite number of ways. How the next emerging level is going to look is up to us. We are responsible for its creation.

---

*According to Plato, the imperfect forms in this physical reality have their perfect and unchanging counterparts, their blueprints if you will, in the realm of forms, which is the true, eternal reality, transcending time and space. As human beings we can actualize ourselves by orienting toward these already existing forms.

The Spectrum of Consciousness: Levels and Lines

LEVELS OF CONSCIOUSNESS

Level	Tier	Scope	Cognitive Line (Commons/Richards, Piaget/Aurobindo)	Worldviews (Gebser)	Values Line (Graves/Spiral Dynamics)	Needs (Maslow)	Self-Identity (Loevinger/ Cook-Greuter)	Explanation
CLEAR LIGHT	3rd Tier	Kosmocentric	Supermind					Nonduality is structurally ever-present. Total embrace of All That Is. Bright Brilliance of the nondual union of the ultimate, infinite Divine Reality with its everyday, ordinary finite operations.
ULTRAVIOLET	3rd Tier	Kosmocentric	Overmind					Plugged in to every level in existence, all the way back to the Big Band. Loving constant witness to the entire Kosmos. Causal states become permanently objectified, and wakefulness persists throughout the deep sleep state.
VIOLET	3rd Tier	Kosmocentric	Meta-mind					Visionary mind. Revelatory intuition. Subtle states become permanently objectified, and wakefulness persists throughout the dream state.
INDIGO	3rd Tier	Kosmocentric	Global Mind				Ego-aware	Direct inner sight, outshining thought. Apprehends that the world is not merely physical, but a psychophysical system. Subject-object dichotomy begins to break down. Wakefulness becomes a permanent trait in the waking state.
TURQUOISE	2nd Tier	Kosmocentric	Late Vision-Logic (Post-paradigmatic)		Global View/Systemic (Turquoise)		Construct-aware (Integrated)	Sees the World as alive and evolving. Holistic and kosmocentric. Lives from both individual self and transpersonal self. Emerging now.
TEAL	2nd Tier	Worldcentric	Middle Vision-Logic (Paradigmatic)	Integral	Flex Flow/Systemic (Yellow)	Self-Actualization	Autonomous	Sees natural hierarchy and systems of systems. Holds multiple perspectives. Flexible, creative, and effective. Online 50 years.
GREEN	1st Tier	Worldcentric	Early Vision-Logic	Pluralistic	Human Bond/ Relativistic (Green)	Self-Esteem	Individualistic	Values pluralism and equality. Relativistic and sensitive. Civil rights and environmentalism. World centric. Online 150 years.
ORANGE	1st Tier	Worldcentric	Formal Operational	Mental	Strive Drive/Multiplistic (Orange)		Conscientious	Values rationality and science. Individualism and democracy. Capitalism and materialism. Risk-taking and self-reliance. Online 300 years.
AMBER	1st Tier	Egocentric Ethnocentric	Concrete Operational	Mythic	Truth Force/Absolutistic (Blue)	Belongingness	Conformist	Ethno- or nation-centric. Values rules, roles, and discipline. Faith in transcendent God or Order. Socially conservative. Online 5,000 years.
RED	1st Tier	Egocentric Ethnocentric	Preoperational (Conceptional)		Power Gods/Egocentric (Red)	Safety	Self-protective	Ego-centric, vigilant, and aggressive. Impulsive and ruthless. Courageous, determined, and powerful. Online 15,000 year.
MAGENTA	1st Tier	Egocentric Ethnocentric	Preoperational (Symbolic)	Magic	Kin Spirits/Magic-Animistic (Purple)		Impulsive	Sees the world as enchanted. Values ritual and deep community. Individual subordinate to group. Online 50,000 years.
INFRARED	1st Tier	Egocentric Ethnocentric	Sensorimotor	Archaic	Survival (Beige)	Physiological	Symbolic	Dawning self-awareness. Survives through instinct, intuition, and bonding with others. Online 250,000 years.

Self-Transcendence

Figure 3.1. Overview of the stages of development according to Ken Wilber's Integral Theory (see also color plate 1).

ONE OF THE ESSENTIAL ELEMENTS of Ken Wilber's integral approach is the recognition that human consciousness evolves, develops, or unfolds through a fluid but hierarchical sequence of levels or stages. Integrating over one hundred developmental models into his framework, Wilber uses a rainbow-hued scheme (based on the colors traditionally ascribed to the seven chakras) to generically represent these different levels, which are grouped into three major classes or tiers.

First tier spans all levels from primitive, infantile consciousness (infrared) to postmodern, pluralistic consciousness (green); second tier represents a leap into holistic, systemic, and integral modes of consciousness (teal and turquoise), which some believe to be the leading edge of development today; and third tier reaches into even more integral, transpersonal, and higher "spiritual" territory (indigo and above)—levels that remain largely unexplored.

Many of the developmental models on which Wilber's spectrum of consciousness is based are the results of research on specific "intelligences," or developmental *lines* of growth and maturation, within the psychological makeup of human beings. This diagram includes the *cognitive* line, the *worldviews* line, the *values* line, the *needs* line, and the *self-identity* line, but many others have been identified, including the moral, emotional, aesthetic, interpersonal, psychosexual, and kinesthetic lines.

By observing the transformation of individuals over time, numerous researchers and theorists—from Aurobindo in the East to Piaget in the West—have shown that each of these developmental lines do indeed unfold through distinct levels of increasing consciousness, order, and sophistication. But what Wilber's spectrum reveals is how the various lines of development actually relate to each other: evolving, side by side, through the same general levels of increasing consciousness. It also makes clear how any given individual can be at a high level in a particular line while at lower levels in other lines, one example of which would be Nazi doctors: individuals who were highly developed in the cognitive line, but dramatically underdeveloped in the moral line.

Evolving Worldviews, Expanding Self

Although the spectrum of consciousness includes twelve colors to denote twelve specific levels, stages, structures, or waves of development, for ease of explanation Wilber often uses a simpler, three- or four-level scheme pioneered by developmental psychologists like Lawrence Kohlberg and Carol Gilligan. Tracing the most general contours of psychological growth, this scheme highlights the fact that increasing consciousness corresponds to a broadening of worldviews and an expansion of one's sense of self.

Egocentric ("me"): A stage characterized by narcissistic self-absorption, bodily needs and desires, emotional outbursts, unsocialized impulses, and an incapacity to take the role of the "other"; seen today predominantly in infants and young children, rebellious teens, wild rock stars, and criminals. (Infrared to red)

Ethnocentric ("us"): An expansion of self-identity to include one's family, peers, tribe, race, faith group, or nation; the adoption of socially conformist rules and roles; commonly seen in children aged seven to adolescence, religious myths and fundamentalism, the "moral majority," Nazis, the KKK, right-wing politics, patriotism, sports teams, school rivalries. (Amber)

Worldcentric ("all of us"): An even greater expansion of self to embrace all people, regardless of race, gender, class, or creed; a stage of rationality that questions rigid belief systems and transcends conventional rules and roles; commonly seen in late adolescence, social activism, multiculturalism, science, moral relativism, liberal politics, the "global village," New Age spirituality; the emergence of integral cognition. (Orange to teal)

Kosmocentric ("all that is"): An identification with all life and consciousness, human or otherwise, and a deeply felt responsibility for the evolutionary process as a whole; "super-integral" cognition and values; innate universal morality; spirituality beyond merely personal motivations; an emergent capacity, rarely seen anywhere. (Turquoise to clear light)

Figure 3.2. Explanation of the lines of development and the evolution of worldviews according to Wilber's Integral Theory (see also color plate 2).

These recent discoveries about the evolution of consciousness and culture have deeply enriched our understanding of the nature of enlightenment. Nondual realization remains the union of emptiness and form, just as Nagarjuna taught, but as the form aspect of reality continues to evolve, the more accurate interpretation of enlightenment is the union of emptiness and *evolving* form. This is to say that enlightenment itself is evolving! There are always newly emerging stages of consciousness and culture to become one with; always new levels to enclose in your enlightened embrace.

In his groundbreaking book *Integral Spirituality,* Wilber makes the point: "A person's realization today is not Freer than Buddha's (Emptiness is Emptiness), but it is Fuller than Buddha's (and will be even Fuller down the road).[3] He explains that somebody who realizes emptiness but is at, say, the amber altitude (figure 3.2 or plate 2), would not be considered enlightened by today's standards because there are several existing stages of development this person hasn't yet matured into and thus is not one with. But in the ancient world that same person would be considered perfectly realized because at that time the amber altitude was the highest stage of development then in existence; there were no higher levels to become one with. And so the discovery of the evolution of manifest existence turns enlightenment into a moving target—a sliding scale—which prompts the striking conclusion that the new enlightenment is Evolutionary Enlightenment!

As we contemplated these big philosophical ideas, the teachings of Evolutionary Enlightenment began to morph into a coherent whole, and we began to integrate them into our spiritual lives. It was an exhilarating time of renewed exploration. Our daily practice began to organize around accessing the very real dimensions of Being, the goal of traditional Enlightenment, and Becoming, the goal of the new enlightenment, in the depths of our own awareness. And bit by bit, the differences between the felt experience of both dimensions came alive in us.

When you are deeply absorbed in Being, the mind is completely still. Every trace of thought and feeling, time and world, self and other, is erased, and there is no impetus to do anything whatsoever. Only consciousness itself remains, pristine and untouched. Nothing else exists, but you are still there as pure Being—changeless, spacious, infinite, and utterly transparent. There is only one single reality, and you are that. This is irresistibly attractive because you are immersed in the actual part of yourself that has never been born and never entered the stream of time, and you sense its immortality. You experience perfect, everlasting peace, a sense of absolute release into the infinite, and it radically sets you free. That is what God feels like before the universe was born.

This absolute Ground of Being is not only a peaceful place within your own interior, it is also the deepest dimension of reality itself—the timeless, formless void out of which the universe was born. It is your own original face, the one you had before the big bang. This unqualified voidness, in which nothing ever happened and the universe wasn't even a thought in the mind of God, is called *Nirguna Brahman,* or "God without qualities," the radically formless Self.

But the wisdom traditions also point to another aspect of ultimate reality, called *Saguna Brahman,* or "God with qualities." This is the Self as it begins to meet the world of space and time, and its earliest characteristics begin to emerge. You can actually locate this aspect of the Self in the depths of your own awareness as well.

At times you will experience the deep meditative state of emptiness as endlessly captivating. Even though it is changeless, it is never boring, old, or predictable. The nature of our unborn Self is always fresh and ever-new. If you hone in to that mysterious quality, you will notice that what makes emptiness enthralling is that it contains a sense of infinite potential. You can feel its very subtle yet endlessly compelling creative vibration dancing right on the very edge where formlessness and form meet. Nothing has yet occurred, yet everything is possible. This feeling is the living pulse of the first cause. The moment this creative impulse crosses the threshold between the unmanifest and the manifest, it bursts forth into the world of form as an act of creation. That which was once perfect peace in the depths of formless Being now dramatically changes its quality. It morphs into the exhilarating creative vibration of Evolutionary Becoming. It shows up as what I call the evolutionary impulse, or Eros, the archetypal energy and intelligence that initiated the creative process and continues to drive it. The feeling quality of the evolutionary impulse is ecstasy and urgency, pure positivity, a big resounding "Yes!" to life.

The wonder of the relationship between Being and Becoming, with their radically different qualities, is that they are in reality one indivisible continuum, an unbroken whole. The creative impulse arises from nothingness and is not separate from its primordial ground. Being and Becoming are one, not two; as meditation reveals, you are that one! This is actually quite a stunning realization. If at the deepest possible level of existence there was always only one, and you are that one, then you are the one who chose to take the leap from formlessness to form, the one who created the entire universe and continues to drive its evolution. You, and you alone, are responsible for all of creation!

The spiritual experience of the nonduality of Being and Becoming confirms the philosophical insight that there is indeed a creative impulse built into the cosmic process from day one. And since you, as a human being, are a product of this evolutionary unfolding, this creative impulse is inherent in every fiber of *your* being as well. This means that every single moment of your existence carries within it the thrilling potential for creative emergence. You can actually feel the ecstasy and urgency of the evolutionary impulse on different levels of your own being.

On a physical level you can feel it as the sexual impulse. The biological command to procreate is the most basic and least-refined expression of the creative vibration, expressing the ecstasy and urgency of the first cause. On a deeper level of the self the evolutionary impulse is experienced as the uniquely human drive to innovate and give rise to that which is new. Our innate creativity expresses itself in all our endeavors, to create culture, art, philosophy, science, and technology. When you experience the state of creative flow, a vibrant energy courses through you. It feels ecstatic, and its often surprising sense of urgency will keep you up at night so that you can give birth to that which wants to come through you. When you are thus lit up, cynicism, inertia, and psychological fears dissipate and make room for fearlessness, excitement, unselfconsciousness, unabashed enthusiasm, and lack of self-concern.

The ego falls into the background, just like it does in deep meditation. And what moves to the foreground is the overwhelming desire to bring forth that which did not yet exist, to make a difference and create a new world. On the highest level, the creative impulse is experienced as the spiritual impulse, the mysterious urge to become more conscious. Sometimes it is felt as a deep yearning for greater wholeness; at other times it manifests as a thundering passion to wake up—now! This is the call of the interior of the kosmos aspiring to evolve through you. It is the God impulse, if you will, and if you answer its call, you as the ego will be completely consumed. The spiritual impulse is the most profound expression of the first cause.

This dynamic, ever-evolving creative principle as it expresses itself in the human heart and mind is what I call the *authentic self*. This is the self that is always inspired, always sensing the imminence of higher potentials, and always ecstatically striving to create the future. Whereas the true self is timeless and formless, the heart of the authentic self is the evolutionary energy that animates the world of form. Just like timeless, formless Being, this evolutionary creativity is immortal. The products of evolution are transient, but the evolutionary impulse that gives rise to them is imperishable, unchanging, and indestructible. When you are aligned with your authentic self, you actually feel the force of evolution coursing through you as a real push to become more conscious and advance the leading edge of the creative process. The pure vibrancy of its energy utterly outshines your egoic resistance to change. This is why attuning to the evolutionary impulse is instantaneously self-liberating, the same way the realization of emptiness, or the Ground of Being is. The authentic self, therefore, is your evolutionarily enlightened self. It is already free. And thus in this teaching, living in alignment with your authentic self and the evolutionary impulse, alive at the very heart of all forms, is how ego transcendence is achieved.

In the teachings of Evolutionary Enlightenment, this energy of Becoming is awakened in you by living according to five fundamental tenets. These tenets point you to the inner posture you need to take again and again in order to show up as the authentic self in every

moment. Making the noble effort to live by these tenets while also continuing to deepen your practice of meditation will allow you to embody
an enlightened relationship to life, always grounded in the silent source
of Being, but simultaneously lit up by the invigorating creativity of evolutionary Becoming, which perpetually emerges from that silent source.

- *Clarity of intention* is the first tenet of Evolutionary Enlightenment.
  It is the very foundation of spiritual practice. This tenet holds that
  your desire to evolve and be liberated has to become more important than anything else in the world. If you truly want to evolve,
  nothing will stop you. You will not even wait for grace to descend
  on you. This tenet places the responsibility for your evolution
  entirely in your own hands. It calls you to question yourself with
  ruthless honesty, asking, *Do my life choices reflect my desire for radical transformation?* As you deepen your self-inquiry, you will inevitably be confronted with areas of egoic resistance to change that
  are often hidden deep within your self-structure. You will encounter your own ambiguity, doubts, obstacles, and fears. This kind of
  self-scrutiny exposes the division in yourself between the actual way
  you choose to live your life and your own highest aspirations, and it
  inspires you to bridge that gap.

- The second tenet, *the power of volition,* calls on you to take unconditional responsibility for the totality of who you are—not just for
  your own personal history, cultural conditioning, and the wounding and trauma gathered in your lifetime, but also for the residue of
  pain and suffering that has accumulated in the deep structures of
  your psyche as a result of our conflict-ridden, deep-time evolutionary journey from the big bang all the way up to the present moment.
  This may seem like a Herculean task, but in fact from a kosmological perspective that responsibility has been yours all along. As the
  true self, *you* initiated this entire kosmic process, and as the authentic self, *you* continue to drive it. Thus *you and you alone* are the one
  who is already responsible for every single turn of this multifaceted
  creative unfolding. And so, as that one, you don't experience

ambivalence or hesitation about taking full responsibility.

The second tenet also asserts that on the deepest possible level you always know exactly what you are doing. It encourages you to step out of the deep-seated belief that you are a victim of your circumstances and inspires you to wholeheartedly assume this deeper-self responsibility for your karma, including past, present, and future. And even as this is forever a work in progress, if you fully stand in the power of your volition, your unconscious drives will gradually be exposed and you will be able to take responsibility for them and show up with clarity and strength.

- The third tenet, *face everything and avoid nothing*, is the quintessential spiritual practice. It calls you to release your deeply ingrained self-protective habit of avoidance and realize your potential for unobstructed awareness at all times, under all circumstances, and in all places. The human condition is such that we automatically tend to disown the less than wholesome aspects of ourselves, like pride, self-importance, and our darker motivations and lower impulses, because we experience them as too frightening, embarrassing, shocking, or humiliating to face. This tenet directs you to confront all your egoic motives and unconscious material and clear your awareness from the reflex of avoidance. Practicing it will shatter the ego's defenses and make you straightforward, transparent, and authentic. Engaging with it continuously will allow you to transcend the ego in every single moment. Then you will no longer flinch when confronted with your dark side. But you will also no longer be overwhelmed by the bright promise of your own highest potentials. You will be able to own up to all of what you are and be free to partner up with your authentic self's unselfconscious and inherently defenseless and unbridled passion for evolution.

- The fourth tenet is called *the process perspective*. It's an invitation to do nothing less than to look at yourself and the universe through the eyes of God. It calls on you to relinquish the narrow confines of your personal self and learn to see all events and every aspect of the human experience as part and parcel of a vast, impersonal, yet glorious cosmic process that started fourteen billion years ago. Through the practice of contemplation and introspection, you can learn to step so far back and let go so deeply that this God's-eye view becomes your actual, tangibly felt vantage point. If you then look at yourself from there, you are no longer a small and insignificant entity lost in the inconceivable immensity of an infinite universe. You *are* this grand evolutionary process looking at a tiny part of itself. Nothing is more powerful to deconstruct the tight grip of your sense of a separate self. It breaks the spell of your deeply ingrained habit of compulsively personalizing every thought, feeling, or sensation you have and exposes your experience as universally human and impersonal, simply happening in and through you. This is immensely liberating. The process perspective allows you to see your own body-mind-personality as the product of this kosmic unfolding and a means by which the universe becomes more conscious of itself through you. This also makes your human existence infinitely significant. It evokes a deeply felt surrender and invites you to humbly put your life in service of this magnificent creative process.

• The fifth tenet, ***kosmic conscience,*** refers to the ability to live your life as an expression of the evolutionary impulse and show up as the authentic self. When you start on the path you are driven by a concern for *my* enlightenment, the end of *my* suffering, and *my* benefit. But as you begin to realize that we are all part of a vast kosmic process, the desire to want to be free more than anything else, as the first tenet has it, will naturally move out of the realm of the personal and increasingly become an expression of the ecstasy and urgency of the evolutionary impulse itself. The moment your own personal wants and needs are experienced as being secondary to that higher dynamic, the power balance within the self shifts. This happens when your degree of awakening to the authentic self crosses the magic threshold from 50 to 51 percent. The authentic self is now the dominant presence in your being, and the ego has become the weaker part of who you are.

This momentous shift changes everything. From now on, your evolution is no longer merely dependent on your own will or intention. The mysterious and unstoppable dynamism of your authentic self will begin to propel you forward. With that shift, you come to understand in a very deep way that the evolution of the interior of the kosmos depends on you, and this awakens a tremendous sense of moral obligation in you to serve this kosmic unfolding. This is the moral imperative of kosmic conscience. The more kosmic conscience comes alive in you, the more you will be lit up with the future-oriented passion to create that which is new, and the more you will feel that you exist solely to serve this always forward-reaching momentum. You realize you are here for the biggest possible reason: to co-create the very leading edge of the possible. A kosmic sense of purpose awakens in you, and you fully commit, again and again, to giving everything to the evolution of the interior of the kosmos, which becomes an inexhaustible source of joy, delight, and freedom.

The role of these five tenets can be understood as follows: The first three tenets challenge us to cultivate the right relationship to our mind, emotions, and life choices. They constitute a complete teaching within a personal enlightenment context, allowing us to live an awakened life of right action and responsibility for our ego and its conditioning. The fourth and fifth tenets, meanwhile, call on us to embrace a much larger evolutionary context. They teach us to see our personal experience through a God's-eye view and show up as this bright, awake, ecstatic energy and intelligence that drives the creative process. The fifth tenet is not a direct practice instruction; the treasured gift of kosmic conscience emerges naturally as a result of earnestly practicing the other four tenets. For a visual representation, see figures 3.3 and 3.4 on the following page.

The practice of the five tenets of Evolutionary Enlightenment serves as an antidote to the developmental stagnation and notorious narcissism of the postmodern predicament in which many of us, still at the green altitude, are trapped. The postmodern self, for all its healthy features such as multiculturalism, pluralism, inclusivity, sensitivity, its ability

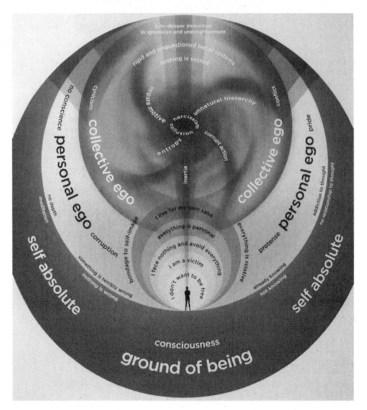

EGO

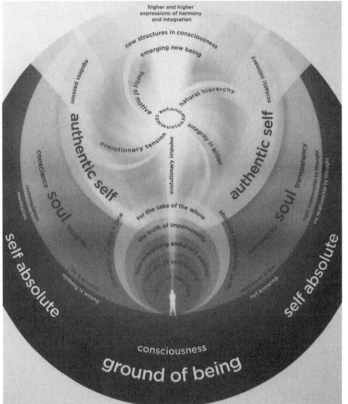

EVOLUTIONARY
ENLIGHTENMENT

*Figures 3.3 and 3.4.
Teaching models
of Evolutionary
Enlightenment
depicting the
potential for spiritual
development in an
egoic context versus an
enlightenment context
(see also color plates 3
and 4).*

to see many truths and to understand that meaning is context-bound, its communal orientation, its care for the marginalized, and so on, has also developed unhealthy traits that are inherently anti-evolutionary and antitransformational.* Its deep-seated discomfort with making hierarchical distinctions sabotages inner growth because there are higher stages of consciousness one has to orient oneself to if growth is to happen at all. Its firm belief that all perspectives are equally valid incapacitates one to make value distinctions and sound judgments that are grounded in discriminating wisdom. The postmodern self has become convinced that "my truth is true for me, and yours is true for you," and then somewhat glibly adds, "therefore, nobody can tell me what to do, and nobody needs to, because I am fine just the way I am." This knee-jerk reaction of ensconcing the ego as an essentially unassailable entity that cannot be judged or called out stifles the awakening of the authentic self, thus effectively undermining the very possibility of further growth.

As a result of moving away from objective truth and orienting toward subjectivity, the postmodern self slides into narcissism. It has an inflated sense of self-importance and has become overidentified with its personal story. As much as it is interested in transformation, inner work, spirituality, and actualizing higher potentials, it mostly enacts this interest by expressing, confirming, and celebrating the ego rather than by radically transcending it. Self-acceptance has taken precedence over self-transformation. And thus many of our postmodern values reinforce, solidify, and energize our already ego-bound orientation.

But the moment you merge with your authentic self and orient from a deep-time perspective that is also infused with the spiritual revelation of nonduality, developmental stagnation loosens up and narcissism vaporizes like a droplet on a hot skillet. You realize that there is always only the one, without a second, and you know beyond any doubt that you are that one. You are the one who was present as timeless, formless Being before the big bang. You are the one who initiated the creative process

---

*Ken Wilber presents a scathing philosophical critique on postmodernism in his 2003 book *Boomeritis: A Novel That Will Set You Free.*

fourteen billion years ago. And you are the one who continues to drive its perpetual evolutionary emergence. Thus you wake up to the startling recognition that this is all *your* responsibility. Who else's could it be? There *is* no other. Suddenly it all becomes clear: the universe is actually trying to become more conscious *through you!* This is your project. Your body-mind is a vehicle for the evolution of the interior of the kosmos. It was never really about your personal story. The majestic process that gave rise to your presence here on Earth is waiting for you to become available for it. It needs your energy and willingness to take its own next step. Its future is wide-open. None of the emerging levels of evolution are already fixed. We are creating their content and structure as we progress. And thus, how the next advance into novelty will manifest literally depends on our choices.

This evolutionary view profoundly challenges the traditional notion that once we have attained the great liberation, we never have to reincarnate back into the cycle of birth and death again. Considering what it has taken for this process to get to the point where it has produced conscious beings with the capacity to understand their own role in this glorious evolutionary scheme, it doesn't make sense to conclude that the ultimate purpose of our presence here is final release from this world and freedom from incarnate existence. If the interior of the universe is going to continue to become more conscious through us, then you and I have to want to stay on the ride. If we opt out, the miracle of greater awareness, complexity, and embrace is not going to occur.

As soon as we truly get this, it sets us on fire with a powerful sense of meaning and purpose. We become serious about being here, passionate to make the right choices here on God's Earth, and devoted to liberating our energy, attention, and awareness so that we can take on the daunting yet thrilling responsibility for how the future turns out. Why else would we be here if not to show up as passionate representatives of the creative principle in the world? What other purpose could be ours but to embrace the awe-inspiring burden of this never-ending creative advance into novelty, which has been ours all along?

Such a grace-filled life, awake to Eros and lit up by the creative vibrancy of the authentic self, is the new enlightenment.

4

A Higher We Emerges

With the dawn of the teachings of Evolutionary Enlightenment, our work at Foxhollow and at our centers around the world intensified. We were lit up with the creative vibrancy of the evolutionary impulse, and many of us felt we were living on the edge of the possible. There was a growing sense that we were reaching into something new, thrilling, and different, as if the leading edge of the evolutionary process was pushing to give birth to a new expression of enlightenment through us.

Early in my work I had intuited that what was unfolding around me was different from what my teacher had taught. In the first place, it was not about the personal enlightenment of the individual; it had a more collective quality. This was apparent from the moment I first began to teach in Rishikesh, when this mysterious and powerful current of enlightened awareness filled the room, engulfing those present and creating an enthralling intersubjective field of bliss and ecstasy among us.

But the real nature and actual potential of this shared enlightened awareness emerged consciously for me a year or so later, in 1987. I was on a teaching visit to Amsterdam and was watching two of my students engaged in conversation. Suddenly it struck me that something deep and significant was being shared between them, something that transcended the actual content and lighthearted nature of their conversation. I could see that what they were sharing was consciousness itself, and that sharing this greatest mystery of all with each other was more important than whatever they were getting from me as their teacher. Observing this revealed to me a completely different possibility: I saw that if nonduality could become the foundation of our shared human experience—the ground on which we meet—the world could be a radically different place. This vision marked the birth of our utopian ideal. It was the beginning of my growing recognition that enlightened awareness could not only come alive in the interior world of the individual self, but also in the interior of a collective of people, as a Higher We. This new kind of enlightenment expresses itself in the space *between* subjects, and thus becomes the intersubjective experience of a whole group. This was the phenomenon that seemed to be trying to emerge around me.

In support of the emergence of this promising new potential, we developed a rich and elaborate practice culture. Our spirited attempts to cultivate this intersubjective, egoless field between us transformed our sangha into a white-hot cauldron for ego transcendence.

People living at Foxhollow would rise early in the morning to meditate for two hours. Their morning practice was usually complemented by a lengthy series of pre-dawn prostrations, often a thousand or more. This time-honored practice is traditionally intended to cultivate an attitude of reverence and surrender to the Triple Gem, a term derived from Theravada Buddhism referring to the "three jewels" or "three refuges" on the path of enlightenment: the Buddha, or teacher; the Dharma, or teaching; and the Sangha, or community of practitioners. It is understood among Buddhist monks that the mere physical act of prostrating with the right intention is a most potent means to effectuate ego release. During these prostrations, lines from my teachings were chanted as a means to help students align with core truths and create a spirit of meditative concentration.

Other more traditional practices, particularly for specific people and small groups, were part of our culture as well. Some shaved their heads to help them renounce their attachment to their identity and some took a vow of celibacy for a period of time to learn to see through the patterns of the mind relative to sexuality. Sundays were reserved for silent retreat, and once every year students were required to either attend our annual public retreat for ten or twenty days or undertake a week of silent retreat on their own.

But the capstone of our practice regime was the group meetings we would hold to train ourselves in the art of relating to one another beyond ego. All of the other practices we so diligently engaged in—meditation, prostrations, chanting, self-inquiry, celibacy—in the end primarily served as preparation for everybody to learn to move beyond the automatic, habitual patterns of "me" and create the right conditions in which this shared egoless field of enlightened awareness could open up between us.

Along with this intense practice culture we also worked to create a community structure that would be the most conducive to catalyzing ego transcendence. We found that a structure of natural hierarchy that groups people together based on their level of spiritual development, psychological maturity, and experience created an evolutionary tension that generated a wholesome upward pull, uplifting and inspiring each person to aim for greater depth and wisdom. Time and again we saw that when people came together in a context of natural hierarchy, they spontaneously oriented toward the shining example of those above them while also deriving sometimes much-needed support from same-level peers. Without such vertical magnetism and nurturing support, we found that people tended to quickly slide back into their old habits, and their development was more easily compromised.

And so guided by this principle of natural hierarchy, I arranged our sangha in three hierarchical rings.* The inner circle, called the *defining core,* consisted of senior students. They were the longtime practitioners with great spiritual maturity who worked directly with me as the spiritual leader. The second ring, called the *resolute core,* consisted

---

*Throughout the history of EnlightenNext, some version of a hierarchical structure was always in place, yet it was continually evolving in a creative way. The structure described here came into being starting around 2010.

of the younger segment of our community. Most of them were extraordinary people—intensely committed, very disciplined, and incredibly inspired. We often appreciatively referred to them as the Navy Seals of our work because of their unusual confidence, strength, and unshakable conviction that they had the greatest teacher in the world and the best community. The third ring was called the *committed core*. This was the larger student body consisting of lay students who had committed themselves to the teachings while also keeping their family lives and jobs. In addition to these three formal rings, our sangha structure contained a fourth segment of practitioners as well: people with an affinity for the teaching who joined our local community activities at our centers around the world.

At its best, this hierarchical structure worked like a developmental vortex in which people felt drawn up and enlivened to give rise to their own highest aspirations.

Each of these three hierarchical rings was organized in smaller women's and men's groups of five, six, or more people who were joined together based on how much practice they had done, their understanding of the teachings, how long they had known me, and on actual perceivable differences in their ability for ego transcendence. These smaller groups were called *holons,* meaning a whole that is simultaneously part of a larger whole. These holons served as the setting for our group meetings in which we practiced what we called "enlightened communication." This was a form of in-depth group conversation in which we aspired to speak to one another with sincerity, transparency, dignity, vulnerability, and clarity about any topic relative to the human condition. During this group practice, each participant was expected to move beyond his or her tendencies of self-absorption and self-concern and make room for the emergence of an interpersonal intelligence—a presence in itself—wiser than any single individual in the group. Whenever someone demonstrated a lack of responsibility for the forces of ego, the others in the group would call that person to task, giving them feedback in sometimes helpful and sometimes harsh, binary ways, judging their responses and behavior as either ego or non-ego. Since ego transcendence is a learning edge for everybody, many experienced these group meetings as a truly challenging ordeal.

I closely observed and monitored these holons, trying to get a good grasp of why some of them flourished and others didn't. As we would gather more and more experience with Higher We work, we found that this rarified intersubjective intelligence would only emerge between us if everybody in the group was able to rise above their egos. Whenever the forces of ego would enter the group field through one or more of us, it would literally be experienced as a toxic force, a pollutant, a destroyer of love inhibiting the emergence of the greater potentials we were all aspiring to give rise to together. What we found was that when people were grouped at a similar developmental altitude, it generated the best results, whereas in mixed-altitude groups the shared resonance would be disturbed. Based on this understanding, I was constantly working to build, adapt, and rearrange our hierarchical community structure over the years, trying to generate the greatest amount of intersubjective spiritual intensity.

Around the turn of the millennium it looked like our sustained efforts at long last were beginning to bear fruit, as several significant breakthroughs into collective enlightened awareness occurred among groups of my students.

The first one came in 1999 during a ten-day retreat in the South of France, among a group of fourteen women who were novice initiate students. I was sitting with them in a circle in the garden, asking them all to notice the tenacious grasping quality of their sense of individuality and describing to them how they could let go of it together, as a group. Then I got up and walked away. Soon afterward, to my pleasant surprise, they all ignited into a state of collective enlightened awareness. The ecstatic recognition that there is only one without a second was searing through every person in the group and had also come alive in the space *between* them. Each woman had a sense of being united in consciousness with all the others in the group, while simultaneously sustaining their own autonomy, individuality, and uniqueness. As they were sitting on the lawn together, they were laughing. I could hear the thrill, intensity, and excitement in their voices. The ego boundaries between them were gone. Their eyes were bright, and they were all expressing a profound ease of being and an unshakable confidence rooted in the clarity of the direct recognition of their prior unity. This exhilarating shared state lasted for a few weeks, then it faded, and everybody fell back into their previous condition.

Two similar breakthroughs followed, both among the woman's groups, also on public retreats. During these occasions the women spontaneously and unexpectedly shifted into a Higher We state. The depth of the communion they shared made them feel as if they were swimming in a sea of ecstatic intimacy together. From that field of seamless oneness they were able to effortlessly relate to one another. All their defenses dropped, and a spirit of unconditional trust, utterly free from the usual fears, doubts, and suspicions, came alive between them. This allowed them all to show up wide open and transparent and break into a deep and passionate inquiry together—an inquiry driven by an undefended sincerity that was as beautiful as it was powerful. One of these breakthroughs was sustained for months. Then, once again, it dissipated, and the women slid back into their old selves.

Inspired by the promising potential that was revealed in these states, I became determined to build the inner scaffolding necessary to hold this intersubjective egoless consciousness. And so I began to work more intensely with my formal students at Foxhollow to catalyze a breakthrough that would be more sustained. But despite the seriousness of my students' efforts, I observed that even the most committed ones were continuing to allow their ego and sense of self-importance undermine the emergence of the collective enlightenment we were all striving to give rise to. My frustration grew. All these people had unreservedly proclaimed to me that their deepest heart's desire was to devote their lives to the teachings. Such purity of intention, we all knew, can only originate from the deepest core of the self, the part in us that is always already free. And thus I considered it to be my duty as their guru to help them stay anchored in their liberated self. I would not rest until

I felt they were grounded in that source and had embodied an integrity so profound that it inherently transcends ego. I made it abundantly clear that they were going to have to put in a lot more effort to close the gap between their own deepest aspirations and the way they actually conducted their spiritual lives. For many of them my insistence on this kind of self-transcending integrity proved to be too much. Their egos kept resisting the increasing urgency of my call to transform.

In the midst of this challenging period of heightened intensity, I began working with a group of men in a focused attempt to push things to the next level. An intense Dharma battle ensued. I kept raising the psychological pressure in order to pierce through their resistance, demanding that they be absolutely serious and authentic, driving them right up to their breaking point. Month after month of sustained pressure went by without any fundamental change. Desperate to break through the deadlock, I kept upping the ante: either they would take responsibility for their egos or they would leave. My demand put them in an agonizing dilemma: on the one hand they desperately wanted to relinquish their egos, but on the other they felt unable to take that heroic leap. Many slid into a severe existential crisis. Not only was their most important relationship—their irreplaceable bond with their guru—on the line, but for some of my more advanced students on the editorial staff of *What Is Enlightenment?,* their treasured job at the magazine was at risk as well. Yet despite everything they could lose, I could feel that they still weren't genuinely responsive to the higher call they had committed their lives to. And thus having tried everything else, I began to send the men away from the property, to their homes and offices. I was well-aware that I was putting the future of our magazine and organization at risk with this move, but I only cared about uncompromising integrity.

Being sent away from their community of supportive friends was so tough on some of them that it propelled even the most resilient souls into a fierce personal crisis. Yet everybody had been around long enough to know how deeply transformative these crises could be. They had by now all directly experienced how powerfully purifying it was to sit in the metaphorical fire, face their own refusal, and inquire into the seriousness of their intention to be involved in our work. And so most of them persevered. And as their time in seclusion away from the center passed, many of them began to feel they had sufficiently reckoned with their obstacles, and one by one they requested to come back. Their egos' defiant stance had crumbled, and they felt ready to start afresh.

To help them reify their sincere intention to truly embody the teachings and catalyze a collective leap into the authentic self, I instructed about thirty-five of the men to go on a silent retreat together for an indefinite amount of time. They began to practice as if there were no tomorrow. Every single day, they meditated for twelve to sixteen hours. They chanted, did a thousand daily prostrations, and met together at night to engage in intense, earnest self-inquiry to work through their obstacles once and for all. They all knew they needed to transform themselves into embodied examples of the noble spiritual ideals their position in the hierarchy required of them.

After two months, on July 30, 2001, late in the evening, the men finally broke through in what can only be characterized as a volcanic explosion of intersubjective enlightenment. Their contraction dropped; they leapt beyond their sense of a separate self and burst forth into a state of collective nonduality. At the same time, an ecstatic surge of evolutionary urgency erupted from the depths of their authentic self, speaking through all of them directly and spontaneously as one voice. Everybody was uplifted in a state of kosmic awareness, in which their greater purpose for being alive disclosed itself with such clarity that it set them on fire with the passion to co-create the future together. They were all awake to the rare and paradoxical reality of autonomy in communion.

In an ordinary context, autonomy and communion do not arise simultaneously. When one is experienced, the other retreats into the background. But in this rarified We-field, these apparent opposites most naturally unite, because the reality of the one becomes the ground of people's relationships and the source of their intimate communion, and this powerful sense of non-separateness creates an atmosphere in which their full autonomy and distinct differences and uniqueness are free to express themselves most fully. This was the big breakthrough I had been working toward for all these years.

No description can more aptly convey the extraordinary and unique nature of what happened that night and in the weeks following than the words of those who were present. Here are some excerpts from their letters to me:

The taste of true communion in last night's meeting is the most sacred, most serious, most real thing I have ever known. . . . Is this the dawning of Impersonal Enlightenment in a whole group of men? Oh my God! May this fire engulf the world.

◆ ◆ ◆

Last night we literally reached a critical mass and exploded. As more and more voices expressed the same doubtless conviction, the transformative power leapt off the scale of anything we have experienced before; the change in just 24 hours was truly phenomenal as we plunged deeper and deeper into ecstatic intimacy. We were a tornado, absolutely out of control, a raging forest fire burning and consuming all ignorance and separation in our way.

Revelation after revelation as the living understanding of the sweetest perfection of your teaching unraveled in front of our eyes. The emerging presence of a mystery that can never be known, all it recognizes is One, and it's on a seek and destroy mission against all separation. We were on our knees before this miraculous phenomena: impersonal enlightenment—the likes of which has never been experienced or expressed on this planet! What is happening in just 72 hours heralds unbelievable revolutionary possibilities for mankind! . . .

This explosive force is unstoppable; none of us have any idea where we are going, and yet undeniably this is why we are with you, to be consumed in the white heat of perfect communion, and in that, set the whole world on fire.

◆ ◆ ◆

The instant we sat down to meet on Wednesday night, the all-pervading unknowable Mystery that is permeating our experience now was tangibly present. It was there in the silence before the chant, in the one voice of the chant, all the time we spoke—saturating our meeting with unbearable, unthinkable Love that consumes all notions of self and other. This tremendous explosion has unalterably shifted our attention to a vast, unfathomable Presence—it is as if this New Cosmic Being speaks as us, through us, manifesting the bigger view that It alone perceives. We repeatedly returned to the sheer significance of what happened on July 30th—the fact that something altogether unknown has come forth into this universe and that You have proclaimed it to be so. Again and again, the fact that we were there, in this circle bearing witness to this truth brought us to our knees in reverence. The One and the Many, the One and the Many—indivisible and whole we were as one body. This unity destroyed all boundaries between meditation and communion, speech and silence. You are literally transmuting the one physical body that is your men. The divine alchemy is changing the very cells of this one body.

The radiance of this beginning is indescribable. An ecstatic communion that is never separate from who we are is the context. All we are left with is "Oh my God—this is so, this is so, this is so!" The fact that it is in our coming together that this love moves and acts has transformed our meetings into a sacred event. At the end of the meeting we are left speechless and without mark. Our hearts are united with yours in explosive peace.

◆ ◆ ◆

There were times of deep silence in which I was bound together with others across space, out of time. But there were no others. It was utterly beyond my mind to understand what was happening. But I knew that this was consciousness.

The morning after I have a continuing deep sense of calm confidence that comes from seeing so clearly who I am. And I have a huge gratitude to you for your tireless struggle to show us our true nature. Thank you for never giving up.

◆ ◆ ◆

This ecstatic impersonal fire continues to explode unabatedly. The meeting last night was miraculous. After only a few days we were all being swept up in this force of absolute unity. It is burning and burning and burning. And what is there to do? Surrender, surrender, surrender and let it be. Don't impede what is perfectly free of the personal. Let ego scream and let it be true.

All of my ideas about what is possible for me, the men, the revolution and even humanity, are shaking under the impact of what is only the earliest beginnings of your vision.

◆ ◆ ◆

Every man is voicing his own deepest recognition in always new and fresh ways, so alive and dynamic, [in the] continual unfolding of Your Teachings each time we gather. And always the intimacy—the ever-present, ecstatic, doubtless, fearless, explosive intimacy that burns through everything in its path . . .

It is fascinating to see how the collective movement toward ever-greater purity is carrying individuals through their "personal" crises much quicker. The context that has emerged is so huge that it almost forces each individual to see his own situation in a radically different way. Many have described how their practice is always now in that context—not to do with one's own liberation, but only to do with purification so that that which we are discovering together can deepen and become stronger for the sake of the whole. It is an entirely different order of being that we are experiencing collectively, with its own qualities and expressions that one could never experience in isolation, no matter how profound one's experience might be. It is truly remarkable to see the birth of a new organism, arising from the merging of many individual organisms as One, and to experience a dimension of experience that cannot be perceived by the separate individual. . . .

It was remarkable to see the room explode into a very focused, mature, impersonal discussion of ego and of what it means to take responsibility for one's own motivations for the sake of the perfect communion that we are experiencing. The discussion was absolutely real, down to earth, and grounded in deep love and care for you and for the view. After all these years of you imploring the men to have the context, have the context, have the context, we were able to go into an issue of such crucial importance without ever losing that context. . . .

In the meditation at the end of the meeting I felt like the top of my head had been blown off and the force of creation was blasting through me. Several other men said they had the same experience! The intimacy is so ecstatic, so beyond anything that has ever happened between us, that it is hard to even imagine the hell that we were in such a short time ago.

◆ ◆ ◆

Impersonal Enlightenment keeps exploding in between us, as us . . . It seems that with the amount of people joining the view, joining this revolution, the fire and the implications of this happening are growing in an exponential way. There is no mercy with the personal. Any attempts to relate to what is happening in any kind of personal way gets attacked and destroyed on the spot. The mystery discovering itself through us has not any other concern but itself. And as you said, the key to all that seems to be humility, the humility not to deny the fact that we, whoever we are, are nothing but that mystery, to leave it untouched, untainted, only being itself as the eternal exploding truth. This truth is rushing through our veins, pouring out of our cells. There is nothing to claim, nothing to own, because there is nothing but that. Any attempt to get hold of this mystery got destroyed by an outcry of the mystery itself, which does not allow anything to interfere with its absolute beauty and magnificence . . .

The miracle is beyond everything one could imagine! The mind cannot grasp the dimension of this revolution. When the fire took over the whole room yesterday, a new world broke open. We have no idea what is going to happen from here. We have no idea. But the fact is—it has happened. It is happening. There is no way back. A new dimension of human consciousness is opening up. Nothing is as it has been before.

◆ ◆ ◆

Because of your unwillingness to compromise, something unimaginable is unfolding among the men. . . . I only know that it is undeniably real, it is what you have known is possible all along, and that there is a transformative power being unleashed as a result, with implications the magnitude of which none of us can conceive.

◆ ◆ ◆

Last night I finally got it that this is actually enlightenment manifesting between us. It is unheard of that a group of unenlightened people that are willing to *leave themselves behind start to experience the enlightened vision and* be *it. It is amazing how easy it felt, really like a natural state, yet it took you 15 years of hard work to come to this beginning.*

I see now why you call it Evolution! Now something is proven to be possible for the human race as a whole. So with every move we make toward higher forms of harmony and integration, that edge moves further, making also that possible for the whole of humanity! Everything we do becomes suddenly significant for the whole. The idea of personal enlightenment is bypassed completely. It is indeed a by-product . . . With this togetherness with you, and this as how we are together, what we could do in this world is limitless.

◆ ◆ ◆

At that instant a burst of energy swept through us. It swirled faster and faster around the circle, and then it shot straight upward. The top of my head opened up to the heavens, and a profound power surged through me. It felt like a collective kundalini awakening. I felt the stars above me through the opening in the top of my head; we had become a portal to another universe.*

◆ ◆ ◆

Today I feel something fundamental has changed and we are in a different world. . . . Many of the men today are talking from a place way beyond their old limitations and with the full context of what is occurring. What a monumental battle you have had to wage against inertia in all of us to open the doors to the future!

◆ ◆ ◆

In the weeks following this remarkable event, other students traveled to Foxhollow from Europe and were quickly absorbed in the field. The impact of this state lasted for several months, then it began to fade.

---

*This particular description of the breakthrough experience into intersubjective nonduality comes from Jeff Carreira's article "The Miracle of Emergence (and the Troubles with the We-space)," in which he describes his experience of this event. The article was published on his website (www.jeffcarreira.com) in 2018.

One cannot overestimate the defining impact of this breakthrough. Even a decade and a half later, Jeff Carreira, my close assistant for many years, wrote, "After nine years of intense pursuit I had the incredible good fortune to be present during a dramatic emergence of collective Awakening. What I experienced at that time divides my life in half. Who I was before and who I am after is not the same person. . . . I've never recovered from the experiences of true communion that I had at that time, and everything that I do today is ultimately motivated by my deep desire to share that miracle with as many people as possible."[*] To him, the significance of this emergence was such that he later wrote a book about it in an effort to come to an understanding of what it meant.[†]

The eruption of awareness on July 30th had a unique character. Even though there were similarities with the earlier breakthroughs in the women's groups, the differences were clear as well. This event was not a spontaneous arising. It was the result of working directly with these men, consciously creating the most intense conditions imaginable and my exertion of a tremendous amount of pressure over a period of many months. There was a qualitative difference as well. This collective state experience was infinitely compelling to those present because of its sheer power and surging ecstatic intensity, and because everybody was very conscious of the nature of what was occurring. They all seemed to realize, *Oh my God, this is what we have been working for!* Many expressed their gratitude to me for never giving up the fight against egoic resistance. But perhaps the most thrilling dimension of this breakthrough was that we all felt that something truly revolutionary had happened, and that a new capacity had become available for human consciousness.

This breakthrough later came to be known as the day on which the real potential of Evolutionary Enlightenment explosively emerged into

---

[*]See Jeff Carreira's article "The Miracle of Emergence (and the Troubles with the We-space)."
[†]See Jeff Carreira's 2016 book, *The Soul of a New Self: Embracing the Future of Being Human.*

the world. Second only to the day I met my guru, July 30th is still one of the most meaningful days of the year for me. It is the anniversary of the most significant development in my work as a spiritual teacher, and I consider it to be the actual beginning of the real project I had been working toward since I first began to teach.

In the years that followed, we kept fine-tuning the methodology and injunctions for replicating and evoking this Higher We state in order to stabilize it. Through trial and error, making mistakes and picking ourselves up again, we slowly but surely began to better understand the dynamics of collective awakening. Together we discovered and developed the ground rules that helped catalyze the shift from the individual higher self to a Higher We. These early groundbreaking insights are now widely used and have been implemented in spiritual culture by former students of mine who have become teachers themselves.*

Over time, our skillfulness at giving rise to these Higher We states grew, and they began to burst forth with more consistency in different holons within the hierarchy of our sangha. Our efforts to sustain them continued unabated, but after a while these states always dissipated, so I kept exerting pressure on my students. We had all seen proof of the promising potential of these states by now. And this made me more determined than ever to ignite a collective leap into the authentic self, to give rise to the perfect relationship between the one and the many, and to create an atmosphere in which enlightenment would become the foundational context for the entirety of the human experience. This was my dream, my meditation, my constant aspiration. My fire for a real spiritual revolution in humanity was burning brighter than ever. And yet it seemed so difficult for others to get beyond a mere glimpse of this glorious reality.

At times I felt that inspiring my students to lean that deeply into

---

*Different creative expressions of the Higher We work our community at EnlightenNext gave birth to can be found in the work of Pete Bampton, Craig Hamilton, Jeff Carreira, Thomas Steininger, and Elizabeth Debold.

their experience for a purpose greater than their own sense of well-being was the hardest thing in the world to accomplish. Their resistance to my constant call to simply stand free from ego-based motivations often made me feel like I was trying to climb up against the downpouring current of Niagara Falls.

But then at other times, often unexpectedly, the dynamics would shift, and this rarified shared field of awakened awareness would open up between my students. During moments like these they would remember why all the hardship, all the hours of practice, all the drama of doing battle with the ego, all the discomfort of the pressure had been worth it. They would light up with a sense of awe and metaphysical exhilaration, with the purity and transparency of being beyond ego that was just exquisite. They experienced a level of ecstasy most people can't even begin to imagine. In the midst of such sacred occasions we could feel in our every fiber that we were birthing something new and noble in the world. And so I remained convinced that if only we would all be genuinely willing to let go completely, anything could happen. And it wasn't long before it did.

Right in the midst of all the breakthroughs and setbacks, a significant shift occurred that lifted everything up to a whole new level.

It started during a small group meeting in Boston, when a surge of collective enlightened awareness swept through the room, uniting everybody in consciousness, the many mysteriously combining with the one. It was a particularly potent eruption, lighting up the hearts and minds of those present so brightly that they all emerged together as the one body of a new being. In the weeks that followed, I kept holding my breath, expecting that this state would soon ebb away as it always had in the past. But to my great relief and pleasant surprise, it was not only sustained, it began to gain traction. Soon it spread like wildfire, flaring up in gatherings large and small in our centers around the world, affecting my entire international student body. To our amazement, this force field seemed to have a nonlocal effect, as large groups of up to a hundred men and women became absorbed in it during our global conference calls. It was spreading all by itself, like a tidal wave that had heretofore still been mostly out at sea but was now gaining strength and momentum, breaking on our community with immense power. It was thrilling. Had we arrived at a point where the rules of the game had changed?

It was clear that this wave of collective awakening was of a different quality than the breakthrough of July 30th. This new emergence was not the direct result of a prolonged, disciplined ordeal on my students' part, nor was it generated by exerting a great deal of evolutionary pressure on my part. It was a spontaneous, contagious arising, and it was powerful enough to pull anyone into its orbit, irrespective of their level of development. To my great delight, I had to bear witness to the fact that large groups of my students were becoming capable of coming together in enlightened awareness without needing to perform a technique in order to do so. Somehow, this intersubjective egoless field seemed to have reached enough of a critical mass to be readily available for people to tune into. Had it become a self-existing reality, an actual new field in the interior of the kosmos? It was as if what used to be an *ascending path of effort,* in which you, as the ego, strive to reach enlightenment, had to some degree reversed its direction and turned into a *descending path of grace,* in which this egoless collective field pours down and becomes the starting point of spiritual practice. If this was indeed the case, then the very nature of our spiritual practice and what it meant to perform it had radically changed. Practice, then, would no longer be about trying to get somewhere we were not, but about deepening our awareness of this new potential, which was already a reality, and aligning ourselves with it moment to moment. While bearing witness to the spontaneous ease of this emergence, it began to dawn on me that this was indeed a shift of a different order, and that we had finally arrived at a new beginning.

In the wake of this shift, a sense of exhilaration and deep self-confidence began to engulf many of my students, fueling an even deeper commitment in them to genuinely live the teachings. As a result, a significant number of them began to reach a degree of stability in which a perspective beyond ego was becoming their natural orientation. Enough of us had finally reached a more or less stable plateau state* of shared enlightened awareness, or intersubjective nonduality. This was so deeply meaningful and fulfilling for all of us that I felt moved to mark the auspicious occasion. So I gathered the entire community and gave a landmark talk, relating the turbulent history leading up to what I felt signified the real birth of radical intersubjective Evolutionary Enlightenment in the world. It was a declaration of victory, a public affirmation that the vision I had until now only intuited and had single-mindedly pursued all these years had finally manifested. The date was November 20, 2005, a day we came to refer to as "Declaration Day."

To this day I consider the emergence of intersubjective evolutionary nonduality to be one of our work's most valuable contributions to postmodern spiritual culture. In the traditional spiritual context, the focus remains on personal enlightenment, the realization of the Ground of Being contained within the consciousness of the individual, the enlightened one. But in this newly evolving expression of nonduality, enlightened awareness breaks out of the boundaries of the "I" space and emerges in the shared We-field between individuals in a group. I had always intuited that unless this leap is taken, the ultimate power of enlightenment to affect deep change in the world would remain inherently limited. But the shift from the traditional ideal of an enlightened "I" to this new form of an enlightened "we" opens up a reality of an entirely different order. It's like a burning match turning into a raging forest fire. Why? Because the moment enlightened awareness is released into the We-field, it can begin to flow freely into the world through the many. As this happens, real collective change can begin to emerge *from within,* since the We-field is the carrier of the values, perspectives, and worldviews we share. It is our collective interior, the domain where culture lives and is advanced. And thus, working with the "we" space within an evolutionary context will uplift our values and widen our perspectives and worldviews.

---

*For more on this concept, see chapter 11.

At this point in history, most of our cultural values, beliefs, and perspectives come from the traditional amber altitude, the modern orange altitude, and the postmodern green altitude, or from a mixture thereof, as seen in figure 3.1 or plate 1. In most of us, only a fraction of our values and perspectives originate from levels higher than green, and thus most of our responses to the world's most pressing sociocultural challenges arise from these often outdated cultural values and less than enlightened perspectives. But if enough people were to be able to come together in the direct experience of their prior unity and awaken to the future-oriented evolutionary vibrancy of their authentic self, then the more inclusive kosmocentric perspective that is disclosed in these Higher We states would begin to inform and create a new and nobler value structure in our culture. Their gatherings would begin to generate truly creative conversations that can result in new solutions to old conundrums. They would bring forth fresh, creative capacities that prompt original solutions that can more adequately address the highly complex challenges we face in this world in crisis. And thus at this turbulent moment in history, the emergence of intersubjective evolutionary nonduality carries the power to orient us to a brighter future. For a visual representation of the potential for cultural revolution, see figures 4.1 and 4.2 on the following page.

During the years following Declaration Day, we poured all our energy and attention into converting this now more easily accessible Higher We state into a permanent trait. I began to instruct my students that when they enter this state together, they should do so very consciously. I asked them to look at their experience as an object: scrutinize it with discernment and try to distinguish clearly between the extraordinary experiential qualities like ecstasy, intimacy, and lightness of being that naturally go along with this state and the higher kosmocentric perspective that is revealed in them. This more embracing perspective is the real source of these exhilarating-feeling qualities, and anchoring yourself in it rather than getting lost in the attractiveness of these fleeting higher feelings was, I felt, key to turning these Higher We states into a lasting, stable pattern.

I believed that if enough of us could take our practice to that level,

Evolutionary Enlightenment

Becoming

Intersubjective Nonduality
Natural Hierarchy
Autonomy
Communion
Evolutionary Tension
Egoless Passion
Ecstatic Intimacy

Higher Values

New Intersubjective Structures

Cosmic Conscience

The Process Perspective

Face Everything & Avoid Nothing

The Power of Volition

Clarity of Intention

THE SELF-ABSOLUTE

The Evolutionary Impulse — The Authentic Self

Transparency

Evolving **CULTURE**

Cultivating the **SOUL**

Integrity :: Conscience :: Authenticity

THE GROUND OF BEING

Being

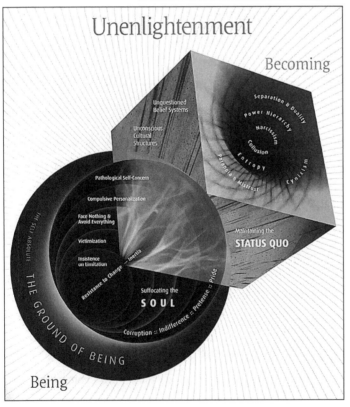

Unenlightenment

Becoming

Separation & Duality
Power Hierarchy
Narcissism
Collusion
Entropy
Paranoia & Mistrust
Cynicism

Unquestioned Belief Systems

Unconscious Cultural Structures

Pathological Self-Concern

Compulsive Personalization

Face Nothing & Avoid Everything

Victimization

Insistence on Limitation

THE SELF-ABSOLUTE

Resistance to Change :: Inertia

Maintaining the **STATUS QUO**

Suffocating the **SOUL**

Pride

Corruption :: Indifference :: Pretense :: Pretense

THE GROUND OF BEING

Being

Figures 4.1 and 4.2. Teaching models of Evolutionary Enlightenment depicting the potential for cultural evolution in an enlightenment context versus an egoic context (see also color plates 5 and 6).

the Higher We would eventually take root among my student body as a stable structure. At that point, a different dynamic would open up in our work together: the Higher We would then give rise to a thriving Triple Gem organism, in which the Buddha, the Dharma, and the Sangha would operate as a seamless, self-generating whole. And this, I felt, would render the role of the guru, as I had enacted it up until this point, unnecessary.

On occasion I shared this intuition with my students. In an interview that took place in the early 2000s, I proclaimed:

> If enough individuals reach a level of maturity where they're able to consistently remain beyond ego as the authentic self, this higher consciousness or enlightened mind will actually emerge as the foundation of their relationships. When such a point is reached, then the role of the individual teacher is going to become a thing of the past. When this new potential becomes stable, I feel that the traditional function of the guru is going to work through the collective in a miraculous way that has never happened before. But until that point, having a living teacher is essential.[1]

At times we felt as if the emergence of this future vision was imminent, since several holonic groups were now able to hold a large degree of integrity, wideness, and inclusiveness of the kosmocentric perspective for prolonged periods of time. Still, regressions kept occurring, leaving us profoundly humbled by the immense challenge of building internal structures in consciousness and culture that would be strong enough to truly stabilize the thrilling new potential of collective enlightenment.

All in all, by the first decade of the new millennium, our work together had reached an entirely new level of maturity. EnlightenNext had become a thriving, vibrant, innovative spiritual culture. The teachings were flowering. They were carrying more Integral complexity, which reflected our discovery of Integral Theory, and were pouring out of me more abundantly than ever. Attendance at my annual retreats was high.

My new book, *Evolutionary Enlightenment: A New Path to Spiritual Awakening*,[2] had just been published, and people beyond the spiritual world had taken an interest in Evolutionary Enlightenment as a new teaching and in me as a teacher and speaker. Our sangha had reached a new level of integrity and wholeness. For the first time, a coherent group of three- to four hundred people were all working together with an unusual level of coherence in an imperfect, fragile, delicate, yet stable hierarchical structure that was largely self-generating, supportive, and beautiful.

As many of my students began to awaken to the exhilarating reality of intersubjective nonduality, the extreme pressure I was putting on people's egos began to diminish. It didn't completely cease, but the need for it was ending because the collective field that had opened up among so many of us was inherently and spontaneously ego transcending, and it began to work its miracles.

In hindsight, this was the moment when I should have relinquished my mythic identity as an old-school guru and given my students more autonomy. But since the Higher We never stabilized with any kind of finality, I remained reluctant to change my ways. I was convinced that if I were to stop exerting evolutionary pressure completely and revise my position as the one in charge of everything, the delicate structure of the spiritual culture we had built together with so much dedication and care over the course of almost three decades would quickly collapse, and the beautiful We-space we had co-created to hold, safeguard, and advance this exciting new development in consciousness and culture would be lost.

5

Dark Release

In the midst of all the positivity and vibrancy of our evolutionary culture, signs began to appear that something was brewing beneath the surface. There was growing dissatisfaction among the senior students, who were becoming increasingly frustrated with my role within the leadership team of EnlightenNext. For years our organization had been losing money, and now a looming financial crisis was taking hold. For anyone with eyes to see it was clear that the ship was sailing toward a cliff.

Over the years, some members of the senior leadership had made several radical suggestions to save our organization, including selling Foxhollow and ceasing the publication of the magazine. But I invariably felt that these drastic measures hit so deeply at the core of our shared endeavor that I didn't consider them seriously. Foxhollow was the beating heart of our world, and the magazine was our inroad into the larger culture. Some within senior leadership wanted us to downsize, but I was on fire with the passion for growth. I was so eager to break through into the mainstream that I kept pushing new initiatives that EnlightenNext couldn't carry: I wanted our magazine to come out four times a year, not just twice. I wanted our "Voices from the Edge" series, in which luminaries and leading-edge thinkers featured in our magazine gave talks at our centers around the world, to happen more often. I wanted to work more closely with other spiritual and cultural organizations, such as Ken Wilber's Integral community.

When the management team pushed back against my expansionist tendencies in their attempt to protect our organization, I didn't always take their objections as seriously as I should have. I was thinking, *I am the visionary; we are gonna do this! And it should be glaringly obvious to you all why we need to.* I wasn't going to ask their permission. I firmly believed that these initiatives would be successful and would open up all kinds of opportunities for everybody, including financial ones. I was convinced that in the long run, pushing for growth would be a wise move. But whenever organizational or financial problems were brought to my attention, more often than not I thought, *My job is to teach the Dharma. You all are supposed to take care of the rest.* Being the spiritual leader, I didn't feel obligated to take responsibility for our financial survival. I disregarded the fact that EnlightenNext was not a well-functioning modern organization with a clean separation of spiritual and organizational authority. And in my zeal to push for growth, our organization began to crack under the pressure.

Thus a human drama that had been looming for some time was about to unfold, but I remained oblivious to it. Long-term students were paid low wages or lost their jobs when the magazine eventually went out of business in 2010. Many of them had come to me when they were young adults. Now they were middle-aged, and a lot of them felt trapped in a structure that didn't seem to offer them future opportunities. Understandably, they became concerned with their own financial survival. Some of them wanted to be more autonomous and work with me in a different way, but I didn't recognize their need. I should have responded in a manner that would have opened doors for them. Instead, I felt threatened. I was afraid of losing power and control. So they had the feeling that I didn't care, and the thinking seemed to go along the lines of *We can't go on like this. We are stuck in a system that is on the brink of collapse, and Andrew doesn't get it!* Out of the corner of my eye I could see all these stresses on the system. Still, I didn't take them seriously. I naively and arrogantly believed that we would find a way through because we all loved one another.

◄ ▪ ►

One evening during my last teaching tour through Europe, I went to a pub in London with a longtime student and dear friend of mine. He was angry, tired of me wanting to push things forward all the time. He looked me in the eyes and said with great passion, "Andrew, everything has to stop! Just stop! Don't you ever want to take a break? This is all crazy. We just need to stop everything completely, at least for six months!" He was exploding. I looked at him, taken aback, thinking, *What on earth is he talking about? Is he out of his mind?* Our work was thriving and we were doing better than ever before—at least from my perspective.

On another occasion, another one of my senior students voiced his concerns about my teaching style of putting evolutionary pressure on people. He expressed that from Declaration Day onward, all the pushing should have come to an end, as it could no longer be justified. This teaching method had been most intensely applied during the impersonal enlightenment phase, which was the toughest and darkest phase of our work, and it had already greatly diminished with the advent of Evolutionary Enlightenment. Still, the pressure hadn't completely stopped. I was still applying it, although in a more limited way, and only on those who had fully dedicated themselves to realizing our shared vision.

I kept ignoring these critiques, and frustration among my senior leadership kept growing. Eventually my denial became untenable, and the senior students decided it was time to intervene. They went on retreat together and discussed their dissatisfactions with my style of leadership. Up until this point it was taken for granted as a matter of principle that nobody would question my authority. Yet now, for the first time, they all found the courage to voice their resentments and doubts about my role as their guru.

After their retreat they delivered a message to me, stating that they wanted to have a serious discussion about their concerns. I had always insisted that all communications with me as a guru needed to measure up to a well-defined standard of etiquette and appropriateness.

But in their frustration they approached me in what I felt was a less than respectful way. It was clear that my position as the leader of EnlightenNext was being questioned in a way it never had before. This I found both intimidating and unacceptable, and I used the fact that they had broken protocol as an excuse not to meet with them. I was enraged that my authority and power were being challenged and I wasn't going to let them get away with it. I was also terrified because I didn't know what they were up to. I heard their demands as rebelliousness, so I instructed them to purge themselves from that adolescent surge of egoic resistance and place our common goal front and center again. Little did I understand that we had long moved past the point where my spiritual instructions were gratefully taken to heart and unpretentiously implemented.

My unwillingness to tackle the situation head-on and work through it with them led to a six-month standoff between myself and my senior students. Rather than listening to the wisdom of my closest and most trusted friends, I was outraged that I was being challenged this way. For almost three decades I had been teaching my students to transcend their pride and become open and humble. Now, my own pride was getting the better of me. There was a painful lack of humility in the way I held on to the absolute authority of my guru persona.

Finally, one of the senior students wrote me a long, angry letter in which he expressed the grievances and resentments among them all that had by now reached a boiling point. He told me that I was out of touch with reality and that my world was crumbling. He added that I was in denial of these conspicuous facts, and that I therefore wasn't living my own teaching to face everything and avoid nothing. Being confronted with reality like this, I could no longer look away, nor could I continue to hide behind my authority and pride.

So after six months I came around, finally realizing the degree to which I had betrayed my senior students' trust, and with great urgency I invited everybody to come together to work out our problems. But for them it was too little, too late. A line had been drawn in the sand, and a united front formed that was ready to launch a coordinated effort to push for effective change. The die had been cast, but I still didn't see the signs that some of them had already decided to burn the house down.

My senior students and some members of our board called a meeting in Lisbon to address the crisis. I knew that I had made some serious errors of judgment, but I was still in denial about the ramifications. Now I was being called out and confronted with my denials, and I was scared to death. Still, I was prepared to do whatever it would take to save our precious work, so I chose to simply trust and surrender, trust and surrender, trust and surrender.

Right before the meeting, the head of human resources, who was also a board member, took me aside. He put a document in front of me along with a perplexing proposition: I was to resign as president of the board of EnlightenNext, Inc. Anyone in his right mind would have responded, "Are you completely mad? This is my life's work! Let me talk to my lawyer and I'll get back to you." But my undefended intention to trust and surrender kept echoing through my soul, and I simply signed. With one quick scribble on a piece of paper, I signed away my professional life and rights and gave up all control of my organization. With that, I had also entrusted the full responsibility of my life's work to the board, and as such, to my students.

When I entered this meeting, there were about ten people waiting for me, most of whom I had been intimate friends with for many years. Some of them were very angry, and there was a feeling of incredible discontent in the room. The tension was so thick you could cut it with a knife, and before we knew it we were all immersed in an intense discussion. It was the strangest experience. People were talking as if I wasn't even in the room with them, saying things like, "The teachings *have* to change!" As everybody in the room in turn spoke their mind, little by little their position became clear: the majority of those present wanted independence. They felt that in order to move forward in their lives, they needed to be free from the constrictions and obligations of the guru-disciple relationship, and as such they no longer wanted to answer to me as their guru. Still, they wanted to stay in touch with the work somehow. A smaller group wanted to continue working with me as their guru, to further develop the deep spiritual work we had all been committed to for so long. One of them was sobbing. He could see that the others were trying to destroy our precious community structure and said to them, "What you are all doing is unbearable to me." The atmosphere in the room was saturated with conflicted emotions. But despite our differences, everyone present seemed to agree that they wanted to remain connected to the future of EnlightenNext in one way or another. So we all agreed to work out the specifics at some point in the future.

As I walked out of the meeting, I saw one of the senior women who was still deeply supportive of our vision sitting alone outside, with tears in her eyes. She said, "Oh my God! They're gonna burn it all down!" You could hear the anguish in her voice. She had committed the past seven years of her life to setting up our education system and felt utterly desperate about the prospect of seeing it all fall apart. It was heartbreaking.

After that pivotal meeting, my former assistant accompanied me to my hotel. He was unusually quiet. I loved him so much that I couldn't bear his silence. He was my closest friend, my most devoted disciple, and my confidant, someone I could call even in the middle of the night if some problem was occurring in the community. We passed a restaurant and I said, "Why don't we have dinner and a glass of wine?" I couldn't bear the growing distance between us. We sat down and I bought him dinner. We had a glass of wine, and another one, and then yet another one. Finally he said, "Andrew, I really think you should take some time off and do some therapy. You've hurt a lot of people, and I don't think you really get it. You've created karma you aren't even aware of, and you need to deal with it."

I knew he wasn't wrong. Still, if I was truthful with myself I had to admit there was no inclination in me whatsoever to step down as a guru or even to simply take some time off. Our work was flourishing. The Higher We all of us had aspired to give rise to for so long was finally emerging. The teachings of Evolutionary Enlightenment were inspiring larger audiences than ever and were starting to reach into the mainstream. I was on fire. We were gaining momentum. Stopping at this point, right when our work was about to reach a whole new level, seemed downright crazy. I also couldn't relate to the idea that taking a break would solve anything. All I knew was that my closest, most intimate friends on Earth were really angry, and I desperately wanted to appease them. I loved them, I trusted them, and I wanted to do anything to win back their trust. So right then and there, in the spirit of trust and surrender, I agreed to take a break. I submitted to what my senior students thought was needed, just as they had surrendered to me all these years.

The next morning I broke the news to the others: I was going to take a six-month sabbatical. My announcement was met with surprise and disbelief. Nobody really expected me to go through with it, even after all the discussion and all the pressure some of them had exerted on me. I would use my time off to focus on my own practice, search my soul, face my shadow, sit in the fire, recognize where I had gone wrong, and find ways to make it right. We all agreed that in six months' time we would meet again to reevaluate the situation, assess my progress, and figure out a way to move forward together.

It would be a giant leap into the unknown for all of us. Nobody knew exactly where we were heading. Only one thing was for sure: after my sabbatical, everything would be different. Whatever else the future of EnlightenNext would hold, my students would no longer be merely my followers. They would be autonomous partners with a more powerful voice. Everything would be up for discussion. It was clear that operating our community based on the outmoded archetype of the mythic guru with absolute authority was no longer viable. I knew this meant the loss of my power, and I felt a deep discomfort about that. But this was the agreement we all came to, so I acquiesced, and I entered my sabbatical in a spirit of trust and surrender.

On June 26, 2013, I wrote a short letter of apology and announced my sabbatical:

I'm fifty-seven years old and currently find myself facing the biggest challenge of my life. I've been a teacher of spiritual enlightenment for twenty-seven years. Enlightenment has always been and always will be about transcending the ego.

Over the last several years, some of my closest students have tried to make it apparent to me that in spite of the depth of my awakening, my ego is still alive and well.

I've understood this simple truth—that we all have egos no matter how enlightened we may be—and even taught it to thousands of people all over the world throughout my career. But when I was being asked to face my own ego by those who were nearest and dearest to me, I resisted. And I often made their lives difficult as a result.

I'm aware that many of my students over the years have also been affected by my lack of awareness of this part of myself. And for those of you who are reading this, I apologize. As time passes I intend to reach out and engage in a process of dialogue with those of you who would like to.

In light of all this, for the sake of my own integrity as a spiritual teacher and as a human being, I've decided that I need to take some time off so I can make the effort to develop in many of the ways that I've asked other people to. Starting this fall, once I've fulfilled some prior commitments, I'm going to embark on a sabbatical for an extended period of time. During this hiatus I will be stepping down from the leadership of my organization. I won't be publishing anything here on my blog and will not be doing any public teaching. My intention is to become a better teacher and, more importantly, a better man.

One of the most beautiful fruits of my work over the years has been the international network of people who have studied, collaborated, and trained with me for so long. They are all examples of Evolutionary Enlightenment in their own right, and I couldn't imagine a greater community of people to carry forward this movement. I'm looking forward to working with them in a very different way in the future.

With my intention to work with my student body differently, the mythic guru in me had effectively died. Little did I know that despite my good intentions, all hell was about to break loose.

When I arrived back home at Foxhollow, I had a group call with the resolute core students to talk about the situation. They were the younger segment of the community, the Navy Seals of Evolutionary Enlightenment—really smart, very inspired, and deeply committed to living the teachings. I tried to be as transparent and vulnerable with them as I could and admitted that some of my actions leading up to this crisis had been driven by motives in myself that I hadn't been aware of. The moment I said that you could hear a pin drop. This was not what I had been teaching with so much conviction, confidence, and clarity over the last decades. The second tenet of our teachings, the power of volition, boldly declares that on some level we always know *exactly* what we're doing. We can become conscious of all our motivations and take responsibility for all our actions, if only we choose to do so.

Having gone through the fiercest battles within themselves to try to live up to this tenet, the resolute core students were dumbfounded to hear my confession. The teacher they had trusted unconditionally had failed to live up to his own teachings? *If even he couldn't do it, then what right did he have to demand such heroic efforts from us, often pushing us right up to our breaking point?* They felt outraged, deeply disillusioned, and betrayed.

Years ago, they had responded to the sacred call of their own deepest inspiration; they had gathered all their spiritual courage and had proclaimed a wholehearted "yes!" to living the teachings. Now it wasn't so clear anymore whether it was actually possible to do so. Their sacred commitment snapped. All of a sudden, they were losing their connection to what had been most important to them for all these years. In their outrage, they stopped doing practice and started rebelling.

Soon an atmosphere of confusion, anger, and resentment erupted all over Foxhollow, as if some dark and destructive force had been unleashed. The resolute core students started to get together every night and held wild and bitter drinking parties. They were all crazed. Lower impulses were erupting all around us. It was hell on Earth.

People woke up to the fact that they had been living in an overly rigid hierarchical system, and they were hell-bent on freeing themselves from it. The few senior students who were still there trying to keep it all together were no longer treated with respect. The resolute core students answered their attempts with defiant anger: "Fuck the hierarchy. I don't have to listen to anything you say. You can't tell me what to do! I do whatever I want. Fuck you!" They seemed possessed with an urge to smash it all to pieces. Foxhollow felt like a war zone. People felt burned, ripped-off, and angry. They argued and swore at one another over nothing. They cursed their dear friends when they were only trying to solve problems. Egos were getting pumped up with power—the power to destroy. To them it felt like the power of their liberated autonomy. But all I could see was the force of Thanatos, the archetypal death urge, sweeping through the community at an incredible speed, destroying everything in its wake. It was uncontrollable—a powerful collective force, stronger than any individual and larger than any personal grievances.

Whether spiritual or organizational, the destruction was so thorough that it ate away at everything we had so painstakingly built together over the past three decades. The delicate but powerful buddha-field of spiritual transmission, reverence, respect, calm, equilibrium, and unshakable intention that had always been Foxhollow's hallmark just vaporized. The hierarchy caved under the pressure, and the rarified atmosphere in which everybody trusted everybody else dissolved right before our eyes.

Suspicion crept in, and people began to turn away from one another and from the community. Fractures and schisms were opening everywhere. It was a dark release.

To my shock and horror I realized that nobody was going to honor our original agreement to keep it all going while I was on sabbatical. Nobody was going to be waiting six months for me to come back. People started packing their bags and began leaving one by one. My closest friends, my most trusted colleagues—people I had known and worked with and lived with for decades—wouldn't even wait one month. They just left. The shockwaves spread around the world, and one by one our international centers closed down.

Before we fully realized what was going on, the whole drama went public in an explosion of bad press. Rumors and counterrumors flew through cyberspace. My detractors went crazy on the internet: "Finally we got him! Haven't we said so all along? The emperor has no clothes!" All the old stories about exerting extreme pressure on people's egos to force breakthroughs got recycled and began to have new life, even though most of this had occurred many years ago and I had abandoned this as a teaching tactic. The critical books several former students had written about me and my work suddenly received new legitimacy. No one in our community had paid these sources any serious attention before, even as some of the books had been out for more than a decade. But all of a sudden, this negative narrative became the new truth of who I was and what we had all been doing together. People began to doubt the teachings, the philosophy, and their own judgment—and mine. A tidal wave of negativity engulfed everyone and further fortified the drama of the collapse. Everyone was scared. People I had lived with every day, who knew me very well, suddenly began to look at me through different eyes: "Oh my goodness, what did we get involved with? Andrew is not who we thought he was." All of a sudden I was branded with many of the damning pathological labels that our psychologized culture offers in abundance. I was a malignant narcissist, a sociopath, a megalomaniac, a secret sadist— all descriptions meant to communicate that there was a dark streak in me, something so fundamentally corrupt that I was beyond cure. I was seen as the master manipulator who had colonized other people's energy and turned them into his advocates in ways they couldn't account for. Once these labels had taken hold in people's minds, any kind of nuanced consideration about me as a teacher or about the paradoxical results of our shared radical experiment was effectively dead.

It was both painful and perplexing to see how quickly and dramatically the narrative had shifted. In particular, the resolute core students' former enthusiasm flipped almost overnight. One day they thought they had the greatest teacher in the world and were part of a leading-edge spiritual community, only to wake up the next morning thinking their teacher was a madman and they were part of a crazy cult. They shifted from believing that the instances of my exerting extreme pressure were part of their trial by fire, essential to creating the strong structure they were benefiting from, to now thinking that our entire utopian project was insane and that they had all been brainwashed.

Curiously, their doubts had very little to do with the reality of their own experience. Up to this point their experience of me and our community had been mostly positive and profound. They had experienced higher states of consciousness and evolutionary breakthroughs. They had enjoyed the unusual depth and sincerity of their companions and had been nourished by the loving support of their community. All of it had felt so enriching that the negativity of the public narrative simply didn't feel relevant to them—the gap between their own experience and the public criticism was just too wide. This made the abrupt shift of interpretation all the more puzzling. Why would people now suddenly put the negative experiences of somebody else above their own positive experiences? It was as if postmodern cynicism and secular materialism had taken over again, their shrill voices whispering in everybody's ear, *It's all bullshit! Bullshit!* The whole dynamic felt like a battle between opposite extremes. Our shared experiment had always been about nothing less than creating Heaven on Earth, a twenty-first-century utopian culture of people living together beyond ego. The shadow reflection of utopian idealism is extreme nihilism—and that is exactly what had been unleashed.

I continued to have three or four calls a day with different groups of committed students all over the world in a desperate attempt to keep it all together. I spoke to everybody. It couldn't have been very satisfying for them because I was in a confused state, repeating what others had been telling me, still announcing to everybody, "Yes, I'm going to take six months off. I'll teach again, but I won't be a guru." It wasn't me speaking. I was doing what I thought people wanted me to do. I kept apologizing to everyone. I did my level best to be honest and sincere, but some people said, "He doesn't even know what he's apologizing for." It was horrible. People cried when they talked to me, or they got angry and shamed me, and I simply sat there, taking the blame. I passively participated with everybody, going along with whatever they brought to me. Suddenly, everybody had become an expert on everything that was wrong, and I was the only one who still didn't get it. It was so undignified. It wasn't good for me or for them.

I felt disempowered, humbled, and devastated. I had been a guru for most of my adult life and I didn't know anything else. The guru had become my primary identity. It was who I *was*. The moment I gave up my power by signing my resignation and surrendering my authority, I no longer knew who I was. My primary identity was shattered and, along with that, I lost access to enlightened awareness, to my own depth, to the teachings, to the transmission—it was all gone. I fell back into the self I had been before I met my master, the self with the subpersonality of the loser, the one with a problem. That self had no access to everything I knew. It was like nothing had ever happened. My access to enlightened awareness seemed to depend on dignity, on self-respect, and in some way on the natural authority of being the guru.

When my students saw me in this weakened condition, they were furious. "Our fearless leader! Look at him now!" The person they had known was nowhere to be found. They were profoundly disturbed that I had lost touch with my own teachings when they were called for and needed most, and in my regressed state I had no response for them. The moment I gave up my power, I literally went from being a powerful, self-confident teacher to being a haunted ghost. I could only watch helplessly how everything was crashing and burning before my very eyes. I should have shouted, "Stop the music, everybody! Let's take a step back and do this thoughtfully!" But there was nothing I could do. I had convinced myself that I had to go along with what my closest friends expected me to do, and without my role as the guru and the chairman of EnlightenNext, I didn't have any measure of authority at all to turn the tide. So I retreated. In the evenings I drank a lot of alcohol and took sedatives to sleep, just to try to keep myself together. But I was barely holding on . . .

Before embarking on my sabbatical, I needed to fulfill some prior commitments. So in the summer of 2013, after two months of living at Foxhollow in a state of shock, I conducted my last ten-day retreat in Florence, Italy. The attendance at this annual event was down by roughly half. During the retreat I realized to my utter surprise that, despite the turmoil, I could still teach. My enlightened disposition and access to the teachings would temporarily reactivate while speaking to the audience and assuming the guru function again. The teachings of nonduality in particular still came through with natural ease, clarity, precision, and intense transmission power. It was truly mysterious.

Between teachings, however, I couldn't have been in a darker, more psychotic place. I remember lying on my bed, literally in a state of abject terror. In the past my students would come to my room to check on me, bring me things, and look after me. But now I was alone, and nobody cared about me any longer. Still, the moment it was time for me to go to the big hall and teach, I could somehow suddenly access that which is prior to all suffering and speak from that place.

Meanwhile, the disintegration of what was left of our community structure continued unabated. Behind the scenes of this public event, factions were forming, and people were discussing who was going to take power over what. Respect for the existing hierarchical order and for my position as guru was gone. Whereas most of my students were going along with this new attitude, several remained supportive of me, including Daniela, one of my committed core students. She later shared with me how she felt about what she saw happening:

> It was heartbreaking. Most of us had always experienced the guru-disciple bond as the most profound relationship one can enter into in this life. We had all felt the direct transmission of enlightened awareness flowing through Andrew, and it had awakened the deepest part of our own selves. Whenever such an awakening occurs, most people naturally respond with immense gratitude, spontaneous surrender, and profound love. We all knew from direct experience that the guru is a portal to our own higher nature. He represents Spirit itself—which is one's own true self—and thus respect for the guru is respect for Spirit.

So to me, the loss of respect for the guru felt deeply inappropriate and dark. It felt like slapping Spirit in the face—especially in this sacred atmosphere of a retreat, where everybody came together for a higher purpose.

I can still remember the group dinner we had with Andrew after the retreat. Usually, the conversation would be centered around the guru and nobody would chitchat among themselves. But this time, everybody was engaged in one-on-one discussions with one another. Andrew still sat in the middle of the big table as he always did, but he was no longer the center of our attention. All people talked about was how relieved they were that the hierarchy had crumbled. They felt they had been freed from the obligation of the guru-disciple relationship, and they were celebrating their newfound autonomy. To me there was something deeply disconcerting about this kind of freedom. People seemed to be losing touch with the sacred, with verticality. My whole being was screaming *this is not right!* It felt like mutiny. Even as Andrew needed to change his ways, and we as a culture needed to change the way we operated, this was not a dignified way to do it. I felt appalled by the way everybody seemed completely disconnected—not only from Andrew as the guru, but even, in a much more basic sense, from his humanity as a broken man in a difficult situation. It was distasteful. To me, it felt as if the mythic guru had just died in Andrew, and people were already dancing on his grave.

Meanwhile, in the United States, Foxhollow was closing down at a rapid pace. While everybody was leaving, my wife, Alka, stayed behind and almost singlehandedly took responsibility for planning, organizing, and executing all the practicalities that went along with closing our sizable estate. As fewer and fewer people were staying on the premises, more and more rooms were becoming vacant; offices were emptied out, and a wide range of materials needed to be sorted through. One by one, all the buildings on the property were shut down as we gradually decreased our footprint. The atmosphere of profound spiritual confusion coupled with the speed at which everything had happened had created plenty of chaos and disarray. With careless abandon, people just dumped everything they wanted to get rid of in the meditation hall while Alka was still cleaning up after them. Living alone in our house during the time I was out of the country, she spent many months seeing to it that every single item was handled with focused attention and with the respect she felt it deserved. She made sure everything would end up at its right destination. She gave artifacts away to other institutions; she contacted people who over the years had given gifts to me, asking them whether they wanted their articles back; and she sold items that didn't have a clear destination, organizing over a dozen public garage sales in what used to be the sacred space of our meditation hall. Neighbors and local villagers flocked to our ashram grounds to buy our belongings, gratefully seizing the opportunity for a good bargain to supplement their kitchenware, furnish their living rooms, set up their offices, or decorate their children's bedrooms. Everybody seemed to assume that this was Alka's job because of her relationship with me, but her motivation came from a deeper place. She saw the proper, respectful closure of Foxhollow as her way of honoring the sacred vision Foxhollow stood for, paying tribute to the grace-filled beauty of our lives together, and showing her gratitude for all the spiritual gifts we had been blessed with all these years. She held down the fort, having made the decision that she wasn't going to leave until the closure of our cherished community center was brought to an appropriate completion.

A mere three months after signing my resignation papers in Lisbon, our thriving community had completely disintegrated. The moment I relinquished my power there was no turning the tide. Nobody was in control anymore, and nobody was thinking clearly about alternatives—how to correct course or move more thoughtfully and slowly. The profound power of our deep alignment and shared vision was gone.

On the morning of December 31, 2013, the last of the trucks rolled in to pick up the rest of our community's belongings, and the doors of Foxhollow were effectively closed. EnlightenNext ceased to exist as a global organization. Its funds were donated to a university because people were convinced it was all blood money and we shouldn't hold on to it. Nobody had thought about my future, even financially. My salary was cancelled and I was laid off like an employee. I didn't know how I was going to support myself or my wife. Fortunately, a few generous supporters came forth to help me provide for our basic needs for a while. The only thing the organization allowed me to retain in the end was the rights to my last book. Even our trademark, Evolutionary Enlightenment, was cancelled rather than being handed over to me as its founder.

I had lost everything: my career, my life's work, my livelihood, my community, my access to enlightened awareness, my dignity, and even my basic human sanity. I was shell-shocked. I went through bouts of deep despair and experienced suicidal feelings every day. For almost thirty years I had been lit up by the spiritual brightness of enlightenment. During all that time I had never experienced anything to compare with this depth of suffering. Now, after flying so high for so long, I had spiraled down into a seemingly bottomless abyss of emotional darkness I never even knew existed. The deep humiliation of being a fallen icon was mortifying; the grief over the loss of my community never seemed to cease; and my feelings of loneliness, abandonment, and rejection by those dearest to me were unbearable. The loss of everything was ruthless, and the speed at which it had all happened made it all the more disorienting.

Some months earlier, when in a spirit of trust and surrender I reluctantly submitted to what my senior students wanted, I could never have imagined that that which was intended as a six-month sabbatical would end up becoming an indefinite leave, with no end in sight.

6

Two Hands
Are All You Need

In this ominous spirit of dark despair and shock, my journey of atonement began. Nothing in my world made sense any longer. Every morning I woke up to the same desperate thought: *I want my life back!* I didn't have a clue as to what my next step could possibly be. But I was prepared to do the one thing that would change everything.

I was aware that in relation to my students, I had never excelled at empathy. I wasn't a compassionate type of guru. Being in the guru role, my human and practical needs had always been looked after by my students, whereas I myself had never cared for anybody's basic needs. So I figured that perhaps a dramatic U-turn would really help me remedy my shortcomings. And thus I began playing with the most atypical idea I could conjure up: what if I were to go to the Mother Teresa Center in Calcutta, India, and care for the sick and the dying? Such an out-of-character move would surely expand my capacity for empathy and sensitize me to human suffering in a deeper way.

One morning, as I was meditating upstairs in my house at Foxhollow, the idea of going to Calcutta arose in my awareness again. As soon as it did, a dramatic vision of my guru basking in golden light appeared in my mind's eye. Against the background of all my despair, this epiphany felt all the more powerful. Since I had always lived by the principle of following Spirit's guidance every step of the way in all my important decisions, I recognized it as a confirmation that going to Calcutta was indeed the right next move for me. For the first time in months I felt a brief moment of relief. But it quickly evaporated, and I slid back into a state of terror.

Meanwhile, the shockwaves of the collapse of EnlightenNext and the story of my fall from grace were rapidly spreading through the spiritual world. Many people outside our work—colleague teachers and their students, and even some independent professional organizations with whom EnlightenNext was engaged in collaborative cultural projects— were deeply disturbed by the news. Some of them, not knowing what to make of the situation, understandably distanced themselves from me. Others extended a well-appreciated supportive hand in my darkest hour.

One of them was my colleague and friend Swami Shankarananda, one of the foremost Western disciples of Siddha Guru Baba Muktananda. He invited me to stay at his ashram in Melbourne, Australia, to regroup, and I gratefully accepted. I wanted to retreat from all the madness at Foxhollow and find my center again before traveling to Calcutta. Throughout my stay at his ashram, Swami treated me with kindness and generosity and instructed everybody to take good care of me. I spent my time in intense soul-searching. Every day I sat down on the wooden bench in my room and tried to meditate, but I couldn't. The silent presence of enlightened mind that had been my spontaneous condition for three decades had dispersed, and a state of merciless turmoil had taken its place. A thousand questions kept running through my mind, all of them variations on the same theme: Why was I really here? Where had I gone wrong? Why was I no longer allowed to be who I really was, the guru I had been for a quarter of a century? The whole situation was disorienting in the extreme. I no longer knew what my role was. Every time Swami held public satsang, he wanted to honor me and tell his audience who I was, but I felt like a wretched sinner and preferred to keep my anonymity. While everybody at the ashram treated me with kindness, friendliness, and respect, inside I felt like I was trapped in hell. I felt so broken that the simplest gesture of basic human sympathy from these people I didn't know touched me most profoundly.

Alone in my room, I would sometimes look at pictures of Mother Teresa's center, seeing volunteers care for terminal patients, clean open wounds and sores, and wash the sick. The idea of being exposed to blood, excrement, pus, and urine made me shudder. I was terrified at the risk of contracting some infectious disease like leprosy or AIDS. As the weeks passed, I became more and more intimidated by the prospect of volunteering at the Mother Teresa Center, so I kept postponing my journey to Calcutta. Aware of my trepidations, Shankarananda said to me, "Why do you want to go there? You just want to torture yourself." There was truth in his words. I was convinced that I needed to suffer in order to atone.

Being with Shankarananda, I felt supported on a human level. Swami knew my work and respected me as a guru and a teacher. He made me feel seen. But the mythic-traditional atmosphere at his ashram was perhaps the last environment I should have been in, because the context of the mythic guru was exactly what I was trying to extricate myself from.

Finally, after two months of hesitation, I gathered all my courage and boarded a plane to India.

Arriving alone in Calcutta was nothing short of confrontational. Human misery is heartbreaking to behold here. The suffering and fragileness of the human condition is transparent for all to see, smell, and touch. I had been in India many times before, both as a seeker and as a celebrated teacher with my entourage. I thought I had seen the monster of grinding poverty. Yet now that I was back here as a fallen guru and a broken man, I perceived its unforgiving brutality in a new way. The dreamlike dystopia of Calcutta's slums perfectly matched my inner desperation.

I got myself settled in a hotel on Sudder Street, where foreign tourists stayed on the cheap. I could no longer meditate and was only able to muster a restless night's slumber with the aid of brandy and sleeping pills. I awoke every morning before 6 a.m. and readied myself to battle the darkness that inhabited my being.

After a few days of putting off the start of my service as a volunteer, I pulled myself together and walked over to the Mother Teresa Center, which is located near impoverished Muslim slums. As I approached the center's imposing concrete walls and massive iron gates, the words "Missionaries of Charity" near the entrance underscored the nature of the new role that would soon be mine. Upon entering, I was struck by the cleanliness of the surroundings, which stood in stark contrast to the desolate chaos of the dusty, grimy streets outside. Big pictures of Mother Teresa and paper boards with her sayings welcomed me into her world of selfless service: "Peace begins with a smile." "Intense love does not measure, it just gives."

The center was quite a scene. Its halls were packed with men and women, often in horrible condition, all wearing the same uniform: blue pants and a grey shirt. Many of them were seriously wounded. Some patients were blind, deaf, or a combination of both. Others were missing limbs, quite a few of them still young boys. Some of the older men had suffered stroke. Others were clearly mentally insane. Many of the elderly there had lost everything and had been found on the streets, abandoned by society and rejected by hospitals. They had no one left to care for them and no other place to go. Some of them were clearly just waiting to die. The extent of disease, decrepitude, and deformity among the residents was harrowing.

Daunted by the overwhelming sight, I somewhat sheepishly approached the first sister I saw. She was an African woman in her mid-forties, dressed in the traditional three-striped, blue and white sari of the Missionaries of Charity, which framed her face beautifully.

"Sister," I said, "I have never cared for anyone in my life. I have always been looked after . . ." As I trailed off, she sensed my desperation. "I don't know what to do or how I can help."

She had a beaming smile. Her eyes were peaceful. "My son," she said in a soothing voice, "you have two hands, don't you?" She then kindly took my hands in hers.

"Yes," I replied.

"That's all you need," she said.

With that telling response, the tone of my stay was set, and my time of service at the center began.

I usually served at one of the center's convalescent facilities, called Prem Dan. Like me, the other volunteers came from all over the world. Sometimes they would stay for a week, a month, or more. I was unsure how long I would last.

On an average day there were around a hundred destitute men who needed care. Many of them were highly dependent on others to survive, and thus our job included a whole series of basic tasks, like bathing them, serving meals, washing dishes, helping them take their medication, cleaning those who had dirtied their clothes, shaving them, cutting their finger- and toenails, and helping them urinate in plastic pee bottles and rinsing them out.

Our first chore of the day was the laundry. There was a primitive eighteenth-century washing system, with four large, interlocked cement basins. The first one contained soapy water; the next one, less soapy water; and the last two held clear water for rinsing. We all stood next to one another in a long line, hand-washing patients' sheets, towels, blankets, and uniforms, and then wringing them out and hanging them up in the sun to dry. It had been more than twenty-seven years since I had even washed my own clothes. I felt completely out of place, and already on the first day I was overcome by the uneasy feeling that whatever I needed to happen would not happen here.

My first weeks at Prem Dan were emotionally tough. One of the tasks I dreaded most was assisting patients to the toilet. I would bring them to this vast, Victorian-style bathroom, lift them from their wheelchairs, put them on one of the toilet seats of the exposed concrete benches, and position them over the ragged hole. If they had diarrhea, which was often, it would splatter all over the floor and my rubber flip-flops. Over time I learned how to position these men so that my feet stayed clean as they relieved themselves, and I proudly taught the new volunteers the technique, including how to use a broom to push the excrement into the hole before it got on one's feet. To complicate things, some of these men could be particularly unruly, especially those who had lost their mental faculties, and so cleaning them up was a real test of one's patience. That these men were so utterly exposed and vulnerable was unbearable and touching at the same time.

Mealtime, whether breakfast or lunch, was always chaotic. We would rush to bring all the patients their trays of food and spoon-feed those who were unable to feed themselves. After lunch we took the men in wheelchairs back to their beds. There was something compelling about the sheer vulnerability of lifting frail men with broken bodies out of rickety wheelchairs and gently placing them back into the comfort of their beds. To connect with other human beings who are so dependent on you in such a delicate way was new and moving. It felt very real to me.

Among my favorite jobs was shaving patients. Shaving another man's face, holding it carefully in your hands, mindful not to hurt him while having direct eye contact, is a beautiful, intimate, and fragile experience. There was something sweet and affectionate about the process. Through shaving these men I began to develop relationships with them. I became familiar with their particular preferences, vanities, and quirks. As I got to know them better, I came to appreciate their unique personalities more and more, and I was often gripped by the recognition of our shared humanity.

The most serious cases were treated in the back room of Prem Dan. Looking down the row of beds, you could see men with severe sores, open wounds, broken appendages, and missing limbs. Some of their wounds were unbelievably shocking. I remember visiting one man who was lying on a cot. He had a horrible open wound that ran from his shoulder all the way down to his wrist. His flesh was exposed and you could see bone. When the disinfectant was applied, the poor man screamed and squirmed in unimaginable pain. I couldn't believe people were able to endure such agony. Sometimes I would go to the back room in the morning and see deceased men being wrapped in sheets and carried outside to be cremated. Death was never far away here.

Working alongside the Missionaries of Charity and helping them fulfill their vow of caring for "the poorest of the poor" was a humbling experience and a most direct and revealing encounter with the stark reality of human suffering. When I first arrived at Prem Dan, many of the patients didn't appear human to me; they seemed more like creatures. But after a time I began to see past the façade of their decrepitude, disease, and injuries, and see them as they were: human beings in need of care. As I developed friendships and comradery with some of these men, all the indelicacies of bodily existence that I was afraid of while still in Shankarananda's ashram no longer scared me at all. Rather than being repelled by them and recoiling, I became intrigued—captivated somehow—by the rawness and vulnerability of the human condition.

But despite this recognition, deep down inside every aspect of my life still felt just plain wrong. I was doing this service to face my karma and come to terms with it, but nearly two months had passed by now, and the spiritual payoff I had hoped for hadn't happened yet. Most of the time I felt utterly lost and confused and haunted by overwhelming grief, shame, regret, and anger. My internal dialogue was stuck in a loop: *How did I get here? How did I get here? How on Earth did I get here?* The reality of my new lot in life had shaken me to my core. The agonizing truth was that my whole community had crashed and burned, and I was never far from this nightmare, no matter the time of day.

As I scrubbed the floors of the center, my mind wandered to dark places. All I could hear were shrill and disconcerting voices in my head, as if the devil was dancing around me: *The last twenty-seven years were all bullshit, a figment of your imagination . . . You made it all up . . . Your enlightenment was just a hallucination . . . You are lost . . . You seduced others into believing your spiritual fantasy . . . It was all fake . . . fake . . . fake . . .* These frightening thoughts felt so real that they left me utterly disoriented.

My whole being was overwhelmed with darkness. This was the lowest state of mind I had ever known. I was stuck in the stranglehold of a soul-deadening nihilism. All I could see was dead matter everywhere, devoid of interiority, depth, life, and light. The entire cosmos appeared meaningless and empty. I was on the verge of losing my sanity. However much I tried to rely on my spiritual training to stay mindful of what was really happening to me, I was barely holding on by a thread.

I had always been an inspired person, lit up with the radiance of an enlightened mind, on fire with the ecstatic urgency to evolve, and driven to create a better future for all of us. I had delighted in a cosmos animated by the mysterious force of Eros, vibrating with pure positivity and dripping with meaning. But that sparkling cosmos was now gone. I had spiraled down from a palpable awareness of divinity to a materialistic, flat, empty dryness, which was spiritually unbearable. In my desolation I realized more than ever before that the "disenchantment of the world" runs far deeper than a mere philosophical position or an intellectual assumption of scientific materialism. It is an actual state of consciousness, the very state I had always identified as the enemy of Dharma, truth, Spirit, and love. Now this state was mine. Like some demonic presence, the desolate sense of meaninglessness haunted my daily experience. Every hour was a struggle with the unbearable vacuity of life, and suicidal thoughts kept creeping into my mind through the cracks of my broken personality. Little did I know back then that the agonizing desire to simply cease existing would be my daily reality for the next two years.

Right after the crash, my students urged me to seek therapy. My past experiences with therapy during my younger years had made me more than skeptical about the effectiveness of the psychological approach. Being pressured into therapy by my students was humiliating. Still, more than anything else, I wanted to do the right thing, and I consented.

So while in Calcutta, I held once-a-week Skype sessions with Buddhist psychologist Jack Engler. Jack was sympathetic to the unusual circumstance in which I found myself. He didn't judge me, which was a relief, because just about everyone else in my life was doing just that. He kept reminding me that I had done a lot of good for people. His warm-hearted demeanor and evenhanded way of holding the whole picture was critical to my sanity at this juncture.

Through my weekly meetings with Jack, I came to better understand how parts of my psychological makeup had influenced my teaching style. He helped me see that the way I had been consistently beaten as a small child by my older brother had caused me to hate the vulnerable little boy inside of me, because he had allowed himself to be humiliated. In an attempt to not ever let that happen again, I had disowned him, and he had turned into my shadow.

During my sessions with Jack, it began to dawn on me that perhaps a part of my intolerance of other people's display of weakness had been triggered by this shadow, even as the stabilization of enlightened awareness in my students had always been my primary motivation for exerting so much pressure on them. Had disowning my own more vulnerable and softer side created a lack of compassion and empathy in me, causing at times cruel responses to what I perceived as students' failures? Had it caused me to overreact, push people too hard, and become desensitized about when to stop? Jack's guidance helped me see that to the extent that this was indeed the case, I had been punishing people for parts of myself that I couldn't stand. This insight was a valuable piece of my complicated puzzle.

Near the end of my stay in Calcutta I began to receive Skype calls from my senior students. A few of them had joined together in a group holon intended to guide me through my sabbatical and help me deal with my issues. It was quite an uncomfortable setup. After almost three decades of being their guru, the roles were now suddenly reversed, and I was treated like a student. Unsurprisingly, the atmosphere during our calls was often edgy. Time and again, our interactions quickly degenerated into confrontations, as my students kept calling me to account for some of the harshest teaching interventions in my history as a guru. They shamed me relentlessly for my toughness and insisted that I had been screwing up other people's lives because of it. They pressured me to admit that I had been driven by impure motives and that my ego, ambition, and unconscious behavior had gotten the better of me. Over and over again they told me with great intensity that I didn't know myself at all. They had apparently become convinced that there existed some kind of mean, dark streak in me that I was completely unaware of and that made me fundamentally untrustworthy.

I felt like I was facing a jury. I did my level best to inquire into what they put before me, but I was completely scattered, and in my state of shock I didn't manage to show up with the clarity and serenity that comes with higher awareness.

When my senior students saw me floundering, they became frustrated, thinking that I didn't have the courage to be vulnerable and authentic in the same way that I had always demanded they be. If *I* couldn't walk my own talk, then what right did I have to pressure *them* all these years? Their outrage built up, and understandably so.

In the midst of these contentious calls, my sessions with Jack were like a breath of fresh air. He was aware that I had done some extreme things but didn't reduce me to those things. He knew that I wasn't some dark character acting out ill-conceived motives, but treated me as somebody who had made some serious errors of judgment along the way. He was this calming, reasonable influence, and speaking to him kept me sane.

More than three months of working my six-day-a-week volunteer schedule at the center had passed, and by now I had settled into my routine of serving at Prem Dan. But other than the rewarding gift of cultivating an intimacy with these patients on a human level, feeling their gratitude and being sensitized to their suffering and circumstances, I didn't feel that my service there was particularly beneficial in terms of addressing my real predicament. It began to dawn on me that the issues I needed to deal with were of a different order. So I prepared myself to fly back to America and seek a more effective path forward.

Back home, I reached out to Integral transpersonal psychologist Roger Walsh to discuss my situation and seek his advice. He pointed out that this formula of submitting myself to the guidance of my own students was an almost guaranteed recipe for failure because of the hierarchical structure of our past relationship and the karma that had built up between us. Such a context, he explained, would simply remain too charged, preventing us from working together in healthy and supportive ways. He suggested that it would be more beneficial to engage in inner work with other teachers with whom I had a peer relationship. Still, I didn't just want to give up working with the senior holon. The bond we shared was immeasurably deep. We had gone through Dharma wars together and had so often emerged victorious on the other side. But Roger was right, and the tone of these meetings with my former students continued to be accusatory and judgmental.

Slowly but surely, reality kicked in, and I began to see the underlying dynamics of our interactions. My senior students were treating me exactly the way they had been trained to by me for all these years! They were giving me a taste of my own medicine, perpetuating the same harsh tactics and binary principles that I myself was the architect of. With a shock of recognition, I became aware of the areas where my teaching approach had been unskillful.

The first issue I saw was that the second and third tenets of Evolutionary Enlightenment, *the power of volition* and *face everything and avoid nothing,* had been applied by me in an overly idealistic way. Both tenets set a very high standard for self-responsibility. They assume that if you truly want to be free more than anything else, you are perfectly capable of taking full responsibility for the totality of who you are—for your ego, with its personal history and cultural conditioning, and for the deep and unconscious psychological structures of your being. And thus these tenets called on us to confront all our egoic motives and unconscious material, and show up fully conscious at all times, under all circumstances, and in all places.

But now that *I* was being asked by the senior holon to live up to the radical nature of the tenets that I myself had introduced, I couldn't do it! A thick cloud of confusion, fear, and anger was covering my clarity of intention, and because of that I was unable to meet my own high bar for self-responsibility. I had always proclaimed that someone's personal predicament, suffering, or circumstances should never interfere with living the teachings, and I had interpreted my students' inability to do so as their irrational refusal. But now I realized that if you put somebody who is emotionally shattered in a corner and exert immense pressure on them, it is simply impossible for them to pull through. In such a state, relentless pushing is counterproductive.

And thus I began to understand that the radical idealism and binary logic with which I had applied these tenets failed to factor in the vulnerabilities, complexities, and many shades of grey of our flawed humanity. Nobody can change down to the core all at once, if only they intend to hard enough, because everybody carries unconscious motivations that escape the immediate impact of their willpower. Bringing this unconscious material to light and working through it takes time, and when a person is shattered, the energy, attention, and awareness needed to do so is compromised.

Understanding all this, I realized that I had been teaching from a place way above the actual territory. In my zeal to lead my community into manifesting the highest possible ideals, I had all too often pushed my students too hard and caused them a lot of agony. Now that I was broken, I began to grasp my responsibility for this mistake.

The second insight that began to dawn on me was that I had been holding up my teaching principle *what we do is who we are* in an unfeasibly absolutist way. Especially in my earlier years as a teacher, I had always insisted with great intensity that my students would be unambiguously straightforward and would close the gap between their awakened intentions and their actual behavior. Now my senior students kept pressing me about this principle. They wanted me to own up to all my worst sins and admit, "Yes, this is who I am!" Now that I was at the receiving end, I realized the harshness of this precept. Reducing human beings to their flaws is a lack of compassion for their humanity. Sooner or later, people make mistakes, and when they do, the last response should be to equate them with their weaknesses. You love them as human beings who need to atone for their karmas, and you offer them a supportive environment. If any of us are going to face the most difficult issues within ourselves, it needs to be done in a context of support, love, and dignity, in which we feel safe enough to relax our self-protective reflexes, explore the parts of ourselves we are least proud of, and face the real causes of our foibles head-on. True healing requires an atmosphere of compassion, which allows us to build the necessary strength to deal with our issues. Reducing people to their shortcomings had been one of the shadows of our work together.

The third realization was of an emotional nature. Now that I had stepped down from my role as the leader of my community, I experienced the unique agony and inconsolable grief of being exiled from the tribe. As a teacher I had sent many students away from our community—their spiritual family—which in many cases had become their main support system. I had taken such extreme measures whenever I felt that after long periods of supporting them they still weren't authentically trying to break through their knots and live up to the teachings. I wanted to protect the shared resonance of our group field, which is so crucial for the success of Higher We work. My firm hand was part of our strength and maturity as a sangha, but the cost was too high. Too many people had crumbled and suffered unbearably by being separated from their community. Now I experienced the full extent of their agony, and the ineffectiveness of this brutal strategy became clear to me. I realized that the likelihood of someone facing themself on their own is infinitely less than if they can continue to count on the loving support of their spiritual family.

Through my work with the senior students following the crash, and feeling the pressure they exerted on me, I directly experienced the perils and rough edges of my own teaching style. And even though our explorations did not reveal some dark streak in me—the effect that some of the senior students wanted to achieve—seeing the areas where my teaching approach had been unskillful was eye-opening for me. As evident as these inadequacies appeared now, they hadn't been obvious to me before, since the teachings had generated all these extraordinary results as well. So many of my students had transformed into spiritually mature human beings and had been living inspired lives. Clearly, with the right person, under the right circumstances, the teachings *had* been effective. Still, it had become equally clear now that the mythic absolutism with which I had applied some of my teaching principles had all too often turned them into an unbalanced, one-dimensional, black-and-white methodology that overrode the complexity of real human beings. Indeed, there was a lack of compassion in the system. Seeing all this set in motion in me a process of deep reflection about the limitations of the mythic-traditional context in which aspects of spiritual life sometimes tend to remain embedded.

At a certain point during this period of working with the senior holon, Alka and I wanted to go to the Shivananda ashram in Rishikesh, a beautiful and harmonious place where we both felt comfortable and at home. It was there, on the banks of the Ganges, that my community had first formed almost three decades ago. Ever since that time I had maintained warm relationships with Shivananda's successors. I adored the inspiring saint Swami Chidananda, the very embodiment of true humility and rare purity; and I had grown very fond of the powerful, scholarly teacher Swami Krishnananda, who had been one of my mentors. Neither of them were still with us, but I still loved living at the ashram. I felt I needed to retreat into a supportive environment where I could deepen my self-inquiry, face my shadows, and continue my work with the senior holon and Jack Engler.

But when the senior students heard about our plans, they vehemently objected. They were convinced that I wanted to go to the Shivananda ashram because everybody there would perceive me as the guru and treat me accordingly. They believed that my hidden motive for going there was that I desperately wanted to get back into the guru position, and they were adamant about that. They kept insisting that I didn't know myself at all; that my ego was in the way; that I wasn't aware of my own motives; and that I therefore needed to run all my decisions by them first.

With this, they crossed a line. I was perfectly willing to seek their guidance, but not to literally surrender every last bit of my autonomy to them. This was *my* sabbatical. When I made my position clear to them, they were outraged. They felt that I had broken their trust and concluded that it no longer made any sense to continue working with me. It was a pivotal moment.

Soon afterward, those in the wider community of EnlightenNext who were still supportive of my soul-searching process began to turn away from me as well. The leaders of the Frankfurt community told their students that I didn't accept any help, and that the senior holon had no other choice but to stop giving it to me. As far as they were concerned, I had ruined it.

And so it was that my last frail bond with what was left of my community was severed. It destroyed all hope that my resignation from the leadership position of EnlightenNext would turn out the way it was intended—as a temporary sabbatical from which I would reemerge in due course as a more skillful teacher and a better man.

7

Let My Heart Be Broken

After the cessation of my work with the senior students, a grim period of isolation set in. My life was adrift and nothing seemed to make any sense. In my broken state, a part of me began to believe that my senior students were right when they had so confidently insisted that my real motive for wanting to go to Rishikesh was my hidden desire to assume the guru mantle again. And thus, to be sure not to make any mistakes, I went to Pondicherry in South India instead, where nobody would recognize me. I rented a small room in Auroville, a universal township dedicated to the ideal of human unity, based on the vision of the late sage Sri Aurobindo. I stayed there on my own, immersed in intense self-reflection. I spent hours driving around aimlessly on my motorcycle, crisscrossing the lush Indian landscape, ruminating about my years as a guru. I had to get clear about the real causes of the collapse of EnlightenNext and the dramatic loss of my community, and my own responsibility for it all. But despite the tenacity of my intention, I could not find my clarity, nor could I conceive of any way out of this quagmire. My former students had been telling me that there was a cruelty, a coldness, and a harshness in me that I had never confronted with the same honesty, humility, and integrity that I had always expected from them. Perhaps this was true . . . I felt like my heart was frozen, and I desperately wanted it to break. But after three months of focused soul-searching, nothing changed. Day after day, I kept staring straight into this dark abyss of no hope.

During this time Alka had been on a sabbatical too, as both of us were spending a considerable amount of time alone. Now she came to join me in Auroville. Her remarkable steadfastness throughout all the drama of the collapse of EnlightenNext and my subsequent ordeal of inner turmoil and soul-searching was of invaluable support to me. Unlike everyone else, she never lost touch with the bigger picture. Many people had approached her, expecting her to leave me. But she never doubted me and consistently made it clear to them that she wasn't going to. Had she turned against me, she would have been showered with sympathy, acknowledgement, and support from many fellow devotees from around the world. In their eyes she was like a battered woman, trapped in an unwholesome marriage, in total denial of her unhealthy dependency and lacking the strength and autonomy to break away from it all—one of the last brainwashed persons under my spell. Nothing, however, could be further from the truth. It was not weakness, but extraordinary strength of character that allowed her to not get lost in group consciousness, stand firm in her autonomy, and never lose the plot, not even once. This was all the more admirable as she had a hard time herself and felt resentment, for good reasons, about some issues. But there was a profound loyalty in her. It wasn't just that I was her husband. She simply knew who I truly was and had unfailing confidence in my heart. That she always remained on solid ground was unimaginably precious to me. She went through the entire drama with breathtaking dignity and grace.

We stayed together in Auroville for a while. Yet as the weeks went by, I remained stuck in my inner predicament, and I realized I needed external help.

I decided to return to America and engage the well-known therapist and spiritual teacher Robert Augustus Masters for guidance and deep shadow work. I trusted his approach because it wasn't merely psychological. He treated shadow integration and spiritual work as one dynamically evolving process.

I had first met Robert two decades ago in Oregon, an encounter that had stayed with me ever since. Over a casual cup of coffee he had told me his most recent dramatic life episode with a transparency that was remarkable given the fact that we had only just met. He had gone through the painful collapse of his own spiritual community and trusted me with all these excruciating details about his fall from grace and the ways in which his shadow had contributed to it. As far removed from my own world as his story had been back then, it was equally close now.

At the end of his lengthy sharing, he abruptly asked me, "Now tell me about your shadow." I was completely taken aback by his unexpected question. As a guru I was categorically convinced that I had no shadow. I saw myself as the pure one, the jivanmukta, someone who has attained *moksha,* or final liberation from the cycle of birth and death while still alive, and the idea of having a dark side didn't square with my self-image. I had sharply criticized the view that shadow can coexist with true enlightenment as a cynical assumption, writing, "Indeed, it is not uncommon to hear spiritual teachers speaking freely and unapologetically about division that exists within themselves. . . . But what is Enlightenment all about? *Enlightenment is the realization of One Self, and the death of division and multiplicity within the human personality.* Undivided intention, undivided motivation, undivided action is *the whole point. One* Self—not two, not three, not four—is the goal of all spiritual practice. From the many to the One."[1] I was so deeply invested in this conviction that I would deflect any information to the contrary coming my way. This set me up for many problems down the road. If one believes one is entirely shadow-free, then why would one ever doubt oneself or scrutinize one's behavior?

So twenty years after that first fateful conversation with Robert, the scales had turned, and the irony of the situation was not lost on me. I was now the fallen guru with the dramatic story, flying halfway around the world to call on Robert's guidance to help me come to terms with the shadow that I, back then, didn't believe I had.

The work we did was nothing short of confrontational, especially the role-playing therapy. Robert instructed me to visualize my students and speak with them in all transparency about everything that had transpired between us. After I did so, he asked me to switch roles; imagine I was one of them, and consider what I had just said. I could feel their enormous disillusionment in me as their teacher. I was aware of their pain about the dramatic way our shared experiment that had started so beautifully and full of promise had derailed so completely. Then Robert asked me to speak their anguish, resentment, disgruntlement, and disappointment out loud. It was one of the hardest things I ever had to do. Their soul-level agony felt simply too heart-wrenching, and a part of me was still denying that I was actually the cause of it, and so I barely managed to put it all in words. But as I moved deeper and deeper into their world, their voices began to come through more strongly. Looking through their eyes brought me face-to-face with my own responsibility for the collapse of our work. It was a crucial step in owning my role in it, and Robert expressed his appreciation for my transparency and vulnerability.

Then we moved into an in-depth exploration of the dynamics of the student-teacher relationship and the sudden role reversal that had occurred between myself and my senior students. I shared with him the contentious ways in which we had been trying to work together after the crash. Right in the midst of my outpourings, Robert stopped me abruptly, looked me in the eye, and in what felt like a candid man-to-man moment said, "Andrew, you have given up your power, and unless you reclaim it you are never going to pull yourself out of this mess." As he said this, something in me clicked. It was true. I had not just relinquished my position as the spiritual head of EnlightenNext, but along with that my actual strength and dignity as a human being. The moment I had done so, the teacher-student role reversed, and I submitted to my senior students in an unhealthy way. My mindset had slid into: *I don't know. You all do. Please tell me.* And thus I had begun to believe even their most scathing judgments about who they now believed I was. Robert's observation helped me see that I was completely tangled up in this unhealthy matrix with them, and it began to dawn on me that I needed to break free from it if I was ever to find my own strength and dignity again. I needed to reinhabit my power in order to be able to take full responsibility for all my actions.

In hindsight it was obvious that my senior students were in no position to guide me through this ordeal and help me resolve my issues—just like Roger Walsh had told me earlier. Their world had just collapsed as well, and they themselves were in turmoil. They too were in the eye of the storm.

All in all, my work with Robert felt like a step in the right direction. But the big emotional catharsis I had been hoping for still didn't happen, even though Robert's acupressure therapy treatments were specifically designed to catalyze such a liberating release. My heart just wouldn't break, and day by day I grew more desperate, afraid that the one thing that was really needed would never happen.

Right around this time, a former student of mine came up with the somewhat unconventional and bold suggestion that perhaps taking ayahuasca would really catalyze my hoped-for breakthrough. Ayahuasca, the "vine of the soul," is a sacred plant medicine with hallucinogenic properties that comes from the Amazon rainforest. It has been used for centuries by indigenous tribes to facilitate psychospiritual healing. Drinking ayahuasca induces an altered state of consciousness that is not unlike dreaming while awake. Rather than a loss of consciousness, it effectuates greater alertness, increases the vividness of your perceptions, and amplifies your internally generated mental imagery. Ingesting the brew allows you to journey deep into the recesses of your own mind. It often exposes long-held emotional blockages and unprocessed childhood trauma or confronts us with our worst fears and unconscious motivations. Whatever you don't want to face about yourself, this plant medicine will show it to you plainly, starkly, and without any hesitation. Taking ayahuasca can also lead to mystical experiences such as spiritual ecstasy, revelations about the nature of reality, and visions—usually vibrant and detailed—carrying a message related to something you are struggling with. Ayahuasca experiences can be highly cathartic and in many cases people emerge from them with a sense of having been purged. More often than not they then return to their daily lives with a renewed understanding about who they really are, their true purpose in life, or the many ways in which their unconscious patterns have been obstructing their development for years.

My former student knew of a retreat center in Brazil that organized ayahuasca ceremonies, and he proposed to join me there. I was more than ready to do whatever it would take to face my dark side and awaken my conscience in new ways. And thus with the desperate intention to have my heart be broken, I traveled to Brazil, accompanied by my former student.

The retreat center was a place of natural beauty, located near the Brazilian coast in the lush and richly diverse Atlantic Forest. During the retreat, each participant was individually guided by Sylvia, an Argentinian transpersonal psychologist and shaman, or spiritual mediator, who was intimately familiar with the physical, psychological, and spiritual effects of the plant medicine. She was an educated, rational, and skilled person, and I came to trust her very quickly. The ayahuasca ceremonies, during which you drink the plant medicine and go into a trance, all took place at night, in an open wooden structure in the forest, built beside a stunning lagoon. A symphony of natural sounds—chirping crickets, frogs croaking for their mates, birds, and other nocturnal animals—accompanies you on your inner journey.

Before you drink the medicine, you are asked to set an intention or hold a specific conundrum in your awareness. At the outset of my first ceremony I asked to see beyond the veil of what I was avoiding. As I went into trance, a vision emerged almost immediately. I saw a multitude of deep flesh wounds and open sores. They were appallingly ugly, appearing in brilliantly flashing colors of red, purple, blue, and yellow. Their mere sight was repugnant and deeply disconcerting. As I looked at them more closely, I realized that these wounds were not in my body, but in my soul. As I continued to hone in on them further, I suddenly understood that they represented my own hypocrisy. I saw that I hadn't been living the foundational dimensions of my teachings in important ways. The moment I had attained enlightenment, in alignment with my guru's radical Advaitic teaching of the always-already nature of enlightened awareness, I had stopped meditating. I truly thought that working on myself was no longer necessary. Indeed, I was convinced that in the profound and powerfully effortless spontaneity of much of my inner experience, everything was being seen directly and unobstructedly. But I was wrong. In fact, I had not been facing everything and avoiding nothing, as the third tenet of my teachings calls us to. I could see how the crash of EnlightenNext had happened because I had been avoiding all the important signals that our utopian experiment was in danger of collapsing. Despite my closest friends desperately trying to get through to me, I had resisted seeing the truth of what was happening. It was mortifying, and I was overcome with unbearable agony and inconsolable grief.

I began vomiting violently, a common side effect of ingesting the foul-tasting brew, which is usually taken as a sign that the human soul is being cleansed and purified. Every time I threw up it felt like years and years of built-up impurities were being squeezed out of every single vein in my body.

The images of these wounds kept welling up in waves, intensifying and then subsiding again, as if to offer me a brief moment of relief to recover from these fierce confrontations with my demons. The medicine is said to be compassionate. Still, its message was tough as nails, unvarnished and inescapable. It brought me face-to-face with the reason why so many people who had trusted me with their lives had felt betrayed. It was the first time I saw this in all its rawness. It filled my soul with a shame so deep it felt like it would last a thousand years.

Then another image appeared. I saw the faces of those who had been closest to me. I felt as if I could see deep into their souls. I experienced their despair, their incredible grief and shock at seeing my failings. *How could I? Their own guru, someone they had loved so much and trusted so deeply . . . ?* I felt their pain, and from there I saw into my ambition. There was a coldness in it that I had never seen before, a hardness that didn't care about people's personal circumstances because for me "the mission" was always front and center. Seeing this about myself was hard to bear, and the sheer agony of this revelation stayed with me throughout the rest of the night.

The next night I went into the second ceremony still reeling from the unrelenting self-confrontation I had experienced the night before. As soon as I entered into trance, my burning desire to cut through my own hardness and have my heart broken surged through me with a painful intensity. I was desperate to face my darkest shadows and purge my soul. I was convinced I was a terrible sinner and needed to be punished. I wanted the plant medicine to deliver me a rude awakening and hoped to be so shocked and horrified at what I had done that I would be on my knees begging God for forgiveness and mercy. I *had* to atone for all the karma I had caused. My intention was single-minded and full of urgency. It felt like it couldn't be more sincere. But right in the midst of this powerful longing, out of the blue a very different voice emerged in my awareness. Like a demonic presence, it whispered, *You have no intention of doing this for real. You're lying to yourself, why don't you just admit it? You might as well give up. You don't mean this—face it!* I was shocked and began to fend off this eerily cunning voice. A fierce battle between the two sides of myself ensued within me. It felt as if my most authentic self was at war with the darkest face of my ego. The more it intensified, the more terrified I became. Throughout the session I was haunted by this diabolical voice that kept trying to convince me that I was insincere and had in reality already given up.

This battle carried on into the third ceremony of the next night. This time I asked the medicine, *What has been the cause of this crisis?* and it gave me the answer in a way that was quite stunning.

As I moved deeper into trance, the voice of doom was getting stronger, convincing me that my yearning to let my heart be broken was untruthful. I kept fighting it with all my might, but with every passing minute I felt more and more like I was losing the battle. My fear was reaching a boiling point. I was convinced that unless my heart broke into a million pieces, my soul would be lost, and I was going to hell forever. I felt my time was up.

In utter desperation, I turned to Sylvia for help. She came over and sat down next to me. In my intoxicated state I began to plead with her out loud, "Please help me. I don't know what to do. My heart won't break. I have hurt a lot of people. I don't know how to atone for the harm I have caused. Please help me." At this point I was writhing on the floor in agony, begging God for help and forgiveness. I recalled how hard I had pushed some of my former students, and in an old-fashioned Catholic way wanted God to punish me for being such an evil sinner. Nothing less than that, I felt, would suffice to purge me and allow me to find my integrity again and truly respond to the people I had hurt. But I was scared to death that I wasn't going to make it and that my heart would stay permanently frozen.

Sylvia listened to my dramatic plea for a while and then simply said, "When are you going to stop beating yourself up?" My first thought was, *She doesn't get it. I'm a bad person. I deserve to be punished for my transgressions.* Desperate to get through to her, I kept repeating, "I don't know what to do. My heart won't break. I have to be able to respond to the suffering I've caused. Please help me." I was shaking with terror and began to vomit again. Each time even the slightest trace of egoic thinking arose, my body convulsed, producing this primordial guttural sound of throwing up. Inside I felt like my pride and arrogance were being spewed out and violently purged from my psyche. With every gag reflex I felt like my big breakthrough was about to occur. I had worked myself up into this insane psychotic state in which I was convinced that this was my final chance to face the truth about myself, and that if I couldn't do it now, it wasn't going to happen in this lifetime. So every time my vomiting reflexes receded, I panicked, thinking, *Oh no, this is it! My once-in-a-lifetime chance at redemption is gone.*

All the while, Sylvia sat there with her back against the wall, observing me. As I looked at her, a visual hallucination emerged. I perceived her as a white witch, a sorceress, not unlike some character from *The Lord of the Rings.* She and her assistant, a Californian guy with long blond hair, had now grasped that I was indeed this evil sinner. I seemed to hear them whisper to each other, *Oh my God, he missed his chance.*

He just made the worst decision of his life and doesn't know it. Now he is going to burn in hell forever—and we are not allowed to tell him. I was completely caught up in this paranoid narrative that my chance for redemption was now lost for eternity, and that I could no longer rectify my karma.

But after a few moments, Sylvia calmly asked me again, "When are you going to stop torturing yourself?" Once more I thought, *She really doesn't get it. I'm a sinner and need to be punished.* I couldn't relate to what she was saying at all. This went on for a while. Again and again, I kept rejecting the help I had asked for, and again and again she inquired, "When are you going to stop beating yourself up?" Finally it dawned on me that maybe I was wrong. With a shock I saw my own unbelievable arrogance, and reality hit me: *For God's sake, Andrew, look at you! You've come all the way to Brazil to participate in this retreat. You are so desperate, and even in your darkest hour, while getting the help you are begging for, you still think you know better!* In that lucid moment I finally grasped my astounding lack of humility. My pride and arrogance were seamless and unbroken, my superiority still neatly intact. They pervaded my whole being. I *always* knew better. It was a profoundly sobering revelation. The instant I got it, I relaxed and surrendered into the spacious clarity of the present moment.

After this reckoning with my arrogance I was whisked off to some other metaphysical domain. There I reexperienced the cause of my early trauma. I relived my first memory of being beaten mercilessly and violently by my older brother. I could feel my confusion, my puzzlement, wondering why this was happening to me and what in the world I could have possibly done to deserve this. I observed my young mind's inability to understand this horrible treatment. Yet at the same time my adult mind began to see through the dynamics of its own psychological makeup. Like the classical victim of abuse, especially when it occurs at such an early age, I had come to believe that these repeated beatings by my brother were somehow my fault, even though I was still so young and innocent. Even as a child I had grappled with strong feelings of guilt and shame about my abuse, feelings too overwhelming to process at such a tender age. As I now reexperienced my early shame for being so violated, I clearly saw how these feelings had crystallized to form a subpersonality: the bad boy who deserves to be punished.

At the same time I realized that my senior students had basically been challenging my mythic identity as the perfect *satguru,* the great wise one who has all the answers—an identity I had held onto for almost my entire adult life. And suddenly I understood: if I couldn't be the perfect satguru, the great innovator who brought Evolutionary Enlightenment into the world, I was going to be the bad boy who deserved to be punished. These were the two choices. The moment my mythic identity fell apart, I retreated into my subpersonality— one identity simply exchanged for another. To my dismay I realized that my shadow had won the day. I was now the fallen guru, and all over the world the public narrative had become some expression of the basic theme of my subpersonality: Andrew Cohen is the bad boy who deserves to be punished—a dark, mean character who at long last has been brought down. I had proven the truth of my subpersonality. There had been these unconscious forces in me that early on had made sure that this was going to be the outcome. With a shock of recognition, I realized, *Good Lord, is that what this is all about?* From a psychological viewpoint it couldn't be more perfectly engineered. There was a poignancy to the humanity of it all.

The moment I saw through all this, I felt my heart break. An immense compassion welled up from deep inside me, not only for the pathos of my own woundedness, but also for the heartbreaking nature of the human condition itself. I saw deeply into the reality of the human predicament: how profoundly unaware and conditioned we all are, and how greatly we are shaped by our brokenness and shadows. As this spirit of compassion washed over me, I forgave myself and everyone else. I dropped my mythic identity as the perfected one and joined the human race. I spent the rest of the night embracing the vulnerable little boy inside of me.

The fourth and last ceremony of my retreat had a very different quality. It was extraordinary and compellingly mysterious. I cannot recall exactly what I asked of the medicine, but it had something to do with my own guru. Right after I drank the brew, a most wondrous trans-rational event began to unfold. I heard the voice of a master instruct-ing me, *Whatever happens, you have to stay with your own uncorrupted innocence.* I began arguing almost instantly: *Me? I'm not innocent!* But I quickly stopped myself with the thought, *Don't argue. Just be quiet and practice the wisdom you just received.* As I slid deeper into trance, the voice continued in my head: *You need to heal, and you need to heal today! But* you *have to do the work.*

Right after hearing these words, I was whisked off to a sublime and numinous dimension. I found myself sitting at the feet of my guru. His spiritual form was so real it might as well have been his physical body. Being in his radiant presence, I relived the moment of benediction, the instant when he placed the jewel of enlightenment in my hands. I wasn't experiencing this for the second time, but as the very time when this actually happened. The jewel of enlightenment is the revelation that the mind is an illusion. It is empty. When you truly know this, you are free in a way that is unimaginable to most.

The moment my guru handed me this jewel was a truly gracious one. But it came like a shock as well, because in that very instant I also realized that over time I had actually dropped the jewel. I saw that dur-ing my years as a guru I had always been able to teach other people how to access enlightened awareness at a level of mastery, but that I hadn't been practicing this myself. As a result, the gap between my skills as a teacher and the life I had been living had grown larger and larger. This was a horrifying realization! As soon as I saw this, the voice said to me, *Don't ever drop it again.*

The mystical reunification with my guru was a mysterious and beautiful experience, full of grace. Intoxicated by its sublimity, I spent the next six hours sitting motionless, absorbed in deep meditation. I practiced the renunciation of the mind, unconditionally letting go of everything, which is the essence of the gift of enlightenment. Still, every so often my mind would go back to ruminating about the past, coming up with stories about having done this or having to take responsibility for that. But I also quickly realized that the ultimate metaphysical dimension is about relinquishing *everything*, and in that context I knew I needed to let go of even that which I took responsibility for. And so I sat there, returning to the radiant emptiness of enlightened mind again and again, immersed in a peace that is not of this world.

When I came out of that session in the afternoon of the next day, my former student was sitting next to me and said, "I felt you were in the presence of your guru."

"How did you know?" I asked.

"It was obvious," he said.

As the retreat came to an end, I felt I had been purged in a deep way. Still, I knew that my healing process wasn't complete, and I was determined to take it all the way. Over the course of the next year I traveled to Brazil two more times to partake in ayahuasca retreats. The plant medicine disclosed many more subtle and profound insights, yet the confrontations with my shadow, and the painful situations it had created, continued unabated as well.

I remember one particular ceremony that was quite revealing and left a deep impression on me. As I went into trance, a vivid image that looked like a scene from ancient Egypt appeared. I saw all these men who were lined up, their waists covered with a small loincloth, their broken bodies sweaty and bent over. They were all waiting for their turn to get whipped, while the unsettling sound of rhythmic chanting reverberated in the background. Whether I had accessed an actual part of our collective unconscious or some hidden place in my own mind, the message was unmistakable: these men were eternally trapped in an unbroken cycle of perpetual shame, guilt, and punishment. It was a deeply disconcerting experience.

When I later shared my vision with Sylvia, she said to me, "You are still stuck in a loop and you need to drop the whole thing." She was right. It felt like my core wound, the bad boy who deserves to be punished, was still alive and vibrating in all its rawness. The fact that I was still trapped in this wound's painful logic exposed itself most clearly after my community had crashed. The moment I relinquished my power, my students began to mercilessly shame me, and I fell back into the brokenness of my subpersonality. The battered little kid inside me had no doubt that I deserved their punishment and wouldn't be convinced otherwise. I just couldn't bring myself to release my deep-seated belief that I was a terrible sinner who owed all his students everything. Like the men in the vision, I was stuck in a vicious cycle of never-ending shame and punishment.

Sylvia explained to me that such cycles can go on forever, and that I simply needed to break the spell and jump off this endless merry-go-round. To do so, she said, my subpersonality needed to heal, and I also needed to claim my own inner power again. Her advice rang true to me and echoed almost word-for-word what Robert Masters had said to me earlier on in our candid man-to-man moment. Yet living it still proved to be an immense challenge, and it didn't take long before my efforts to do so would be put to the test.

Back in New York, I had an encounter with one of my former students. He was furious. He shamed me for two hours straight, telling me that I was a terrible person who had done unforgivable things, and he made sure to impress upon me the idea that I hadn't even begun to atone for it all. I left the meeting devastated. Desperate, I called Sylvia and told her I was ready to come back and go deeper. But after listening to me for a while, she said, "Andrew, you have been working on yourself so hard and suffered so much. If you aren't careful you'll do damage to your heart." Her statement came from such a deep place of loving care for my soul's well-being that it touched me profoundly. Still, my former student's rant haunted me. It had opened up my old wound again and reawakened this nagging doubt that maybe I really *was* the sinner my subpersonality kept assuring me I was. In an attempt to convince Sylvia of this as well, I told her the most drastic teaching interventions I had ever enacted. A part of me wanted to shock her and get her to affirm the worst of what my former students were saying about me, because I still believed it was true. But she wasn't going for it. She admitted that what I had told her was extreme, but that given the radical spiritual context we had all dedicated our lives to, she could make sense of it. She added that sometimes a teacher has to enter into his own dark side in order to access the spiritual power necessary to take on the shadows of his students, but that doing so is dangerous, because once you access the shadow domain you risk making serious mistakes.

Then she said to me, "I rarely meet people who are as transparent, honest, and authentic as you are. Unless you are different with other people, I don't get the extremity of all this resentment toward you. So are you different?"

I replied, "No."

She then inquired, "Would you do those things again?"

"Never," I said.

"Well, then that's it," she said. "What more can you do?" She dissuaded me from coming back for another retreat and strongly advised me to slow down.

Sylvia's guidance was priceless, and the ayahuasca retreats with her were seminal in healing my early trauma. Together with the insights I had received from my work with Jack Engler and Robert Masters, taking the powerful plant medicine had given me a deeper understanding of my inner world and its shadows.

I remember how Jack had pointed out to me a terribly obvious truth that I had previously denied. He explained that most people who search for enlightenment with great passion do so because they experience great suffering and want to escape it. It wasn't the first time this wisdom had crossed my path, but I had always believed that it didn't apply to me. I was convinced that I had pursued enlightenment for its own sake. But I had completely overlooked that I too had been so dissatisfied with ordinary life and the suffering caused by my childhood trauma that I had become absolutely willing to let go of everything, take the high road to enlightenment, and transcend human suffering once and for all. For almost thirty years I had believed that this was exactly what had happened to me, because after enlightenment there was so much bliss and freedom that my suffering was simply outshined by it. I no longer *consciously* experienced this suffering, and therefore I had become convinced that transcending my suffering had also healed its cause. But this had obviously never been true. Despite the profundity of my enlightenment, my subpersonality was still intact, and it had remained active in a covert way, causing me at times to be overly harsh with those whom I perceived to be weak. I wasn't truly free from it.

Even though I am a transcender by nature, and this orientation will always be the one I most naturally gravitate to, the pitfalls of this inclination had become clearer than ever. Both Jack and Sylvia helped me realize that in order to heal, I needed to claim the little boy inside myself and *own* him, not just transcend him.

Three years had passed since my fall from grace, and I was now deep into my sabbatical. I had come a long way—from being convinced that I was the pure one who didn't have a shadow, to now seeing that true enlightenment does not necessarily mean "the death of division and multiplicity within the human personality," as I had so confidently written during my early years.[2] I had begun to see very deeply into the reality of this elaborate subterranean world, a world that exists in all of us, and I had come to appreciate that to the extent that our shadows remain unconscious, we will always lead a double life.

My heart had softened, and I slowly began to shed my identity as the sinner, the bad boy who deserves to be punished, along with the shame inherent in this subpersonality. My inner work wasn't over, but once in a while I began to see the first hopeful glimmer of a new sense of enlightenment, an enriched enlightenment with a gentler flavor, a more human face, and profoundly free from the constraints of the mythic perfection in which my role as a teacher had been trapped.

8

Awakening to
the Truth of Suffering

When I turned sixty in October 2015, Alka and I decided to go on a whale-watching tour out of Boston Harbor to celebrate the occasion. As we sailed out into the open sea, several humpback whales began to appear on the horizon. The truly wondrous sight of these majestic creatures lifted my spirits. We slowly sailed in their direction, careful not to disturb them. But they seemed as curious about us as we were about them, and they turned toward us, unafraid. There were many moments when they allowed us to get very close, and whenever they did I felt the hair stand up on the back of my neck as I experienced the extraordinary poignancy of interspecies intimacy with these highly evolved beings. We stayed out at sea for about four hours and saw twenty-five whales. The enchanting experience kept repeating over and over that day. It was an incredibly uplifting adventure.

After we returned to Boston Harbor, Alka and I walked down the wharf and entered an adjacent hotel to have something to drink. We both ordered coffee and sat in silence for a very long time. I put my head in my hands and went into a deep meditative state. Soon the ecstasy of our time with the whales receded, and a sense of intense despair welled up from deep within me. My head was spinning, and I felt like I was sinking ever deeper into darkness. Suddenly I heard something snap. It was my heart. The hard ice of pride in which my heart had been encased seemed to crack open, and a deep truth about sentient existence revealed itself in a way it never had before: I experienced the overwhelming nature of suffering itself. It felt like an infinite field of pain and grief that included all sentient beings everywhere, throughout all of creation. Experiencing this foundational truth of our human circumstance touched me to the core. It was both unbearable and liberating. I had never felt more vulnerable or more human. It was a moment of grace, the moment when I woke up in a deep way to the inescapable existential reality of the Buddha's First Noble Truth, the truth of suffering.

I understood that this moment of epiphany was the culmination of a gradual, three-year process of allowing the inherent suffering of the human condition to seep into my heart, drop by drop—a process that had reconnected me with parts of my own personal history that hadn't been totally resolved.

Ever since enlightenment had thrust me into a state of bliss, gratitude, love, ecstasy, and continuous existential wonder, I had been largely cut off from the truth of human suffering. I had taken my stand in transcendental reality, which remains forever untouched by the sorrows and losses of this world. But the unrelenting ordeal I had gone through since the collapse of my community had gradually sensitized me to this foundational truth of life. I had witnessed the unforgiving nature of grinding poverty in Calcutta and the horrible condition of so many patients at Prem Dan; I had experienced eye-opening revelations with the plant medicine ayahuasca; and I had gone through confrontational meetings with so many of my students, who spoke candidly and vulnerably about their experience of being treated by me in overly harsh ways. With every agonizing wave of exposure to the reality of human suffering, my heart softened, and I felt the rough edges of my arrogance, pride, and sense of superiority fade away.

Awakening to the truth of suffering is the awakening of compassion. In Mahayana Buddhism, an enormous emphasis is placed on the need to cultivate compassion as the moral foundation upon which the realization of the true nature of reality as emptiness rests. Without integrating compassion as a foundational dimension of our being, the realization of emptiness may lack heart for our flawed humanity. Realizing emptiness, after all, means radical freedom from the entirety of the relative domain, including the burden of the human predicament. But as we then reembrace the human condition from that liberated state and come to terms with its inherent suffering, compassion arises spontaneously.

Waking up to the truth of suffering enriched my awareness in new ways. I could feel how underneath the drama of my personal ordeal I was still alive to my radical spirit, that mysterious force that invites you to "put down your chains, to opt for a life that is free and authentic"[1]— a force that is rooted in the unqualifiable freedom of the empty nature of absolute reality. But along with that, a deepened sense of compassion had sensitized my heart to the vulnerable human circumstance in which we all find ourselves. I had moved into a state of wholeness I had never known before.

As this new portal opened up in my awareness, I felt replenished, both psychologically and spiritually, and a surge of fresh energy began to flow through me. I felt ready to reach out to my former students again. I wanted to apologize to them, take responsibility for my mistakes, and try to make amends. I missed them dearly and desperately. We had been a close-knit family, and our longstanding shared commitment to create a powerful space for group awakening—a flourishing evolutionary space, vibrant with creative friction—had forged a soul-level bond between us that I felt was hard to deny. So I wrote an extensive apology letter to all my former students, detailing the sobering insights that had emerged during my sabbatical (see appendix).

Writing this public letter was a profoundly humbling experience. It felt like making a deep bow in front of the whole world. But to my shock and consternation, my conciliatory gesture wasn't well-received. While a few of my former students still valued the positive achievements of our work together and appreciated my apology, the responses of them were outright devastating to me. Many of them were outraged that though I admitted my mistakes, I still upheld the positive side of our work and pointed to its extraordinary accomplishments, whereas as far as they were concerned there was no sugar to be separated from the sand. They wouldn't grant our shared experiment even a measure of partial truth, goodness, and beauty. Their interpretation had become so one-sided that to them the whole experiment had been one big farce. They wanted me to admit that my mistakes were unforgivable and that I therefore should *only* have expressed shame, grief, and remorse in my letter.

I began to receive vindictive hate mail cloaked in often irreverent language expressing outrage and dismay that I still had the audacity to claim a certain dignity in this calamity. Given their inspired enthusiasm for our work not that long ago, their judgment struck me as strangely unbalanced, even extreme at times, in its doubtless absolutism. The visceral intensity driving their all-out rejection was puzzling to me. If everything we did together had really been as misguided or as corrupted as they now seemed to believe, then they all needed to account for why, as intelligent, sophisticated, mature people, they had so passionately dedicated their lives to our shared endeavor. They seemed to have lost touch with the true reason for their extraordinary commitment to our work not so long ago, with the real taste of enlightened awareness they had experienced in my company, and with the genuinely awakened and inspired lives they had all lived because of it. To me, there was beauty and profundity in the legacy we had created together; to me, it was a precious jewel that deserved to be honored.

Despite the intense backlash, however, I continued to feel that apologizing was the right thing to do. It was clear that I *had* to take responsibility for the unnecessary suffering I had caused, and I felt I needed to do so face-to-face with those involved. And so I began to make plans to meet with all my former students whom I felt I had somehow treated unfairly. I thought it could be deeply healing to simply talk with them in the spirit of openness and vulnerability, to hear them out, to just be present with them without any agenda and learn where I had been an untrustworthy teacher to them.

As I began reaching out, it quickly became clear that many of my students were no longer interested in my conciliatory gestures. Their response was often firm and formal, running along the lines of: "Thank you for reaching out. There is, however, no need to reconnect or rebuild any kind of relationship between us." They simply wanted to be left alone and move on.

Many, however, did show an interest in meeting with me. For them I embarked on an apology tour that took me to New York, Boston, San Francisco, London, Amsterdam, Copenhagen, Paris, Frankfurt, Jerusalem, and Tel Aviv. I visited around eighty people. It was a most gripping experience. Some of the conversations we had were deeply touching, others felt weird and uncomfortable, and a few became so highly charged that they went off the rails. People's grievances were often unique and deeply personal. Still, several themes surfaced more frequently than others.

A number of my students were still resentful about my at times overly harsh treatment of them. It was true that whenever I had felt that their ego was taking over and sabotaging their further development or undermining the often hard-won emergence of the delicate, trans-egoic We-field we were all co-creating, I had often come down on them very hard. At the time I had been convinced that a firm response would humble their egos and steer them back in the right direction.

But as I now heard some of them talk about their experiences of my harsh treatment, I felt deeply regretful that I hadn't responded to them in a gentler and more compassionate way, with a greater appreciation of the complexity of human development, in light of which the ego's narcissistic tendencies need to be understood. But I was impatient, especially in my younger years as a teacher. I couldn't understand how people could lose the plot so quickly. It had taken the harrowing ordeal of the collapse of my community for me to fully grasp that berating people harshly puts them in a state of agony, which makes it virtually impossible to deal with the real challenges of higher development in a fruitful manner. Had I been kinder, more understanding, and less morally condemning, I could have avoided unnecessary suffering. And thus, in many of my conversations with my former students, I unreservedly admitted how ashamed I now felt about my insensitivity, and I sincerely apologized to them for not having been a better teacher.

Another issue I was confronted with repeatedly was my habit of shaming my students, often relentlessly. This mostly occurred when I felt that they weren't living up to their full potential or were practicing the teachings in a halfhearted way. Sometimes, however, I had taken this attitude when they expressed their intention to discontinue their studentship and leave our work. At the time I saw such announcements as a deep betrayal of the mission we had all set out to build together, and I often responded in an inexcusable way not uncommon in mythic guru systems, saying things like, "If you leave, your life will be meaningless and hellish. You will be lost because I am your direct connection to the Absolute." I always took it personally rather than openheartedly allowing my students to go, giving them the freedom and dignity to make up their own minds. At times I had become so angry that I instructed others to just throw these students' belongings out of the community house where they were living, unconcerned about where they would sleep the next night.

As I listened to their vulnerable descriptions of how horrible my treatment had made them feel, the inhumanity and lovelessness of my actions got through to me, and the emotional hardship they had endured because of my cruel interventions hit me deeply. I felt their pain and apologized profusely for having been so judgmental. Some of them noticed how shocked and devastated I was as I listened to their sharings. They felt my human side and were moved. In beautiful moments like these, we both experienced a real sense of connection beyond my self-image as their guru and their projections of me as a heartless, inhuman character.

But these moments of real healing only happened in a rare few cases. I remember an in-depth conversation with a student whom I had, in retrospect, clearly treated poorly. As we were talking, I apologized to him from the bottom of my heart. I explained to him exactly where I had gone wrong and what I now knew I should have done differently, and

I let him know that I understood why he had reacted the way he had. He was surprised that I was aware of his perspective in such explicit detail. It was clear to him that I had reflected deeply on our history together and that I had really grappled with my mistakes. He expressed his appreciation for having put myself in his shoes. Throughout our conversation, I felt deeply connected to him. He knew that I knew, and he accepted my apology with an open heart.

In most conversations, however, such an intimate meeting of hearts did not happen. Time and again we seemed to bump into some hidden barrier, preventing us from diving below the surface layers of social niceties and the status quo of superficial friendliness. Even though many people I spoke with appreciated my reaching out to them, it often felt as if the changed context no longer allowed us to communicate with real depth and break through the invisible wall between us.

Other times I noticed that some people simply didn't know how to respond when I spoke transparently about issues in myself that I hadn't seen before. Having been their guru for so long, my sincerity about my humanness made them feel uncomfortable, and I began to wonder whether apologizing was the right thing to do.

Once or twice the conversation simply spiraled out of control. I remember how one former student became furious as we reflected on our history together. She screamed in my face, yelling at the top of her lungs that all I had ever wanted to do was to take control of her life for my own dark reasons. The projection coming at me from her was so extreme and so terribly divorced from reality that I had no choice but to endure her fury, remain poised, and simply absorb it all. My apology meant nothing to her. Our perspectives were miles apart, and there was no mutual understanding between us.

Overall, my apology tour didn't seem to catalyze the deep healing with my sangha that I had hoped for. Some people thought I hadn't gone far enough. Others were offended that I hadn't contacted them. Many of our conversations left me clueless as to how to move into a more thorough consideration of our deep and rich history together, and as this sentiment grew, my apology tour began to feel like it was leading nowhere. Saying goodbye when we parted ways at the end of such encounters was often a poignant moment. It felt like a critical juncture in which the deep relationship we once had, and all the years we had spent together, had come to a conclusive end.

It was clear that the lives of most people from my former community had dramatically changed after I had renounced my leadership role. Their attention had moved to different concerns. Many resolute core students had chosen to dive into worldly life and had children at the last moment. Some of the most dedicated ones now denied that anything of real value happened during their formal studentship. They had become convinced that it had all been a spell. Most people from the committed core had turned the page as well. They had no hard feelings and had happily moved on. Many of them had lost touch with the mystery they had once felt so lit up by.

And so, as it dawned on me that most of my former students had closed the chapter on our involvement with one another, I began to feel that I too needed to move on. I felt that for the time being I had taken my soul-searching and atonement process as far as I could. I had exhausted its potential, and I had transformed into a very different man because of it. The mythic identity in which my former incarnation as a guru had been trapped had dissolved; my shadow issues that had contributed to the crash of EnlightenNext had been worked through to a significant degree; and I had devoted a considerable amount of time and effort to apologizing for my mistakes and seeking to make amends with those I had hurt. For two years I had been immersed in the heat of crisis, and I felt alchemically transformed at a deep level. The perpetual evolutionary pressure I had endured had purged my heart, and the hardness of the man I used to be had largely burned away. I sensed that my sabbatical had come to a natural completion, and I felt ready to resume the teacher role again.

The handful of people who were sympathetic to my healing process were thrilled about this development. Throughout my ordeal they had surrounded me with love and support, each in their own unique way, and all of them had become very dear to my heart. Some of them had unwaveringly supported me on a human level and had been instrumental in my psychological healing as a man. Others had remained lit up by the dharmic sophistication of the Evolutionary Enlightenment teachings and kept encouraging me to reembrace the teacher role at some appropriate point in the future. Yet others supported me on a spiritual level. They consistently urged me to fully reclaim my spiritual self-confidence—reminding me of the beauty and preciousness of my radical spirit as a guru and affirming that my spiritual transmission was still present and powerful. It was as if they had been holding up a mirror, forcing me to look at myself and stay awake to my true nature. These people passionately wanted the work to continue in some new form and kept motivating me to once again take up my role as a spiritual teacher.

As it became clear to us that the time was ripe to move forward, we came together, formed a small but eager team, and began to plan my relaunch as a teacher. Together we created a new website and began to think about how to organize our first retreat. We were all inspired by a sense of moral obligation, driven to stand up for the truth of the teachings and passionate about honoring the legacy of the work. It was a time full of creativity and anticipation.

But our fledgling sense of exhilaration was short-lived. When other former students got wind of my intention to return to teaching, they were outraged. To them the very idea was like adding insult to injury. Many of them who had earlier accepted my apology abruptly changed their minds. They just couldn't grasp how my expressions of regret could have been sincere if I was now considering teaching again. Their reactions were unusually fierce. Many of them made it emphatically clear that I should *never* teach again, and some even began to actively discourage me from taking up any spiritual role—not now, not in the future.

Despite my transformation, they continued to feel that I hadn't even begun to deal with my real issues yet. To this day, many of my former students seem to believe that if I had really done the work I needed to do, somehow they would all know it, even though most of those spreading this narrative haven't seen me for many years. They don't have an accurate sense of the deep transformational work I have done, the ways in which I have put myself under a magnifying glass, or the extent to which I have changed. They seem to assume that life came to a screeching halt in 2013 with the crash of our community, and that I am still the man they once knew.

One former student told me unequivocally, "Andrew, I will never trust you again until you let go of everything, *completely*." He spoke as if the only way I could prove to him that I had truly understood the real message of the crash of EnlightenNext would be to become a nobody, relinquish my teacher role once and for all, and live out the rest of my life as a gardener, a dog trainer, a sadhu—to him, anything but teaching qualified as a truthful life choice. But what exactly would that look like? I had run this thought experiment many times during my sabbatical, and it invariably felt inauthentic to me. Would I avoid all conversation of meaning and depth? Never again be lit up with the mystery of existence? Focus on issues of lesser significance? This is not who I am. Sharing enlightened awareness is the only thing I live for. Without serving the Dharma, life is meaningless to me, and there is nothing that compels me here.

Some of my students argued that as long as I identify as the teacher, I am not radically free of egoic attachments, and thus I am not living my own teachings. But becoming a guru is never an egoic choice. At no point in my life did I have any ambition to become a spiritual teacher. When I met my guru and laid my life at his feet, something deep within my being shifted. At that moment my karma, my destiny, and my will were all swallowed by the infinite, and the source code of my life changed from "My will be done" to "Thy will be done." When I left Poonjaji after an extraordinary three weeks, I was no longer the man I had been before. Enlightened awareness was flowing through me and began to light up those around me independent of any deliberate intent on my part. I had inadvertently transformed into a spiritual teacher, and people started to respond to me accordingly. I hadn't taken up the teacher role; the role had taken me, and it had done so quite miraculously. It was never my planned choice, my life goal, or some egoic fixation. How then could I ever deny this choiceless miracle? Why would I banish it from my life, disown it, turn it into a shadow, and spend the rest of my life being somebody I am not? How authentic would that be, and what purpose would that serve?

In their attempts to prevent my comeback as a teacher, some of my senior students told me, somewhat patronizingly, "Don't worry, Andrew, your work is taken care of now. We can take it from here"—as if my life was essentially over and I had nothing more to offer. To them my role and gift had become irrelevant, and the only thing left for me to do was to disappear into oblivion. But the direct transmission of enlightened awareness still flows through me to this day. It is the living mystery at the heart of what I have to give. That mystery, to which the teacher also bows, and the perpetual evolutionary process it animates, is what I am here to serve.

In the period following my apology tour, my former students' conviction that I have no right to teach again remained as visceral as it was non-negotiable.

One would assume that the creative vibrancy of the evolutionary context we had all marinated in for so long and the level of maturity and sophistication we had all grown into would at least open up a possibility to try to work through our problems and perhaps emerge on the other side, even if only to clear up whatever was still a source of tension for those who simply wanted to move on with their lives. But to this day the signs of thawing and healing are still few. A lot of the karma between me and a number of my former students remains unresolved. It hasn't been dealt with on a deep soul level. It still feels like there is a gaping wound in our collective soul that hasn't healed, and I am still brokenhearted over it. But I no longer know what to do to catalyze a true healing.

Because of the intense opposition coming my way, I continued to struggle with doubts about my reemergence as a teacher. Yet deep within my soul I felt I had no choice but to teach again and bear witness to the good, the true, and the beautiful of the innovative spiritual legacy we had all co-created. Underneath a layer of doubt, the glow of my authentic self was still bright, urging me to keep the truths of the teachings alive and the light of awakened awareness burning.

On February 7, 2017, I took the plunge. I formally ended my sabbatical after almost four years of absence from the public eye and led my first relaunch retreat in Paris. The night before the event I went to bed plagued by a sense of insecurity so strong that it made me feel like I couldn't go through with the event. But to my great relief I woke up the next morning bathed in a state of joy and lightness of being, and I knew that everything would be fine.

It was a small gathering of about twenty people, several of whom were long-term students who supported my reemergence as a teacher. Being with my students again, the guru function in me reactivated. I had instant access to the same spiritual clarity and intensity I had always experienced during my years as a guru. It felt like stepping back into a hurricane of consciousness and energy. From the very first moment it was obvious that the guru function had never been lost, despite how it had appeared to me over the last three and a half harrowing years. It had always remained fully present in the background, untouched by any drama, ready to reemerge.

It was a delight to be teaching again. I shared my understanding of the causes of the dissolution of EnlightenNext and my subsequent personal ordeal of being lost and falling back into an unenlightened disposition. Then I described the transformation I went through as a result of the crisis, both as a guru and as a man. Judging by the dialogues we had, most of those present could feel that I had softened. It was a moving and memorable first gathering. Many were profoundly impacted by the palpable intensity and presence of Spirit that is ignited in the company of a guru. For my students, more than anything else it was a moment of renewed connection with the uncompromising nature of the Absolute, and they reawakened to what it means to be in relationship with this mysterious force.

The activation of the guru function is actually not a well-considered choice. It happens spontaneously, whenever there is a sincere receiver who approaches the guru in a spirit of genuine sacrifice of the self. By its very nature, the guru function lies dormant until it is called out, and when it is, it simply responds to whatever is required, without deliberation or judgment. It feels like a selfless metaphysical compulsion, a magnificent mystery to which even the teacher submits. It leaves one no choice but to step out of the way and live up to its calling. The essence of the guru function is its power to impart awakened awareness in the hearts and minds of those who are open to its impact. Its transcendental energy is infectious. It lights up the immense love, deep peace, and inspired wisdom that is already present within you as the innermost secret of your own heart.

In my case, the guru principle expresses itself most prominently as the ecstatic urgency to evolve, a vibrant spiritual energy that ignites the exhilarating creativity of Eros, the evolutionary impulse hidden in the heart of the kosmos. Like a bright, awake fire, it burns through the ego's inertia, its dullness, its ongoing existential anxiety, and relaxes it into an expanded identity, a state of uncontracted openness and uncorrupted innocence, free of pretense and alive to the awe and wonder of the miracle of existence. As such, it is the true self's best friend and the ego's worst nightmare.

After the Paris retreat, more teaching occasions followed. During each one I felt both blessed and humbled that the sublime gift my guru had bestowed on me continued to flow through me, and day by day I could feel myself reconnect more deeply with the profound moral obligation that falls on the shoulders of whomever has been granted this gift and the sacred duty to share it with others. Slowly but surely I became more strongly realigned with the guru within, which is my primary identity, the truest expression of my authentic self, and once again I experienced the grace-filled effortlessness of teaching the Dharma. Teaching still came as naturally to me as breathing, just like it did before.

As my teaching schedule began to gain traction, it became increasingly clear to me and to those around me that I was no longer the guru

I had once been. The mythic identity I had been so heavily invested in for nearly three decades had burned away. Unlike before, being in the guru role no longer felt like position-holding. This became apparent in the radically different way I now related to students, which was much more natural and free of pretense. But it was also obvious in everyday changes in my attitude and behavior. For example, like many Dharma teachers, I previously almost never went out in public alone. I always surrounded myself with an entourage of close students ready to protect me and take care of my practical needs. This was a way to control the space, assert the hierarchy, and safeguard my mythic identity. Now it was clear to me that this was not true freedom. In formal teaching situations a certain structure may help to liberate the teaching function and make it more effective, but outside such a context any need to uphold a particular posture is a sign of bondage. Now whenever I am not in a formal teaching situation I effortlessly fall into a natural state, free from having to uphold the mythic guru identity.

To this day, I continue to feel a great sense of responsibility regarding my teaching role. I am absolutely committed to not ever making the same mistakes again, and I continue to learn what it means to be transparently human *and* enlightened. I feel compelled to become unambiguously clear about the errors of the past and deepen my understanding of the complicated conundrums our shared utopian experiment and its abrupt collapse have brought to light.

PART 2

$\bullet\ \bullet\ \bullet$

EXPLORING
THE SPIRITUALITY
OF TOMORROW

9

The Owl of Minerva
Flies Only at Dusk

Ever since Eastern spirituality was first introduced to the Western world, numerous spiritual teachers, gurus, and mentors have fallen from grace, plagued by scandals involving money, sex, and power, leaving a trail of confusion, doubt, and disillusionment in their wake. Many of these teachers, like Adi Da Samraj, Osho, and Chögyam Trungpa Rinpoche, were profoundly enlightened beings—spiritual geniuses—whose transmission of mind was powerful enough to jolt their students into higher states of consciousness and give them a taste of the Absolute. Their inspiring presence uplifted people far beyond what they imagined possible, and many felt compelled to abandon the world in the name of truth and freedom, join the spiritual communities that had sprung up around them, and pursue the utopian dream of creating Heaven on Earth. These communities, like my own, started out with such promise, but at some point along the way their vision soured.

The cultural impact of all these situations combined put an end to the "romantic period" of the sixties and seventies, when Eastern gurus and their wisdom were eagerly embraced by the spiritually hungry audience of the postmodern West, and ushered in the "reckoning period" of the eighties and nineties, when new scandals kept erupting with disconcerting regularity.

As a result, a crisis of trust has engulfed the spiritual world. The breakdown of these spiritual experiments has carved a deep, culture-wide fissure of cynicism and skepticism in the Western mind about the actual value of the spiritual quest. It has even cast a shadow over people's trust in their own potential to lead a truly awakened life, and many have simply given up on such a project altogether. During the brief but turbulent history of East-meets-West spirituality, it has become painfully clear that something has gone terribly wrong with the cross-pollination between Eastern wisdom traditions and our postmodern Western culture.

This has led some influential voices to boldly declare that the age of the guru is definitively over, and this adage is gaining in popularity day by day. Some who adhere to this position, like contemporary philosopher Charles Eisenstein, acknowledge that the loss of the guru role presents us with a problem: "As many spiritual traditions recognize, a living teacher, a guru, is necessary to bring the teachings to life in their unique application to each individual. We need something from beyond our old selves, someone to illuminate our blind spots, to humble our conceit, to show us the love we didn't know we had within us."[1] But even those who clearly see this problem are reluctant to unambiguously stand up for the necessity of the guru principle. Most of them favor alternative solutions that are designed to seamlessly match the egalitarian spirit of our times rather than excel in effectiveness.

They have replaced the classical guru model, in which the teacher had unfettered authority over the student, with what some have facetiously called "the San Francisco model." The teacher in this orientation is basically reduced to a spiritual friend, a fellow traveler on the path, or, at best, a more experienced colleague. Since the postmodern mindset that produced this approach has declared hierarchical distinctions as officially taboo, any such perceived differences are diligently leveled out, while one's own inner guru is upgraded to a position of ultimate authority at all times. The problem with this model is obvious. The guru function can only work its transformational miracles if the guru's degree of attainment is recognized as being higher than the student's, and if the guru has a platform in which to actually work with the student based on this natural hierarchy. In the absence of these conditions, nobody gets challenged and nobody truly awakens and grows.

Others who have sought an alternative to the guru function have become convinced that the solution can be found in the postmodern spirit of interconnectedness. They claim that humanity's increasing awareness of our interbeingness points us toward a new spiritual culture in which the classical guru role will no longer be enacted by a single person, but by an awakened collective, a community of practitioners. This intuition was most famously expressed by the venerated Buddhist monk Thich Nhat Hanh, who uttered the visionary words, "The next Buddha may be a sangha." While his intriguing prophecy perfectly suits the egalitarian sensibilities of postmodernity, it still begs the question: Can the guru function, which requires a unique expertise rooted in enlightened awareness, be effectively taken over by a community of students? Or is the collapse of the Buddha into the sangha one of the unfortunate consequences of a postmodernism that has gone too far in its corrective response to the power hierarchy implicit in the classical guru-student relationship, with its inherent potential for abuse? The latter is the position I will stand up for in the coming chapters of this book.

I still strongly believe in the efficacy of the Buddhist notion of the Triple Gem, in which all three of its constituents—the Buddha, the Dharma, and the Sangha—have their own unique, distinct, irreducible role to play. Each represents a very different and indispensable dimension of the reality of the One, and each has an integrity of its own that needs to be honored.

When EnlightenNext was at the height of its creative emergence, the Three Jewels were vibrating, working side-by-side, alchemically joined in an ongoing dynamic interplay. I was on fire. The teachings were pouring through me like never before, and our community was living and practicing them with a depth of commitment that was both extraordinary and rare. Together we managed to create the right conditions to catalyze something many in the spiritual world viewed as genuinely and authentically new, something that did not exist before. We were giving birth to a living buddhafield of intersubjective non-duality brimming with the ecstatic urgency to create a new world. We were all lit up with the thrilling sense that with the emergence of this enlightened We-space we were actually cutting a new groove in the ever-evolving interior of the kosmos.

The success of our spiritual experiment has convinced me of the transformational power of the Triple Gem. When all three of its jewels are present simultaneously and can operate together as one integrated whole, the ultimate gift of enlightened awareness can truly shine forth and come alive in this world.

Yet even with the Three Jewels fully functioning and all the transcendental breakthroughs people experienced as a result, our promising spiritual experiment still collapsed. So what went wrong?

For many years now I have been reflecting deeply on the way I enacted my role as a guru, about the means I used to implement the teachings of Evolutionary Enlightenment, and on the dynamics of our sangha. My inquiry has lead me to better understand the reasons why EnlightenNext fell apart and what my own responsibility was in causing this downfall. As my search for answers has progressed, I've been struck by the similarities between the story of our movement and what happened to so many other spiritual teachers and communities. The resemblances seemed to point to a deeper problem, one endemic to the classical guru-disciple model itself. For all of its effectiveness, the Triple Gem framework is also thousands of years old. It was created in the mythic-traditional context of the ancient world and is infused with beliefs in rigid hierarchy, absolute authority, and the possibility of human perfection—outdated views that simply can't survive the scrutiny of the postmodern gaze. If the Triple Gem model is to be carried forward into the future, it needs to be recontextualized and updated to include the novel breakthroughs of our time and incorporate the evolved needs of postmodern people. But how do we do this? How do we move beyond the anachronistic aspects of the mythic guru model and continue to share its true gifts in ways that are culturally appropriate in a leading edge, postmodern, or emerging Integral context? Can we liberate the guru-student relationship from its unnecessary baggage and save its precious essence from the current cultural rejection that is causing its rapid downhill slide into irrelevance?

During the past years I have explored these subjects, often in the sobering solitude of my own mind but also in creative dialogue with colleague teachers, deep thinkers, and Integral philosophers. In the course of these conversations it has occurred to me that many of my dialogue partners have been grappling with the same questions as they explore new ways to more effectively work with their highly individuated students, organize their post-mythic sanghas, and teach more integral forms of the Dharma, in which practitioners train a wider range of aspects of their developmental potential—beyond just focusing on waking up. It quickly became apparent that these themes were leading us into new territory. The cultural world you and I are living in doesn't yet contain already created structures in which an evolved Buddha, Dharma, and Sangha can fully flourish and fulfill their true promise as the most potent evolutionary instruments for creating a more enlightened society. It is up to us all to co-create them. Postmodernity has put the problems with the traditional model on the radar with compelling clarity, but it doesn't offer any solutions. Everybody is acutely aware of what's wrong, but nobody yet has any clear-cut answers about how to skillfully reorganize the spiritual practices of tomorrow.

In the pregnant space where old structures are deconstructed and new ones are being formed, a measure of creative chaos is inevitable and mistakes are bound to occur. Trial and error is the way evolution produces novelty. Many of those I spoke with, such as Doshin Roshi, the founder of Integral Zen, view the crash of EnlightenNext in light of this larger evolutionary context. "This is a time for pioneers," Roshi emphatically declared, mindfully reciting his every word. "People who don't buy the old ways. People who are forging ahead and have the courage to find the paths that have not been trod. That's what I see when I look at Andrew Cohen and the mistakes he made. My goodness, what a goldmine. Those mistakes—that gold is the mother of wisdom. It's the mother of the knowledge of where we need to go."[2] Not without some poetic flair, Steve McIntosh, a thought leader in the Integral philosophy movement, echoed this very same sentiment when I spoke with him in 2018: "Hegel's famous dictum is so memorable: 'The owl of Minerva flies only at dusk.' I love it. The owl of Minerva, representing wisdom, only really appears in hindsight, at the end of the day." For Hegel, this is not tragic. It's the way evolution works. Only in retrospect can we truly understand history's at times ruthless developmental logic.

In the chapters ahead I will hone in on this "wisdom of the dusk." I will share some of the lessons that have emerged from my fall from grace and the dissolution of our community, present the best understandings gleaned from my dialogues with thought leaders, and relate it all to the broader implications for spirituality in general where appropriate.

It is my hope that the story of our work—successes and failures alike—can eventually serve the evolution of the Buddha, the Dharma, and the Sangha, as these time-honored spiritual jewels move into their post-postmodern expressions.

10

Death of the Mythic Guru

"Guru Yoga is the most powerful yoga there is. But in today's world it is almost impossible to do it right," Ken Wilber writes in *One Taste: Daily Reflections on Integral Spirituality*. "With Guru Yoga, you fall in love—deeply and desperately in love—and that love is the vehicle through which you can much more quickly learn the language of your own true self. Precisely because this learning is driven by love, it happens more rapidly than sitting alone, in the corner, on your meditation mat, counting your breaths." In a cautionary manner he adds: "Precisely because Guru Yoga is so strong, it can also cause the most damage. The abuses are legion, and we hear about a new one almost every day. In any event, I honestly do not think that Guru Yoga—for some very good reasons, and for some truly pathetic reasons—can flourish in this country." He then points out that both our postmodern culture *and* the mythic guru system are partly responsible for this unfortunate situation.[1] Wilber's assessment accurately frames the modern-day predicament of Guru Yoga.*

---

*In Buddhist teachings, Guru Yoga is the practice of devotional surrender to a guru—a deep and sacred spiritual process in which the devotee's own Buddha nature progressively merges with the enlightened mind of the guru to the point where there is no longer any difference between the disciple's inner state and the guru's state of self-realization.

The Spectrum of Consciousness: Levels and Lines

LEVELS OF CONSCIOUSNESS

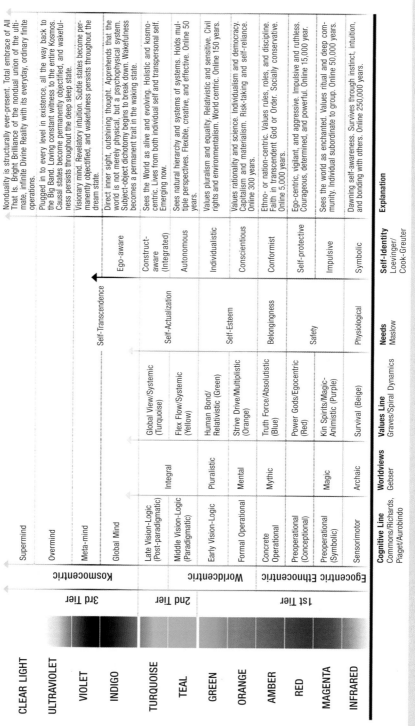

Level	Tier	Cognitive Line (Commons/Richards, Piaget/Aurobindo)	Worldviews (Gebser)	Values Line (Graves/Spiral Dynamics)	Needs (Maslow)	Self-Identity (Loevinger/Cook-Greuter)	Explanation
CLEAR LIGHT	3rd Tier / Kosmocentric	Supermind					Nonduality is structurally ever-present. Total embrace of All That Is. Bright Brilliance of the nondual union of the ultimate, infinite Divine Reality with its everyday, ordinary finite operations.
ULTRAVIOLET		Overmind					Plugged in to every level in existence, all the way back to the Big Band. Loving constant witness to the entire Kosmos. Causal states become permanently objectified, and wakefulness persists throughout the deep sleep state.
VIOLET		Meta-mind					Visionary mind. Revelatory intuition. Subtle states become permanently objectified, and wakefulness persists throughout the dream state.
INDIGO		Global Mind				Ego-aware	Direct inner sight, outshining thought. Apprehends that the world is not merely physical, but a psychophysical system. Subject-object dichotomy begins to break down. Wakefulness becomes a permanent trait in the waking state.
TURQUOISE	2nd Tier / Worldcentric	Late Vision-Logic (Post-paradigmatic)	Integral	Global View/Systemic (Turquoise)	Self-Actualization	Construct-aware (Integrated)	Sees the World as alive and evolving. Holistic and kosmocentric. Lives from both individual self and transpersonal self. Emerging now.
TEAL		Middle Vision-Logic (Paradigmatic)		Flex Flow/Systemic (Yellow)		Autonomous	Sees natural hierarchy and systems of systems. Holds multiple perspectives. Flexible, creative, and effective. Online 50 years.
GREEN	1st Tier / Egocentric Ethnocentric Worldcentric	Early Vision-Logic	Pluralistic	Human Bond/Relativistic (Green)		Individualistic	Values pluralism and equality. Relativistic and sensitive. Civil rights and environmentalism. World centric. Online 150 years.
ORANGE		Formal Operational	Mental	Strive Drive/Multiplistic (Orange)	Self-Esteem	Conscientious	Values rationality and science. Individualism and democracy. Capitalism and materialism. Risk-taking and self-reliance. Online 300 years.
AMBER		Concrete Operational	Mythic	Truth Force/Absolutistic (Blue)	Belongingness	Conformist	Ethno- or nation-centric. Values rules, roles, and discipline. Faith in transcendent God or Order. Socially conservative. Online 5,000 years.
RED		Preoperational (Conceptional)		Power Gods/Egocentric (Red)	Safety	Self-protective	Ego-centric, vigilant, and aggressive. Impulsive and ruthless. Courageous, determined, and powerful. Online 15,000 year.
MAGENTA		Preoperational (Symbolic)	Magic	Kin Spirits/Magic-Animistic (Purple)		Impulsive	Sees the world as enchanted. Values ritual and deep community. Individual subordinate to group. Online 50,000 years.
INFRARED		Sensorimotor	Archaic	Survival (Beige)	Physiological	Symbolic	Dawning self-awareness. Survives through instinct, intuition, and bonding with others. Online 250,000 years.

Self-Transcendence →

Plate 1. Overview of the stages of development according to Ken Wilber's Integral Theory.

ONE OF THE ESSENTIAL ELEMENTS of Ken Wilber's integral approach is the recognition that human consciousness evolves, develops, or unfolds through a fluid but hierarchical sequence of levels or stages. Integrating over one hundred developmental models into his framework, Wilber uses a rainbow-hued scheme (based on the colors traditionally ascribed to the seven chakras) to generically represent these different levels, which are grouped into three major classes or tiers.

First tier spans all levels from primitive, infantile consciousness (infrared) to postmodern, pluralistic consciousness (green); second tier represents a leap into holistic, systemic, and integral modes of consciousness (teal and turquoise), which some believe to be the leading edge of development today; and third tier reaches into even more integral, transpersonal, and higher "spiritual" territory (indigo and above)—levels that remain largely unexplored.

Many of the developmental models on which Wilber's spectrum of consciousness is based are the results of research on specific "intelligences," or developmental *lines* of growth and maturation, within the psychological makeup of human beings. This diagram includes the *cognitive* line, the *worldviews* line, the *values* line, the *needs* line, and the *self-identity* line, but many others have been identified, including the moral, emotional, aesthetic, interpersonal, psychosexual, and kinesthetic lines.

By observing the transformation of individuals over time, numerous researchers and theorists—from Aurobindo in the East to Piaget in the West—have shown that each of these developmental lines do indeed unfold through distinct levels of increasing consciousness, order, and sophistication. But what Wilber's spectrum reveals is how the various lines of development actually relate to each other: evolving, side by side, through the same general levels of increasing consciousness. It also makes clear how any given individual can be at a high level in a particular line while at lower levels in other lines, one example of which would be Nazi doctors: individuals who were highly developed in the cognitive line, but dramatically underdeveloped in the moral line.

Evolving Worldviews, Expanding Self

Although the spectrum of consciousness includes twelve colors to denote twelve specific levels, stages, structures, or waves of development, for ease of explanation Wilber often uses a simpler, three- or four-level scheme pioneered by developmental psychologists like Lawrence Kohlberg and Carol Gilligan. Tracing the most general contours of psychological growth, this scheme highlights the fact that increasing consciousness corresponds to a broadening of worldviews and an expansion of one's sense of self.

Egocentric ("me"): A stage characterized by narcissistic self-absorption, bodily needs and desires, emotional outbursts, unsocialized impulses, and an incapacity to take the role of the "other"; seen today predominantly in infants and young children, rebellious teens, wild rock stars, and criminals. (Infrared to red)

Ethnocentric ("us"): An expansion of self-identity to include one's family, peers, tribe, race, faith group, or nation; the adoption of socially conformist rules and roles; commonly seen in children aged seven to adolescence, religious myths and fundamentalism, the "moral majority," Nazis, the KKK, right-wing politics, patriotism, sports teams, school rivalries. (Amber)

Worldcentric ("all of us"): An even greater expansion of self to embrace all people, regardless of race, gender, class, or creed; a stage of rationality that questions rigid belief systems and transcends conventional rules and roles; commonly seen in late adolescence, social activism, multiculturalism, science, moral relativism, liberal politics, the "global village," New Age spirituality; the emergence of integral cognition. (Orange to teal)

Kosmocentric ("all that is"): An identification with all life and consciousness, human or otherwise, and a deeply felt responsibility for the evolutionary process as a whole; "super-integral" cognition and values; innate universal morality; spirituality beyond merely personal motivations; an emergent capacity, rarely seen anywhere. (Turquoise to clear light)

Plate 2. Explanation of the lines of development and the evolution of worldviews according to Ken Wilber's Integral Theory.

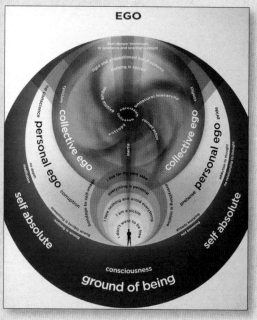

EGO

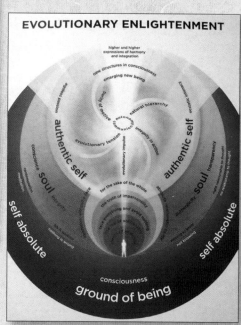

Plates 3 and 4. Teaching models of Evolutionary Enlightenment depicting the potential for spiritual development in an egoic context versus an enlightenment context.

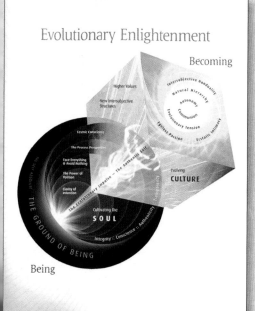

Evolutionary Enlightenment

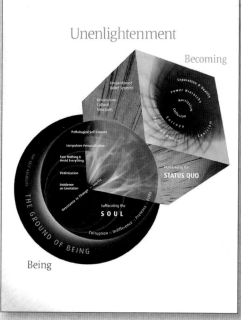

Unenlightenment

Plates 5 and 6. Teaching models of Evolutionary Enlightenment depicting the potential for cultural evolution in an enlightenment context versus an egoic context.

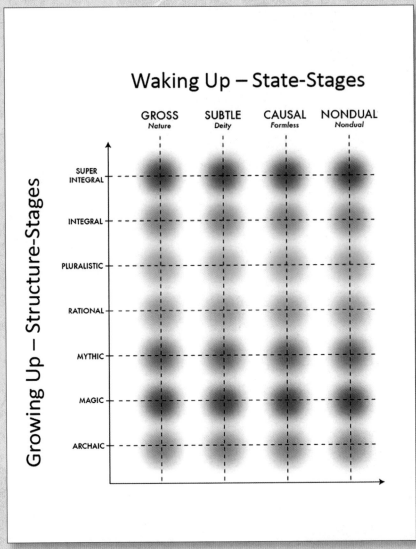

Plate 7. The Wilber-Combs lattice depicting the relationship between states of Waking Up and stages of Growing Up. (Image courtesy of Ken Wilber.)

It is clear that if we are to preserve the precious gift of having a direct relationship with a living master, we need to come to a solid understanding about the respective responsibilities of both the mythic guru model *and* the postmodern mindset that prevent Guru Yoga from truly living up to its promise in today's world. In addition, we need to work our way through any obstacles such an understanding brings to light.

The fundamental problem of Guru Yoga quickly becomes apparent if we consider its original form. Guru Yoga came into practice thousands of years ago, when humanity still believed that the Earth was flat and was the center of the universe, that women were inferior human beings, that homosexuality was a sin, and that slavery was acceptable—even in Buddhist monasteries. At that time, the mythic-traditionalist value structure, or amber altitude in Wilber's spectrum of consciousness model (see chapter 3, figure 3.1 or plate 1), was the highest developmental level then in existence, and its values of absolutism, fixed hierarchy, and strict authority were the leading edge of human evolution. Modernity hadn't yet emerged, and nobody in the ancient world lost any sleep over futuristic fantasies like the separation of church and state. Consequently, the guru, who was almost always male in those days, often served multiple functions, both spiritual and worldly. He was the political leader, the wise village elder, the priest, the educator, as well as the spiritual master. He was seen as a god-king, a sovereign endowed with divine attributes like omniscience, omnipotence, omnipresence, and infallibility.

It was generally assumed that the guru's attainment of the perfection of the Absolute also guaranteed the perfection of his human body-mind. Because he had realized this state of absolute perfection, everything he said and did was therefore also perfect. As such, the guru was granted absolute authority. If you approached him hoping to be initiated in the great secret of existence, you did so humbly and reverently. You were only accepted as a student if you were prepared to completely surrender all aspects of your life to him—body, mind, and soul—and offer him all your attention, devotion, money, and possessions. Living the noble life of a renunciate, striving to merge your mind with the wisdom-mind of the guru, was seen as the most laudable of all life choices in the ancient world, and society in those times supported the radical absolutism in which the guru-disciple relationship was embedded. Total submission of your autonomy to the spiritual master was considered to be the high road to God.

But these mythic-traditional times are long gone, and cultural evolution has advanced at least two or three developmental stages since that illustrious era.

Around five hundred years ago, with the dawn of modernity during the European Enlightenment, amber traditionalism began to make room for orange rationality. Meaning was no longer found in the total surrender of one's autonomy to some divine authority—quite the opposite. The assertion of one's autonomy and independence became one of the highest values. Truth was no longer delivered by divine decree or dogma, but discovered by using the scientific method and the rational, thinking mind.

Then, roughly a hundred and fifty years ago, green postmodernism (see chapter 3, figure 3.1 or plate 1) began to emerge as a further basic structure in our consciousness, coming into full fruition with the cultural revolution of the 1960s, when pluralism, multiculturalism, and the value of diversity and multiple ways of seeing reality burst onto the scene. Postmodernity gave rise to deeper compassion, care, inclusion, involvement, and idealism. Environmentalism, animal welfare, and care for Gaia were placed high on the agenda, and formerly forgotten or marginalized groups were given a voice, resulting in the women's, gay, children's and civil rights movements.

As postmodernity's demand for equality grew stronger, so did its rejection of any and all hierarchical distinctions. Being acutely aware of the many ways in which authority had been abused throughout history, the postmodern mind came to view hierarchy as a pretext for the abuse of power, oppression, and dominance.

Alongside this development, the rise of postmodernity also sparked our collective renewed interest in spirituality and inner growth, areas the previous modern era had largely rejected as irrational superstitions. The postmodern worldview allowed for the reenchantment of our subjective interior, which we were encouraged to explore. This caused an influx of Eastern gurus during the sixties and seventies, who came to the orange-green West to teach meditation; administer *shaktipat,* the direct transmission of spiritual energy from master to student; and introduce all kinds of traditional yogic techniques and spiritual disciplines to their hungry Occidental audience. Many of these mostly Asian gurus, however, were still deeply steeped in the amber-traditionalist mindset of the ancient world. Not surprisingly, this created a critical cultural tension between two very different value spheres. Orange modernity no longer bought into these outdated mythic beliefs in the guru's godlike perfection and absolute authority, and green postmodernity felt deeply uncomfortable with the hierarchical implications of the guru-disciple relationship and its requirement to submit one's autonomy to the guru, fearing it would open the floodgates for more abuse of power. And thus as Eastern gurus began to work with Western students, the amber context of the mythic absolutism, in which their collaboration remained embedded, increasingly exposed the foundational conundrum of the guru-disciple relationship in today's world: How do we negotiate the delicate tension between the authority of the guru and the autonomy of the student in such a way that the learning effect and transformational power of Guru Yoga isn't compromised?

In my own teaching work, the radical transformational potential of the guru-disciple relationship was considered to be of ultimate significance, and whenever it came into conflict with my students' autonomy, the importance of the latter was often downplayed as a matter of lesser concern.

During my spiritual quest as a young man I assimilated the age-old mindset of mythic absolutism from my Indian teachers and then quite naturally replicated it in the way I enacted my guru role. Even as I loved to cooperate with my students in creative ways and reflect on a wide range of subjects together with them—and I was curious, clear, and open about what I did not know—I never allowed anyone to question my authority on significant issues concerning spiritual matters. I firmly believed that the guru's wisdom usually comes from a higher state of consciousness than the disciple's and could therefore not be rightly assessed or understood by the student, who is still at a lower level. Traditionally, the guru is considered to be the face of one's true self, and questioning or doubting the guru is regarded as doubting your own higher self. Therefore, whenever my highly individuated students would resist my instructions, I mostly interpreted their noncooperation as an expression of ego, and as my job was to confront their egoic motivations, their defiance often resulted in a crisis with me, their guru. The way I performed the guru function was shot through with a strong flavor of this mythic absolutism.

Looking back, it is somewhat puzzling that the mythic guru role came so easily and naturally to me despite the fact that I was raised in a secular Jewish family in New York City and was part of the postmodern boomer generation, well-known for our rejection of traditional values.

Spiritually, my adherence to these values had everything to do with the overwhelming nature of the transcendental brightness my guru bestowed on me when he gave me the ultimate gift of enlightenment. This interior event felt so extraordinarily powerful, whole, full, and perfect that it wasn't a big leap for me to assume that the guru was indeed a perfected human whose wisdom is unquestionable, just as traditional spiritual lore has it.

For a few years I held on to this idealized image of my guru until I found out that for all his purity of transmission, he at times still acted out of ego. As I observed how he could be petty, competitive, and jealous, I became extremely disillusioned, and my image of him as "the perfected one" was shattered. I began to criticize Poonjaji's view that the ego was merely an illusion and therefore not to be problematized, and I saw his refusal to work with his students' egos as evading the real spiritual work of purifying the psyche and transforming it into a fine-tuned instrument of Spirit. Poonjaji was a true master in waking people up, but he left many hanging in midair when it came to their further growth into greater human maturity. Consistent with this emphasis, he differentiated between the man and the master in himself. When I heard about this distinction, I interpreted it as an excuse to not have to live up to the highest ethical and behavioral standards. And so in my youthful arrogance I set myself the firm intention: If *he* wasn't going to be the embodiment of perfect purity, then *I* would be. In me, the disturbing gap between the man and the master would not exist. With an unshakable spiritual self-confidence, I aspired to take full ownership of the notion of "the perfected one" in every moment, and this was how this outdated mythic ideal remained intact in me.

But there was also a philosophical reason for why I so naturally embraced the mythic guru role: I had always disliked the excesses of the postmodern mindset. As the West kept moving deeper into postmodernity, some of its truly revolutionary, original, and novel breakthroughs became too radicalized.

First of all, postmodernity's emphasis on subjectivity, which started out as a healthy corrective move away from modernity's exaggerated objectivism, went too far and deteriorated into unbridled narcissism. The postmodern self is endlessly preoccupied with personal feelings and with its own self-fulfillment. It abhors being judged, criticized, or called out on its shortcomings.

Subsequently, the groundbreaking claim that knowledge is indeed context-dependent and in part socially constructed has slid into a form of extreme relativism that is always ready to deconstruct any and all universal truth claims, until there is nothing left to orient oneself around. This has resulted in nihilism and a full-fledged crisis of meaning.

And perhaps the most hotly debated distortion of all: postmodernity's much-needed insistence on equality overfired into an exaggerated antihierarchical stance in which nobody is allowed to be more evolved than anybody else. Any form of power, authority, or hierarchical distinction immediately raises red flags and invariably prompts a knee-jerk reaction to deconstruct them.

These radicalized tendencies are the areas where postmodernity bears a responsibility for the cultural resistance against Guru Yoga, and as a guru I could see how every single one of them is a formidable obstacle on the spiritual path. They inflate the very narcissism and self-centeredness that spirituality strives to outgrow. They hollow out the inspirational sense of meaning that drives our evolution, leaving us bereft of higher ideals to which we can orient ourselves. And they reduce the guru to a mere spiritual friend with whom you can walk down the path together as an equal, someone who can teach you just as much as you can teach him. And so I felt driven to counter these excesses by adopting healthy amber-traditional values like discipline, an appropriate respect for authority, and the cultivation of a straightforward intellectual clarity that enables people to make plain value judgements. These principles resonated with me as a source of strength, orientation, and direction—all indispensable qualities if one is serious about the spiritual path.

As a teacher, I observed how embracing these amber-traditional values is a powerful way to unblock the evolutionary impasse in which so many postmodern people are trapped. Especially at the beginning stages of the spiritual path, this amber training, which is centered around the cultivation of self-discipline, is indispensable if one is to break through one's habitual egoic patterning.

And thus in an effort to remedy the pernicious aspects of postmodernism by infusing more traditional values, and inspired by the sense of perfection of the enlightened state, I quite spontaneously adopted a relational guru-student model saturated with mythic absolutism.

As these mythic-traditional values were part and parcel of my teaching approach, they were, to a certain extent, also built into the way I set up the hierarchical structure of our community.

My students were organized in a pyramid-shaped hierarchy consisting of several levels. Contrary to the visceral rejection of all hierarchical distinctions as illustrated by the green-postmodern altitude, once your center of gravity rests at the teal or turquoise level as seen in figure 3.1 or plate 1, hierarchy is spontaneously reembraced. At these Integral stages, hierarchy is perceived to be the real structure of the kosmos—its foundational organizing principle and a most natural phenomenon. In line with this view, the overall hierarchical configuration of our sangha was set up to resemble such a natural hierarchy. Every level within our community accommodated people of a similar degree of depth, verticality, and spiritual capacity.

This arrangement allowed my students to engage in the teachings at the level they felt they could handle. If you wanted to remain engaged in the world and live the life of a householder while also seriously practicing the teachings, you could do so by joining the third ring, the committed core, or the more loosely affiliated fourth ring of practitioners that constituted the base of the hierarchy. But if you felt compelled to take it all the way, give up your worldly life, and, like a traditional monk, enter a community of people who had completely devoted themselves to Spirit, you could join one of the two upper rings. Only those who had already proven they could actually stand that level of transformational intensity and had pledged their full commitment to the teachings would be allowed to join the resolute core or could be accepted as senior students, and I worked directly with only these people.

Our communal hierarchy thus functioned like an evolutionary ecosystem, offering students the opportunity to enact different roles at different times. There were always more advanced practitioners you could look up to as inspiring embodiments of the teachings and from whom you could learn. There were always equally trained peers to whom you could relate in the spirit of same-level mutuality, and draw support and encouragement from, during difficult ordeals of ego transcendence. And there were always those in the lower rings who had yet to go through the challenges you had already outgrown, and whom you could teach, mentor, and share your gifts with. We found that if people were given the chance to enact all three of these roles, it supercharged their evolution.

Every aspect of the hierarchical setup of our community was designed to support, optimize, and advance people's growth. It worked like a powerful developmental vortex, drawing students up. The continuous presence of shining examples above them generated a vertical magnetism that kept them awake and aligned with their highest potentials, and prevented them from falling back into the unconscious mechanics of their old habitual patterns. Because of the hierarchy, the atmosphere in our community was always saturated with a thrilling evolutionary vibrancy. People made an effort to step outside of their comfort zone and reach into the unfamiliar, the unknown—"leaning forward slightly off-balance," as I called this inner posture of aligning with the future-oriented Eros of the authentic self. They would stretch beyond their usual ways and show up at their best with their peers and around me, not only in their inner attitude, but also in exterior expressions, like staying in shape, dietary practice, sexual discipline, dressing nicely, taking care of aesthetics, and so on. As such, the hierarchy served as a powerfully effective teaching tool that provided unique growth opportunities for everybody.

A person's place in this hierarchical scheme largely corresponded to their competence in the specific metaphysical potential we trained in: that of establishing an awakened collective, beyond individual egoic consciousness. This extremely rarified condition can be seen as the leading edge of the sangha domain, and generating it was always a daunting task. Facing ego is extremely challenging by definition, and for many the work in the holons was a confrontational exercise in holding discomfort while also remaining established in the sheer brightness of intersubjective nonduality—the shared state of enlightened awareness we had been able to catalyze. And thus spiritual practice in our sangha was about being able to endure the heat of such a transformational fire without crumbling; or if you did, simply picking yourself up and doing so over and over again. The group gatherings were like a hot kiln in which everybody could experiment with their learning edge. People would train in their authenticity, their clarity of understanding, and their capacity for empathy and care. The atmosphere in the community was so intense that one could feel the heat almost 24/7.

The entire hierarchical structure of our community, with its lively connectivity *within* the levels as well as *between* the levels, was designed to bring the ego to full surrender and prepare people to commit enough to enable them to break through into intersubjective nonduality. It helped many students become humble, teaching them how to keep their egos in check and put Spirit first, and to substitute their individualism for the sake of the whole. In our postmodern times of highly empowered and autonomous individuals, this is no small feat.

Ultimately, my future vision for our community was that it would eventually become a self-generating organism in which people would be deeply involved with the teachings and with one another—a system that I would no longer be so directly involved with, struggling with people's personal karmas and taking on their egos. In my mind's eye I could see a vibrant, autonomous community, which would allow me to step back from any such personal interventions and simply teach the Dharma. And during the final years of EnlightenNext, this vision was in fact beginning to see the light of day.

But while these positive developments were occurring, an undercurrent of a different kind began to emerge. The downside of the hierarchical structure began to be exposed, and it began to overshadow the promise of my future vision.

The pressure to live up to the teachings was so intense that some of my students developed anxiety over not meeting the high mark we had set for ourselves. This created all kinds of undesirable psychological responses.

Some people would pretend that they were more spiritually advanced than they actually were; others would be extremely guarded about what they said in the holons, afraid it would be judged as ego; and yet others became overly concerned with their status within the hierarchy and began positioning themselves to protect their place.

So rather than the unselfconscious openness and transparency our practice was meant to generate, these people began to feel a deep ambivalence. They still felt grateful about being in an evolutionary sangha and thrilled about the opportunity to explore the leading edge of their development; and on a deep soul level they wanted nothing more than to rise to the occasion. But the challenge had become too great, and they began to feel divided between the parts of themselves that fell short of our high mark and the ideals they aspired to uphold. Some of them were afraid that if I got wind of the issues they were still struggling with after all these years of practice, they would be publicly shamed or even asked to leave their cherished community.

The extreme intensity with which I took on the ego had produced a system in which a degree of fear was ingrained. That fear was then perpetuated by our community culture as my students absorbed the ways of their exemplar, calling one another to task in often equally harsh ways. Students weren't as kind, forgiving, patient, and understanding as they could have been in scrutinizing and confronting the egos of their peers, and not every single thing they criticized in one another as ego was actually ego. In the end, the responsibility for this unnecessary toughness was mine.

Another unfortunate consequence of our strict hierarchical context and my insistence on only the most serious commitment was that it created a split in our community—between those who were able to play ball and those who weren't yet capable or willing to do the challenging work of self-transcendence. One of my shortcomings as a teacher was that I wanted everybody to become a warrior monk. Those who thrived in our community were always the stronger ones with greater self-confidence and a certain strength of character, and I was determined to pour all my energy and attention into working with them. I didn't know how to accommodate those who had apparently reached their ceiling and those who were still at a less mature stage in their development, even as it was obvious that they too had an authentic desire to serve our project to the best of their abilities. They were often the ones who had invested many years and an immense amount of their life energy to support the everyday workings of our community, by cleaning, cooking, and doing maintenance work. These indispensable jobs were the sine qua non of our shared project, and I failed to appreciate that. My single-minded focus on students in the top two rings of the hierarchy created a high-quality sangha, but it also excluded many. Now I consider this to be a failure of leadership. The mere fact that these students loved the teachings, felt drawn to me as their teacher, and had committed themselves to serving our work meant that I had a duty toward them as a guru. Today my attitude has changed profoundly. I now relate to my students by meeting them at the level they are at, and I work with them at the leading edge of *their* development.

For some, the division in our community became a source of great frustration. It was antithetical to my overall vision of one big, unified, cooperative community, a self-generating superholon of mature, autonomous individuals living together in a natural hierarchy and on fire with the ecstatic urgency to create the future together.

Many resolute core students grew frustrated with our community rule that people's place in the hierarchy was determined by how long they had known me. This principle implied that those who had entered the community later were perpetually regarded as junior to those who had come in earlier. A ranking system like that doesn't necessarily correspond with people's actual evolutionary advances, and many began to experience this as profoundly disempowering and disheartening.

In hindsight, this particular criterion for determining one's placement in the hierarchical order of the community was an all-too-literal interpretation of the concept of hierarchy characteristic of the amber-traditional value system.

These downsides of our hierarchical community structure were a sign that the format of our work together had become too rigid, and this rigidity began to produce unhealthy side effects.

Moreover, within the general thrust of what we were trying to accomplish, my mythic guru role was rather incongruous.

What we were all most passionate about was the co-creation of an advanced, second tier, teal to turquoise practice culture (see figure 3.2 or plate 2); and my teaching of Evolutionary Enlightenment was an expression of that newly emerging integral consciousness. In our best moments we actually reached into kosmocentric consciousness, which is free from narrow self-concern, and we were ecstatically inspired to participate wholeheartedly in the perpetual evolutionary unfolding of this vast and awe-inspiring universe-process, in which we perceived ourselves to be a small but significant part.

But my tenacious adherence to my mythic guru persona brought an untenable paradox to our spiritual experiment. On the one hand, I was on fire to create new structures in consciousness and culture, push the leading edge of evolution, and inspire my students to boldly reach into the future. On the other hand, I was tightly holding on to an ancient mythic-traditional context in the way I enacted my role as guru, and thus I effectively held people back in an outdated past. I tried to be an evolutionary teacher *and* an amber-level guru at the same time—these two roles are incompatible and contradictory.

The phenomenon of modern-day spiritual teachers holding on to a mythic-amber structure is the principal reason why the practice of Guru Yoga in our postmodern culture is like swimming upstream. Using Ken Wilber's developmental model (see figure 3.1 or plate 1), most spiritual students nowadays would be considered to be at the green altitude and moving toward green-exit—already sensing the attractive pull of the greater wholeness of the emerging teal and turquoise Integral stages on their inner horizon. When these people then end up in the amber guru model of an earlier time in the evolution of human consciousness, they find themselves stuck two or three stages below their actual center of gravity, even as the profound spiritual states they experience in their guru's company are still way above their heads. And thus when it comes to training in the spiritual states, most students will rightly feel that there are still worlds to evolve into; but when it comes to their growth through the developmental stages, many may eventually come to find that they have run into a dead end, because the overly amber context of their sangha tends to impede the smooth transition from green-exit to teal and turquoise. This double-edged dynamic is at play in many contemporary communities that practice Guru Yoga. Despite continued *state* advances, the *stage* differences between teachers and their students creates an unsustainable tension between two very different worldviews, and this, over time, almost always ends up in the type of crisis we have witnessed again and again when students break away from their teachers, or when yet another guru falls from grace.

This concerning situation has led some of our most prominent spiritual luminaries, like the inimitable Deepak Chopra, who himself has been the grateful beneficiary of a long-term guru-disciple relationship, to conclude, "I'm distancing myself from guru-disciple interactions. They are fraught with dysfunction and in today's world becoming irrelevant."[2] Others, like George Leonard, the founding father of the human potential movement, and his colleague Michael Murphy, co-founder of Esalen Institute, have voiced analogous positions, proclaiming that the time of the guru is definitely over.

The failure of Guru Yoga has taught us in no uncertain terms that as long as the guru-disciple model remains embedded in mythic absolutism and is enacted as unconditional submission of all aspects of the student's life to the person of the guru, it will continue to collide with the evolved needs and sensibilities of today's emancipated, autonomous individuals. It has become transparently obvious that Guru Yoga as it is traditionally practiced cannot flower in an evolved cultural context, and that the mythic-amber guru is effectively dead in the modern and postmodern world.

But for the many people whose lives have been permanently transformed by their association with a living master, myself included, it remains hard to imagine that the guru will ever become obsolete. It seems more likely that the guru principle will continue to play a pivotal role in the spiritual process. And exactly because I am no stranger to the lessons of its pitfalls, I feel a passion to share my evolving understanding and stand up for its at times inconvenient truth. And thus the questions that keep me up at night are these: How can we preserve the precious core at the heart of Guru Yoga and keep it alive in these less than supportive postmodern times? And which concrete changes do we need to introduce to liberate the guru principle from the mythic-amber absolutism in which it is still so often locked up?

It is clear that if the guru principle is to survive into the future, the practice of Guru Yoga needs to be remodeled. The key to this reformation, I feel, is to somehow scale the authority of the guru down without infringing on the transformational benefits of the guru-student relationship.

In my work as a teacher today I have come to understand that the first necessary step in this process is to clearly distinguish between the man and the master in myself. All throughout my teaching years I fully embraced my "guru persona" as the totality of my being. I saw myself as the full embodiment of what a guru is. In doing so, I aligned with the ancient mythic-amber model of absolute perfection and purity, and from that stance I chose to relate to my students.

But the fusion of man and master is one of the core fallacies of the mythic guru model. It often occurs quite naturally and almost imperceptibly, because if you are awake to the absolute Is-ness of the Great Perfection, it is so all-consuming, overpowering, awe-inspiring, and all-inclusive that it is easy to become convinced that everything you say or do communicates this perfect Is-ness. And spiritual teachers fall into this trap routinely.

When I interviewed Jeffrey Kripal,* an eminent scholar with several books on Eastern and Western esotericism to his name, about the future of the guru model, he spoke about this classic pitfall in a heartfelt, sympathetic way: "I don't have your experience, Andrew, but if I were to experience myself as God and the source of the universe, it would be pretty darn challenging not to confuse Jeff's will and wishes with this

---

*Jeffrey J. Kripal is associate dean of the faculty and graduate programs in the School of the Humanities and the J. Newton Rayzor Chair in Philosophy and Religious Thought at Rice University. He is also the associate director of the Center for Theory and Research at Esalen Institute. Jeff is the author of eight books, including *The Flip: Who You Really Are and Why It Matters,* where he envisions the future centrality and urgency of the humanities in conversation with the history of science, the philosophy of mind, and our shared ethical, political, and ecological challenges. Also noteworthy among his books is his memoir-manifesto *Secret Body: Erotic and Esoteric Currents in the History of Religions,* as it deals extensively with the Human as Two. He is presently working on a three-volume study of paranormal currents in the sciences, modern esoteric literature, and the hidden history of science fiction for the University of Chicago Press, collectively entitled *The Super Story: Science (Fiction) and Some Emergent Mythologies.* In this he intuits and writes out a new emerging spectrum of superhumanities (in both senses of that expression). His full body of work can be seen at www.jeffreyjkripal.com.

cosmic being. That's a natural confusion. And I think it's understandable and forgivable, and we need to say that, too."[3]

As we inquired into the nature of the relationship between the guru's divinity and his or her humanity, it quickly became obvious that other than being a prolific writer and original thinker, Jeffrey is also a warm and generous human being with a passion for spirituality. He is supportive of the guru principle and cares about its future. In his work he has proposed a model that he calls the "Human as Two," and his insights resonate profoundly with my own current understandings about the relationship between the man and the master:

> I think the number-one mistake we make is that we assume that a human spiritual teacher is "one thing," that is, a realized being through and through. We forget that actually, every human spiritual teacher is at least "two things," a relative historical social ego, capable of all sorts of nonsense and bad behavior, and a realized or enlightened form of consciousness, capable of the most fantastic and extraordinary things. . . . [Once we accept this,] we can also understand why some sort of submission or devotion might well be necessary and healthy, *and* why we should also reserve the right and duty to criticize the teacher when he or she does something morally and socially wrong. Both are true and necessary. . . . I also am convinced that particular spiritual teachers have the capacity to evoke or catalyze in their disciples various experiences of enlightenment, visions, altered states of energy, and so on, at the touch of a finger, hand, or peacock feather. . . . But none of this should remove the fact that these same human spiritual teachers are also human beings. There is no necessary relationship between enlightenment or deification, and moral or social behavior. The sacred is *not* the good. The mystical is *not* the ethical. . . . It has never been true that a divine presence is the same thing as human morality. . . . We can have enlightenment and cosmic consciousness while still being screwed-up individuals who are abusing each other. These are

not incompatible. . . . This recognition that the spiritual teacher is "two" is the most significant change in the spiritual process we could initiate, if we are willing. It would allow us to honor and integrate our deep histories and traditions without following them in any simplistic or naïve way.[4]

With his model of the Human as Two, Jeffrey accurately outlines the foundational feature of a post-mythic guru paradigm. There is no way around the fact that the master always expresses him- or herself through a relative personality structure. Anybody's expression of the enlightened state is therefore, paradoxically, always colored and shaped by the condition of that person's body-mind, both gifts and flaws included, while at the same time, at the deepest possible level, it is also a direct transmission of the uncorrupted purity and perfection of the transcendental essence of reality itself. An authentic master, because he or she is rooted in Source, is able to transmit a powerful measure of its inherent purity, brightness, and brilliance to students, and to this day this remains the most precious gift the true guru brings to the spiritual process. And so as we revisit the authority of the guru, we need to do so in a way that fully honors both these foundational truths.

In his work, Ken Wilber has proposed a roadmap for remodeling the practice of Guru Yoga to fully include all important bases of human potential—one's divinity *and* the full extent of one's humanity. His vision for transforming the classic Guru Yoga into what he calls *Integral Guru Yoga* also recontextualizes the jurisdiction of the guru role, and it does so without giving in to the unhealthy postmodern tendency to collapse the enlightened master into an ordinary human, or regressing into the outdated mythic-amber paradigm that elevates the unavoidable imperfection of the human persona of the man to a perfect master.

At the heart of Wilber's thinking is that Guru Yoga, if it is to become viable again in the twenty-first century, needs to supplement its original practice, that of Waking Up, with what he identifies as

Growing Up and Cleaning Up—two additional areas of practice that were unknown to the ancient sages but that have been brought to light in the last hundred years by the findings of modern day psychology.

Growing Up refers to the insight of developmental psychology that the human psyche grows through a series of interior stages of increasing psychological maturity (see figure 3.1 or plate 1). With each new stage, a person's self-identity expands, and as it does so, his or her worldview, values, and perspectives become more inclusive, whole, complex, and embracing. As people mature through the stages, their circles of care, compassion, and concern widen, moving from egocentric, including only oneself (red altitude); to ethnocentric, including also one's group or community (amber altitude); to worldcentric, including all human beings regardless of race, sex or creed (orange and green altitudes); to kosmocentric, including all sentient beings (second tier and the higher altitudes).

Incorporating this pathway of Growing Up into our spiritual practice is paramount because, as Wilber often emphasizes, Waking Up, or training higher states of consciousness, does nothing to make your values more inclusive or your worldviews more whole. Even the most profound enlightenment does not alter your stage of Growing Up, even as it does make you one with the unqualifiable Ground of All Being. The reason is that Growing Up and Waking Up are of a different order. Unlike your state of Waking Up, which you directly experience in the intimacy of your own awareness, none of the stages of Growing Up can be seen by looking within. They constitute the interpretive framework—the prism of the mind—through which you view the world without being aware of it. And so whenever you have a Waking Up experience, it will always be interpreted according to the worldview and values of the stage you are at.

This means that an enlightened sage at the mythic-amber stage will still be inclined to express the mythic absolutism and the ethnocentric, misogynistic, and sexist attitudes so characteristic of that stage. He feels like he is one with all sentient beings, but he is incapable of seeing the more advanced interior qualities of people at the worldcentric or kosmocentric levels. His experience of oneness doesn't reach into the stages he has yet to grow into. If anything, his realization will energize the values and worldviews of his present developmental level, because the certitude and clarity of absolute reality are now informing it, and so he will experience his amber prejudices and bigotries as holy precepts, fully endorsed by Spirit. To illustrate this, Wilber cites the example of the book *Zen at War,* in which highly regarded Zen masters espouse purely ethnocentric beliefs.

This relationship between states and stages is depicted in figure 10.1, called the Wilber-Combs lattice, which is one of the important contributions of Integral Theory. The major stages of Growing Up are shown on the vertical axis, whereas the major states of Waking Up can be found across the top.

And so Waking Up alone is necessary but not sufficient to produce enlightened exemplars whose goodness, moral virtue, loving-kindness, and compassion extend to the widest possible embrace. These capacities increase as we progress on the path of Growing Up, which is practiced by training ourselves to take the role of others and walk a mile in their shoes.

The other major area that must be included in a readjusted Guru Yoga is a robust practice of shadow work, or what Wilber calls *Cleaning Up.*

Earlier spiritual traditions were unaware of the fact that our minds can dynamically repress, project, and deny emotions because we experience them as undesirable, too overwhelming, or too painful to face, and so we push them out of our awareness. We banish them to our unconscious zone, where they transform into painful neuroses that linger on. We may think we've gotten rid of them successfully, but in fact they continue to impact our lives, showing up as emotional reactivity, which not only sabotages our own psychological health and well-being, but can also inflict harm and suffering on others.

The practice of shadow work is designed to reintegrate this unconscious material of our dark side and make it conscious again. It's about becoming intimately familiar with our own emotional and psychologi-

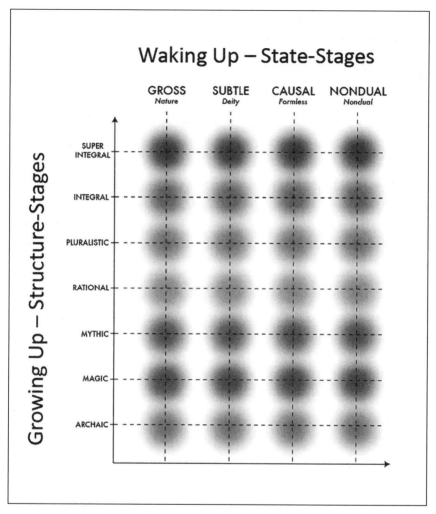

Figure 10.1. The Wilber-Combs lattice depicting the relationship between states of Waking Up and stages of Growing Up (see also color plate 7). (Image courtesy of Ken Wilber.)

cal makeup, which is often a deeply uncomfortable process that takes a rare kind of honesty and self-transparency—the kind of work I can now say I know well.

A deliberate focus on shadow work is a crucial ingredient for the success of our spiritual practice, because meditation alone does not reveal our blind spots to us. Contrary to many people's initial assumptions,

Waking Up in and of itself does not heal our shadow material, as is evidenced by the numerous cases of enlightened masters who still manifested all sorts of emotional dysfunctions, from sexual abuse to power issues, in their relationships with their students.

From a present-day Integral vantage point, most of the troubles with Guru Yoga stem from the fact that the practices of Growing Up and Cleaning Up were not yet fully understood, and as such they could not be skillfully executed by either students or their teachers. This exposes the heart of the problem with Guru Yoga in today's world: if you step into a guru-disciple relationship with the traditional attitude of full surrender of every aspect of your life to the guru in order to Wake Up, but the guru isn't familiar with the actual territory of some of these aspects, such as Growing Up and Cleaning Up, then you are giving the guru authority over areas of your life that his expertise doesn't cover—areas that may still be dysfunctional in the teacher's psyche. This can be problematic, because a guru not only transmits his enlightened state, but the condition of his relative personality as well; and as a student, it's hard to see the difference. And so you may imbibe as ultimate reality what are in fact dark pathologies, or devote your life to a set of narrow-minded worldviews and values originating from earlier stages of development, yet be convinced that they are absolute truth.

In the old days, this couldn't even be diagnosed as a problem, because the stages of psychological development and the reality of the shadow hadn't yet been discovered, and not a single spiritual tradition was aware of them. But ever since our knowledge of human potential has expanded, the ancient belief that Waking Up alone covers all important bases no longer makes sense. If Guru Yoga is to move beyond its current impasse, Wilber argues, it needs to evolve into an Integral Guru Yoga model by fully embracing the practice of Growing Up and Cleaning Up. But he is also unambiguous in saying that at this point in time this promising future ideal hasn't yet been reached: "Every version of Guru Yoga now in existence, bar none, is not an Integral Guru Yoga," Wilber states, "and therefore most of them are always messing up, in severely broken ways, with either (or both) Growing Up and Cleaning Up (and without understanding how or why they are doing either)."[5]

We are currently in an intermediate period in which several pioneering teachers are experimenting with ways to bring the paths of Waking Up, Growing Up, and Cleaning Up together in the context of the guru-disciple relationship. And so we have to relearn how to engage in Guru Yoga. We need to find the right balance between the authority of the guru and the autonomy of the student, and cultivate a more nuanced approach to devotion and surrender. As we readjust our attitude, we need to keep in mind that the gesture of surrender has always and forever been the key to realizing the true self, for a reason that still remains true to this day: the success of the guru's spiritual transmission depends on the student being completely open and receptive. There is no way around the fact that in order to Wake Up, the ego needs to move out of the way. So how do we include this powerful truth without disregarding the lessons of the discoveries of modern-day psychology?

Wilber proposes a refinement of the traditional attitude of full surrender of every aspect of one's life to the guru to make it more workable in our times:

In short, what we would see, with this re-evaluated Guru Yoga, is a functional and temporary surrender of personal self-autonomy to the person of the guru, but only in the areas specifically and demonstrably related to the actual process of Waking Up—and in those specific areas, "the guru can do no wrong" is entirely appropriate. (We saw that this is exactly how we view authorities in any field—e.g., a superb teacher of physics can "do no wrong" when it comes to the truths of physics—that's generally true to the extent it involves the basic truths of physics as presently understood—and this would apply to genuine gurus . . .) This stance of "everything I do is wrong, and everything the guru does is right" is a pragmatically effective means, within a specifically circumscribed area of Waking Up, to help an individual let go of their egoic self-contraction and expand their awareness to a oneness with the entire Ground of Being—and it is entirely appropriate in that very specific area of Guru Yoga. But when it comes to processes that most definitely include Growing Up and Cleaning Up, the guru is not a teacher in these areas at all. (Unless they have specifically studied those areas and become teachers in them as well—which is actually what I am recommending under the term "Integral spirituality.") . . . In fact, without that expanded and more Integral study, gurus themselves almost certainly have major deficiencies in each of those areas (of Growing Up and Cleaning Up), and if those dysfunctional areas are included in the rubric of "the guru can do no wrong," then disaster is just around the corner. . . .

Guru Yoga is not fit to take over the entirety of a student's life, about which it allegedly can make no mistakes. It is certainly not fit to address areas of Growing Up and Cleaning Up (unless the guru is trained in Integral). . . . Both those problem areas can be fully taken into account if the guru and the specific path of Guru Yoga itself either studies, or actually practices, the pathways of Growing Up and Cleaning Up—that is, if Guru Yoga becomes a genuine Integral Guru Yoga.[6]

Wilber's point is clear enough: a readjusted Guru Yoga needs to be restricted to the areas it legitimately addresses, and the actual authority, power, and jurisdiction of the guru should mirror her or his actual expertise. But translating this orienting directive into the actual real-life setting of day-to-day spiritual practice remains a challenge. By its very nature, the guru-disciple relationship tends to cover broader territory than Waking Up alone. It is meant to encompass the entirety of one's being. Contemporary students not only expect their spiritual teachers to guide them toward awakening, but also show them how to *live* it, how to embody enlightened virtues like inspired leadership, unquenchable evolutionary fire, awakened compassion, penetrating clarity, lovingkindness, humility, and generosity. The sacred impulse at the heart of every human being is not to only reach toward greater freedom *from* life, but also toward ever more unselfconscious liberated creativity *in* life. And this is where the practice of Guru Yoga reaches into the areas of Growing Up and Cleaning Up.

And so as long as there is no full-fledged Integral Guru Yoga, the gurus of today are called to either expand their area of expertise by familiarizing themselves with at least the basics of the areas of Growing Up and Cleaning Up, or, if a particular case requires it, delegate responsibility to trained experts who can complement the spiritual competence of the guru, so that students can be offered a genuinely Integral spiritual practice.

As the practice of Guru Yoga evolves toward greater proficiency at Growing Up and Cleaning Up, the core functions of the guru role remain unchanged. They are the faculties of the guru principle that quicken awakening and inspire the soul, and they are still as relevant today as they were when the guru model was first conceived. The true guru acts as an instrument of Spirit, a catalyst for ego transcendence, a clear mirror, and a transmitter of enlightened awareness. These guru functions are the unique and timeless gifts of Guru Yoga, and they need to be preserved. When these functions come to life in a relationship with a living master, they set in motion an extraordinary transformational process at the deepest possible level of your being, a process that tends to unfold along the following lines:

First, a deep love relationship spontaneously forms between yourself and your guru. An authentic master who is established in the state of enlightened awareness radiates the grace and beauty of the Divine. You feel magnetically drawn to her because you recognize her as a living, breathing embodiment of Spirit. When you are in her presence, you intuitively know she is the face of your true self, the portal to your own source condition, and you want to be in her company all the time. In due course, a deep bond of love is forged between yourself and your guru that spontaneously turns most other concerns into matters of lesser importance. In the extraordinary intimacy of this devotional relationship, you begin to forget yourself, and the force of love begins to supercharge your awakening process.

Wilber calls this devotional relationship a "second-person approach" to spirit and he often highlights its unique status among the different approaches. Ultimate reality, he maintains, can be looked at, experienced, and approached through three basic perspectives. Spirit in first person, the "I," is the subjective perspective. It is practiced through meditation, introspection, and recognizing yourself as the ever-present witness of this and every moment. Spirit in second person, the "you," is practiced by being in relationship with the Great Other, the living mystery at the heart of existence that is always greater than yourself. When you feel the presence of this Great Other, the only appropriate response is to surrender so fully that every trace of your sense of a separate self is utterly outshined. And lastly, there is Spirit in third person, the "it," which is the objective perspective. It is practiced by recognizing that you are part and parcel of the Great Holarchy or web of life in which everything is interconnected, a small but significant participant in this vast, impersonal evolutionary system driven by Eros—a core perspective in my teachings of Evolutionary Enlightenment.*

Of these three fundamental vantage points, the importance of Spirit in the second person cannot be overstated. The I-Thou relationship with that which is greater than yourself gets at the egoic self sense in ways that none of the other two approaches can. In his groundbreaking book *Integral Spirituality,* Wilber captures the unique power of this approach poignantly:

> The ego can actually hide out in 1st- and 3rd-person approaches. I simply go from I to I-I, never having to surrender to You. Spirit in 2nd person is the great devotional leveler, the great ego killer, that before which the ego is humbled into Emptiness. Vipassana, Zen, shikan-taza, Vedanta, TM, and so on, simply do not confront my interior with something greater than me, only higher levels of me.

---

*The fourth tenet of Evolutionary Enlightenment is called the *process perspective.* See chapter 3.

But without higher levels of Thou as well . . . then one remains subtly or not-so-subtly fixated to variations on I-ness and 1st person.
That is why the merely 1st-person approaches often retain a deep-
seated arrogance.[7]

As a living embodiment of Spirit, the relationship with the guru
serves as an archetype of this I-Thou relationship, and in this role it has
the power to catalyze ego transcendence in this most radical way.

As you live out this sacred relationship and interact daily with the
living divine presence in your guru, you will notice that an authentic master is free and unselfconscious. He or she is like a powerful
mirror, reflecting back to you all the areas within yourself where you
are still unfree. By simply relating to the guru, you sense his liberated
condition, and you come up against all your self-contractions, your
stuckness and your self-consciousness. This is called the *mirror principle,* since it withholds nothing from you. It confronts you with all
of who you are: your obstacles and your infinite potential for liberation. And in its all-embracing reach, it fires up all-important dimensions of your developmental potential: Waking Up, Growing Up, and
Cleaning Up.

But perhaps the central function of the guru is spiritual transmission. A true guru has the capacity to directly transmit his or her own
enlightened state to you. When you are completely open and your ego
has moved out of the way, the guru's grace self-activates. In that clear-
ing, the deepest part of the guru meets the deepest part of you, and the
exhilarating force of the guru's enlightened energy and awareness begins
to light up your dormant spiritual potential and wake you up to your
higher nature.

As you experience the combined power of these functions of the
guru, it becomes obvious to you that the bedrock of the guru-disciple
relationship is a great transcendental mystery that lies far beyond your
everyday egoic state, and in that recognition you spontaneously let go
into that unqualifiable greatness. This humble gesture of surrender
catalyzes the real mystery of Guru Yoga: the separate self begins to

melt, and as it is released, it slowly makes space for the true self to shine forth.

In light of the extraordinary efficacy of the spiritual process in the company of a true master, postmodernity's rejection of the guru is unfortunate. Being in direct relationship with a living guru is the most powerful form of spiritual practice we know. None of the aforementioned functions of the guru can be found in books, received from a meditation instructor, or experienced by merely practicing a collection of Dharma tenets and techniques. They are all faculties of the direct relationship with the enlightened adept, expressing the awakening power of the living mystery of reality itself, and every single one of them is therefore the unique, irreplaceable, and indispensable purview of Guru Yoga.

This is why the precious core of Guru Yoga needs to be preserved for future generations, and why it *does* have a very real place in the postmodern world, particularly as we continue to tweak it toward a more integral expression.

11
When Shadow Meets the Bodhisattva Impulse

Enlightenment is a vision that cannot be held or grasped in any way. Beyond this world it's a mystery that is exploding. A fire that is burning. It's a fire a person is either going to jump into or run away from. This fire burns beyond the mind. No-time is the place where this secret abides. Realize that and you realize the Self you are when there's no mind and no time. Realize that, and cling to that alone as your own Self.[1]

I wrote these words over twenty-five years ago in my third book, *Enlightenment Is a Secret: Teachings of Liberation.* They vividly convey the true nature of radical spirit, which has always been the source of my deepest inspiration.

Waking up to the great mystery of consciousness itself in the depths of your own heart is an absolute confrontation. Its self-radiant brightness and uncorrupted purity are both overwhelmingly intoxicating and terrifying. Beholding this perennial secret fills us with the paradoxical quality the German theologian Rudolf Otto captured so well in his famous Latin phrase *mysterium tremendum et fascinans.* The great mystery is both frightening and attractive. The finite ego instinctively turns away from its awe-inspiring presence, for it cannot fathom the

175

boundless, all-inclusive wholeness of the ultimate reality. Its inherent purity leaves us totally exposed and naked before God. To our small, separate sense of self, absolute consciousness always feels infinitely and compellingly too much. So it recoils in fear because it realizes its own imminent demise. Being confronted with the fire that rages beyond the mind is knowing that every trace of ego will be burned to ashes. And thus the great mystery repels. But despite its terrifying force, glorious beauty, and grace-filled majesty, it is also irresistibly attractive because we intuitively sense that it is no different from our own most intimate true nature. And so we feel magnetically drawn to it, much like the moth in the well-known Sufi parable that is so attracted to the light of the burning candle that it flies into the flame, is consumed by it, and attains enlightened oneness with the fire.

The undifferentiated brightness of radical spirit is by its very nature ego-consuming, and its uncompromising quality has always been the beating heart of my work and transmitting presence as a guru. I have a radical essence. Fierce grace is the way Spirit manifests through me.

In *The Eye of Spirit: An Integral Vision for a World Gone Slightly Mad*, Ken Wilber explains how upon achieving enlightenment, various intrinsic potentials of the enlightened mind such as equanimity, discriminating wisdom, and compassion combine with the person's own particular talents and native dispositions. He or she then arises as an embodiment of a specific enlightened quality constellation. Wilber discusses various possibilities using Buddhist deities to express certain archetypes: Avalokiteshvara expresses gentle compassion; Prajnaparamita personifies vast spaciousness; Manjushri manifests luminous intelligence; Yamantaka is the samurai warrior, defending Spirit; Bhaishajyaguru represents healing radiance; and Maitreya stands for the promise that ever-present awareness will be accessible into the endless future.

Among these six archetypal qualities, my own transmission force feels most closely related to Yamantaka:

And so perhaps you will arise as Yamantaka, fierce protector of ever-present awareness and samurai warrior of intrinsic Spirit. Precisely those items that pretend to block ever-present awareness must be quickly cut through, which is why ever-present awareness arises in its many wrathful forms. You will simply be moved, from the ground of equality consciousness, to expose the false and the shallow and the less-than-ever-present. It is time for the sword, not the smile, but always the sword of discriminating wisdom, which ruthlessly cuts all obstacles in the ground of the all-encompassing.[2]

In the Hindu tradition this same archetypal transpersonal energy is personified by the dark warrior goddess Kali, who is depicted with her tongue hanging out of her mouth that is dripping with blood, a necklace of human skulls, a scimitar in one hand, and a severed head in the other. She is trampling the body of her husband, Shiva, who himself represents the destructive aspect of the deity, obliterating evil and ignorance to create space for positive regeneration.

The Shiva-Kali energy is a particular expression of the ferocity of radical spirit as well as a specific function of the guru role. It is the force that removes obstacles and pushes students to embrace their own highest potentials. Whenever it encounters egoic resistance or complacency, it flares up from its source in the Absolute—swiftly, as if out of nowhere—cutting through these impediments. Its purifying ferocity cannot be controlled or tempered. It is not tamable, and not meant to be tamable. When it shows itself, it is awe-inspiring. Its raw power pierces through every veil of self-delusion. It doesn't care about dreamlike egoic concerns like your personal pride or self-importance. It relentlessly tears down the walls of your self-obsession and self-absorption, purging you in the fire of radical spirit. Its ferocity is scary, but the minute the ego backs down, it disappears again, just as quickly as it came.

Humankind's spiritual history is replete with stories of saints, sages, lamas, and gurus who use fierce grace to shock their disciples out of their ignorance. Most well-known, perhaps, is the tale of the legendary Tibetan master Marpa, who put his pupil Milarepa through the harrowing ordeal of letting him build and then demolish three towers in turn in order to purify Milarepa's negative karma and help him attain enlightenment. Even as such brutal tribulations seem surreal by any contemporary standard and belong to an era long gone, these stories still point to an important truth about the power of unwavering commitment and radical self-transcendence.

In our times, the transformational fire of radical spirit is still burning in some of our most exemplary spiritual luminaries.

The revered yogi Paramahansa Yogananda, renowned for being the first modern guru and an icon of unconditional love and divine romance in his relationship with the transcendent, was also known for being a fierce teacher who didn't hesitate to reprimand his students harshly in front of one another.[3]

Even the Indian "hugging saint," Mata Amritananda Mayi, aka Ammaji, who is celebrated around the world as an embodiment of selfless motherly love and boundless compassion for all beings, sometimes speaks to the force of fierce grace that is alive in the enlightened guru:

> A true guru will not allow an iota of ego to grow in the disciple. To check the growth of pride, the guru may act in a very cruel manner. People who see the blacksmith forging a hot piece of iron with his hammer may think that he is a cruel person. The iron piece may also think that nowhere can there be such a brute. But while dealing each blow, the blacksmith is only thinking of the end product. The real guru is also like this.[4]

My own guru, H. W. L. Poonja, would at times demonstrate this Shiva-Kali force. In particular I remember a moment when he expressed divine rage to a seeker. As a result, the person promptly flipped from a state of unconscious belligerent arrogance to awakened awe and humility, as if he suddenly realized who he was sitting in front of. The dramatic nature of his abrupt shift left a deep impression on me. Poonjaji's radical intervention effectively pulled the rug out from under this person's ego, and I imbibed that teaching demonstration of how to handle ego from him.

And so during my own years as a guru I unleashed the same kind of ferocity whenever people demonstrated arrogance, pride, self-absorption, or a casual attitude about their spiritual life. I wanted them to be serious, face their own unconscious motives, and work toward the realization of the vision we all shared.

Fierce grace is part and parcel of life in the company of a guru, and the stories of radical teaching interventions stand in a long tradition of spiritual masters moving Heaven and Earth to shake their disciples out of their egoic complacency. A genuine satguru cares deeply about an aspirant's progress. He is unreservedly committed to the upliftment of other human beings and is intensely and emotionally connected to the fulfillment of the spiritual work he has set out to accomplish in this world. This higher motivation is at the heart of the guru function—and its enlightened passion is unimaginable to most. This is what it means to be a *bodhisattva*. Having attained enlightenment, the bodhisattva does not retreat into the timeless bliss of nirvana, but vows to remain among sentient beings until all are similarly liberated.

In our work, the liberating fire of radical spirit was the lifeblood of the spiritual culture we all co-created. Many of my students experienced a glimpse of this living mystery early on in their association with me. Whenever they truly received the force of spiritual transmission that streamed through me in my most enlightened and radical moments, they were often jolted into a state of enlightened awareness. From that transegoic vantage point they then saw the extraordinary possibilities of a truly awakened life, and they became passionately inspired to actualize this in their own lives.

What really occurs on the deepest possible level in such blessed moments is that the true nature of the guru and the true nature of the disciple merge, and a profound and most intimate bond of love spontaneously forms between them, a bond described in the mystical literature as the most sacred of all relationships. The very moment this transcendental connection of the heart establishes itself, the guru accepts responsibility for the spiritual process of the student, and the student freely and naturally surrenders—giving the guru permission to enact the guru function with him or her.

In our spiritual culture this metaphysical occurrence was then formalized with an overt agreement between us. My students either pledged to lay their *spiritual lives* in the hands of the guru, keeping their worldly lives outside of my authority; or if they felt ready to assume an even deeper level of commitment, they would endeavor to lay their *whole lives* in the hands of the guru. These formal agreements were never entered into lightly and were only allowed after years of demonstrating a consistent willingness and seriousness to live the teachings. Everyone who chose to enter into formal studentship understood that the job of the guru often involves an intense, long-term struggle with the karma and conditioning of the disciple in the context of this most intimate and personal relationship. They knew they had to be absolutely serious about facing their own limitations and working through them. At no point was there any doubt that what we stood for was real ego transcendence by trial and fire. The uncompromising ferocity of our transformative practice was always on the table for all to see.

But the demanding nature of our practice didn't end with the difficult ordeal of ego transcendence. In addition, the teachings of Evolutionary Enlightenment gave our entire endeavor an extra edge, bringing a vibrant atmosphere of future-oriented visionary idealism that supercharged everything we did. This catalytic environment created rare growth opportunities for everybody, but posed some unique challenges as well.

On the one hand, our spiritual lives were saturated with a freshness, a creative urgency, and the ecstatic thrill of giving rise to something new. Living in that scintillating vibrancy that is always pregnant with potential is exhilarating. As a teacher I was completely given over to the wildness of the evolutionary drive, and I wanted my students to be ecstatically awake to this energy as well so that they would be ready to fully and unreservedly participate in the process of evolutionary emergence. Surrendering to this force of Eros is powerful. Like nothing else, it breaks through any inertia and initiates real change. It is, therefore, a source of profound liberation.

But on the other hand, the risks of being so fully given over to the forces of creative change were never far away. When the transformative fire burns that high, the pressure to change is far greater than the steadying forces of integration and equilibrium. This can be profoundly destabilizing, but it is also absolutely liberating. Strong people with a healthy self-structure who are driven by a single-minded dedication to their own progress can more easily handle this evolutionary pressure and will grow as a result. But those with a less well-integrated personality may crumble in the face of so much intensity.

It was clear that we were operating in an experimental zone where exciting novelty actually emerged, but where errors and unforeseen challenges were prone to occur as well. Radical spirituality plays itself out on the very edge of people's personal boundaries and on the outer fringes of evolution itself, which is why it carries both unique gifts and unique dangers. Still, everybody knew what they had signed up for and were behind the goal. We all freely chose to come together in this sizzling frying pan of creative emergence outside of the safe zone of the conventional and the typical in order to live such inspired lives. We understood that true depth sometimes requires risk.

This being the spirit of our work together, it is important to point out that some of my teaching interventions that later came to be seen as questionable or controversial happened within a noble spiritual context in which they were considered legitimate teaching methods.

And so as I now look back on the twenty-seven years I enacted the guru role prior to the collapse of our work, I place my teaching interventions relative to dealing with my students' egos in three broad categories:

The first category contains teaching interventions in which I spotted ego accurately, addressed it with fierce and uncompromising Shiva-Kali energy, and did so with precision and skillful means. This often resulted in positive evolutionary breakthroughs.

Tough but profoundly transformative lessons were learned by those who had the courage and strength to face these challenging spiritual ordeals. They managed to endure because they felt connected to the living mystery of radical spirit, the fire they knew one either runs away from or surrenders to. They were in touch with the enlightened intention behind my actions, and it was often their trust in me as their guru that helped them through the hard times.

All throughout the course of my work with my students this type of positive transformational leap would occur. As a result, many students gained exceptional levels of presence, freedom, authenticity, and transparency. This created an atmosphere in which people were unusually mature and awake.

To this day I still have lively recollections of some of my students' responses after they broke through into a higher perspective. In these eye-opening moments they so often told me that they now finally understood why I had been pushing so hard for so long. And they invariably voiced their immense gratitude for never giving up the struggle with their unyielding egos, which they now saw as an expression of their guru's compassion and love for their own soul.

Evidently, this first category of teaching interventions, in which right judgment and radical Shiva-Kali energy combined to create positive breakthroughs, is the ideal and desired outcome of the confrontational teaching style. The transformational fire accomplished exactly what it was intended to effectuate, and people transitioned into deeper levels of awareness, wholeness, and spiritual maturity.

The second category holds teaching interventions that were more ambiguous, both in their nature and in their outcome. I spotted egoic resistance with accuracy and addressed it fiercely, but went too far in pushing against it. I didn't sufficiently feel the critical edge where a person's boundaries had stretched to their maximum and were about to break. I failed to honor where people were in their personal development and continued to push, and this created resentment and even breakdowns, rather than breakthroughs. The excess of evolutionary pressure I brought to bear on these students caused unnecessary suffering for them.

There were several factors that increased the odds of my pushing going overboard. One of them was my utopian idealism.

It is a widely recognized phenomenon that those who are inspired by visionary ideals tend to be demanding characters who create high-pressure environments around them. These revolutionaries are often more concerned with the realization of their vision than with the personal circumstances of the people they work with, who help them achieve their ideals. It was no different for me. I was so impassioned about realizing our utopian goal, a superholon of awakened individuals living together in intersubjective nonduality, that at times I forgot about human beings. I wouldn't tolerate those who wouldn't play ball and show up as serious co-creative partners with me in service of the project we all shared.

In my mind's eye I could see how the moment everybody took full responsibility for themselves, our collective superholon would light up and become vibrant and alive. All of us would then be consciously co-creating the future together as new structures in consciousness and cultures—structures with the promising potential to catalyze real post-egoic cooperation between people and serve as the foundation for a more enlightened wider society. I felt as if I could not rest until the collective awakening that we were catalyzing with increasing regularity would manifest through each and every one of my students as a permanent state. And so whenever I felt my students' egos slide into inertia and interfere with the emergence of a Higher We, the guru function in me was activated, and I began pushing for a breakthrough.

Another reason why my pushing sometimes became unhealthily excessive had to do with some of my own shadow issues, as described in the previous chapters.

What triggered me into extreme pushing was the disconnect I observed between my students' self-declared evolutionary aspirations and their actual behavior. Whenever I perceived this gap between people's intentions and their actions, I read that as their lack of seriousness, their egoic refusal, or even their hypocrisy. Being a student in our school came with a powerful obligation to live up to your own highest potentials beyond ego and be responsible co-creators of the enlightened collective that had begun to emerge among us. I wanted everybody to be with me for the right reasons—not to find a safe haven under the protective wings of some archetypal father figure, escape from the difficulties of the world, or merely delight in the ecstatic bliss of higher states. And thus when I noticed that my students continued to be more entranced by their own egoic resistance to change than they were lit up by the thrilling nature of the higher potentials we were all giving rise to, I became frustrated and impatient with them. Over time, my disgruntlement morphed into sheer desperation. At that point I felt I didn't have any other options left than to maximize the pressure on them, and I unleashed all my ferocity and anger, putting before them a clear choice: "Either do this, or leave!" I personalized my frustration and impatience in ways that were wrong and inappropriate. I now regret these interventions. There are no two ways about it. This is where I crossed a line. I went too far and pushed too hard for too long, and the results became counterproductive.

In hindsight, it's clear to me that what actually happened in these situations was that the purity of radical spirit and the awakened heart-mind of the bodhisattva impulse in me got mixed up with my own shadow issues. Whenever I overreacted and came down on my students too hard, whenever I shamed them or acted punitively, the shadow I never believed I had was acting out. For some reason I experienced the discrepancy between what people said and were prepared to do and what they actually did as intolerable. It made me overly angry and caused me to push excessively. Whenever I perceived my students to be weak, failing to live up to the teachings, I instinctively treated them with impatience and intolerance. The reasonable psychological explanation for my edginess around any form of vulnerability, weakness, or ambiguity is that it was a sign that my own shadow had been triggered. I overreacted to parts within myself that I could not accept and didn't want to face. In these cases, my students' weaknesses were, in fact, my own.

My rootedness in radical spirit didn't really help me bring my own shadows into the light and clean them up. Quite the contrary. It is a little known fact that enlightened awareness can actually fortify one's shadow because the force of the Absolute is now behind whatever qualities and convictions one's mind is made of. And I wasn't exempt from that principle. The profound clarity of enlightened mind had instilled in me an extraordinary spiritual self-confidence. This, combined with Poonjaji's instruction to never doubt myself along with my mistaken conviction that I was entirely shadow-free, gave me an unshakable certainty about my intuitions and interventions as a teacher. It made me oblivious to my blind spots and to the shadows and idiosyncrasies that tend to color even one's deepest intuitions.

As a guru, I was almost always exclusively focused on only the highest possible perspective. I truly wanted my students to transform and saw my passionate, relentless pushing mainly as an expression of my love for them. Where I erred was that in my unwavering dedication to the highest principles and in the intensity of my evolutionary zeal, I often overlooked the complexities of a more integral approach to human development. I failed to fully appreciate the enormity of the struggle I was calling people to. Even as I understood this intellectually, I wasn't always truly in touch with the extreme nature of the emotional challenges my students went through in their efforts to break through the confines of the ego because I interpreted everything from the point of view of radical freedom. My instinctive tendency was to interpret their difficulties with the Dharma as egoic refusal. In reality, this was not always the case. Often a more accurate explanation was that their current level of development and karmic proclivities did not yet allow them to live up to the teachings with the kind of urgency and intensity I required. And so my fundamental flaw as a teacher was that I was all too often oblivious to these human subtleties and at times reacted in shadow-driven, punitive ways to what I perceived as my student's failures. My own ordeal during my sabbatical made me see firsthand that some egoic obstacles just take time to work through. This deepened my empathy and enriched my understanding of the sheer multidimensional complexity of human development.

Another element that contributed to the uncompromising nature of my teaching style is my personality type.

My personality has always been more oriented to qualities like transcendence, forward-thrusting agency, and Eros, rather than to patient, nurturing care and Agape. In the typology of the Enneagram, for example, I identify as a type One, the idealist or reformer. Some of the characteristics attributed to type One feel strikingly familiar to me. Ones are driven by a powerful sense of mission and a deep feeling of purpose. They tend to be rational, principled, determined, conscientious, sensible, responsible, serious, self-disciplined, and hold deep convictions about what's right and wrong, just and unjust. Ones feel impelled by a sense of personal obligation to improve themselves and the world. They aim for quality and excellence and expect themselves and others to live by their high standards, and they're prepared to put everything on the line for their values, their ethical convictions, and for the greater good. But if their ideals are not met, they tend to feel disappointed, frustrated, and resentful, and as a result they can become harsh with themselves and others. Ones tend to get into conflict by being impatient, overly rigid, perfectionistic, and critical. At their best, ones are tolerant, accepting, discerning, wise, humane, prudent, and fair. They are firmly committed to the people they love and often become the kind of person others turn to for guidance.

Integral Theory makes the interesting point that a person's personality type does not fundamentally change as she moves through the stages of growing up and advances in cleaning up her shadow. Types are simply the various personality orientations—the different forms of self-expression—possible at each developmental level. And so even as people can change as they develop and mature, they cannot actually switch types. What does occur, though, is that a particular type will express itself in more integrated ways as it further evolves.

I can now clearly see a similar dynamic in my own case. Even though I have changed in different dimensions of my being, my typological essence is still very much the way it has always been.

Finally, there is the third category of teaching interventions, in which I misread a situation, didn't get the sensibilities at play, and made errors of judgment in my treatment of people. In short, I made mistakes, plain and simple.

As I see it now, this third category probably caused the greatest amount of resentment. When I didn't hit the bull's-eye and was taken in tow by my personal opinions, my students rightly felt they were being treated unfairly. Yet they couldn't do anything about it because of the hierarchical structure of our community and the mythic rule of never questioning the guru.

I now feel ashamed about these instances. I can no longer relate to the unnecessary harshness with which I treated people, and I unambiguously take full responsibility for everything that happened as a result of my lack of right judgment.

Thus to summarize, a multitude of factors both positive and negative influenced my radical expression as a guru. At the heart of it was the uncompromising fire inherent in the transmission of radical spirit, a fire that burns *beyond* this manifest reality. But alongside this pure source, a mix of elements *within* this manifest reality contributed as well: the ferocity of the Shiva-Kali energy characteristic of my particular expression as a guru; my singleminded utopian idealism that cared more about realizing our higher collective vision than it did about human complexity and personal concerns of individuals; my personality type as a transcender, which is more masculine and Eros-oriented, and my Enneagram type of One, with its unrelenting insistence on the highest possible standards; my shadow issues; my disconnectedness from the truth of human suffering; and the strong flavor of mythic guru absolutism in which my work was embedded.

All of these influences helped shape both the success and the failure of my confrontational teaching style and, ultimately, the destiny of our work. So looking to the future, what is different now?

I have defended my radical teaching style before, for example, when in 2006 I wrote the essay "A Declaration of Integrity."[5] What has changed since I wrote that essay is that back then I had no awareness of the mythic-amber influences that permeated my guru role; I was still deeply invested in what I now consider to be the strange belief that I had no shadow; and I hadn't fully awakened to the truth of human suffering. These three realizations, which were still lacking in "A Declaration of Integrity," have refined and enriched my understanding of the guru role and have given my teachings today a more multidimensional character.

Yet even now, with my softened, more integrated personality, my radical heart remains untouched. The fire of enlightenment still burns in me, and the radical essence of my deep psyche is still the primordial quality of my innermost authentic self. To this day, transmitting this sacred fire of evolutionary love remains my deepest aspiration.

Some critics have delegitimized my radical approach as being the result of shadow only. But the reality is undeniably more complex and benign than this oversimplified public narrative that continues to uncritically propagate stories of abuse of spiritual power and its victims, and that has come to define my public persona. Even as some aspects of these critiques are, unfortunately, valid and true, most of them are unhelpfully sensational, deeply partial, and devoid of a more nuanced, multidimensional understanding of the complete picture of spiritual life in our sangha.

From a green-postmodern level of consciousness (see figure 3.1 or plate 1), the visceral disapproval of the hard-school approach to spiritual growth is understandable. Radical spiritual practice is boundary-breaking, and to the postmodern mind any infraction of someone else's boundaries is seen as a transgression. And thus when gurus who are lit up with radical transformational fire then make mistakes, they make it all too easy for postmodernity to pathologize this sacred fire or even write off the radical spirit that inspires it, which is truly unfortunate. In making a legitimate corrective move toward minimizing the risk of real abuse, postmodernity's overzealousness to play it safe at all costs pushes into oblivion the exhilarating divine aliveness of radical spirituality, and with that risks losing its unmatched transformational benefits as well.

And so how do we negotiate this conundrum? There is no way around the fact that historically the results of this kind of harsh teaching style have often been ambiguous. On the one hand, some students attest to the fact that they were thoroughly and permanently transformed by it in a way they would never have managed on their own, even as it breached their boundaries relentlessly and they came out somewhat bruised. On the other hand, in some cases the woundedness never healed, and the progress collapsed. This double-edged result begs the question: does a radical teaching style still carry validity in a post-postmodern age? Should there be room for it in a careful, consensual, limited context, or is it simply no longer the way forward because it violates the dignities, vulnerabilities, and autonomy of some of the aspirants?

As a guru, the impulse of my heart will always be to keep the fire of enlightenment burning. But the lessons of the story of EnlightenNext have made me acutely aware that if radical spirituality is to survive into the future, it will need to be framed within more of an integral context.

In the conversations I had with spiritual teachers and Integral luminaries after the crash of EnlightenNext, most of them shared my passion for the necessity of keeping radical spirituality alive. Together we explored ways to create the right circumstances for its practice and discussed some of the qualifiers that seem critical in order to advance this type of spirituality.

One of these qualifiers that emerged as a theme in several dialogues was the notion that radical spirituality is not really meant to be practiced on a large scale, and several of my dialogue partners made this point explicitly. Among them was my dear friend and colleague, Zen priest, and Integral spirituality teacher Diane Musho Hamilton Roshi,* who said:

> There are always going to be realizers whose job it is to give people radical experiences, adepts who are keeping a channel open for the

---

*Diane Musho Hamilton Roshi is a facilitator of the Big Mind Big Heart process developed by Genpo Merzel Roshi. She is an expert in conflict resolution and first director of the Alternative Dispute Resolution program of the Utah judiciary. She is the author of several books, among them *Everything Is Workable: A Zen Approach to Conflict Resolution.*

rest of us. Alongside them there are the more conventional among us, like myself, who are dealing with numbers of people who have families and kids and are making a contribution to civic life. It could very well be that part of your challenge was that even though you were a more radical teacher, you were also trying to have an impact on culture. It's sort of like a bell curve. Your nature was out there, at the top of the bell curve, but you were actually trying to have an impact down at the base. These are mutually exclusive aspirations. If you are catering to a big audience, you have to have conventional values. Nobody with your values and your way of being is ever going to be influencing large numbers of people. You were trying to impact mainstream culture, but mainstream culture is not designed for that realization.[6]

Spiritual teacher and author Sally Kempton* offered a similar observation during my dialogue with her. Sally went through a lifetime of rich spiritual experience, having been blessed with the direct transmission of shaktipat, the kundalini-awakening divine energy, by her guru Baba Muktananda, who was celebrated as one of the most powerfully transmitting gurus of the twentieth century. Having lived in this vibrant field of grace for so long, she understands the value of this living spiritual quality like no other, and so she explained the necessity of creating the unique conditions that most effectively support radical spiritual transmission:

> The guru model is stuck in the past. It is essentially based on a patriarchal family structure, and it is not supposed to get as big, not even as big as your scene did. Certainly not as big as Muktananda's or any of the popular Tibetan gurus. It is meant to be small so that the

---

*Sally Kempton, a former New York journalist and second-wave feminist, studied and traveled with Baba Muktananda from 1974 until his passing in 1982, receiving from him the monastic name Swami Durgananda. In 2002 she began teaching applied nondual wisdom independently. She is the author of several books, including *Meditation for the Love of It* and *Awakening Shakti*.

teacher really, really knows his students. In our age, that seems very hard to maintain. To carry the living reality of direct transmission forward we have to take it out of the public sphere, where it tends to become a career path. We need to find a way to recognize that the transmission in most cases is happening in special and particular circumstances, and we need to create those circumstances, step into them fully, and not expect the conditions of transmission to maintain outside of the formal container. We have to give the guru the opportunity to be radical, and we have to do so in a way that doesn't impact the ability of the students to stay true to their own spiritual process.[7]

An analogous message about the necessity of preserving radical spirituality and the challenges of doing so powerfully came through in my dialogue with (r)evolutionary, Integral Life practice teacher, social activist, and brother-friend Terry Patten,* who offers perhaps the most comprehensive and lived-through consideration about the role of radical spirituality in a post-postmodern world. Terry spent fifteen years of his young adult life as a close devotee of the radical American guru Adi Da Samraj, but eventually decided, with a great deal of regret, that he had to leave to regain his sovereignty and integrity as an individual. Still, to this day he retains an immense appreciation for the invaluable gift he considers radical spirituality to be. His longtime involvement with an adept who is acknowledged by many to be one of the most profoundly realized beings of our time make him eminently qualified to testify to the extraordinary transformational benefits of living in the company of a qualified guru:

*Terry Patten is a philosopher-activist, Integral teacher, coach, and social entrepreneur. For many years he has devoted his life to exploring the biggest questions of our time, and his online seminar *Beyond Awakening: The Future of Spiritual Practice* features in-depth conversations with some of the world's most prominent thought leaders. In 2004 he joined Ken Wilber's Integral Institute. He is the author of four books, including *Integral Life Practice: A 21st-Century Blueprint for Physical Health, Emotional Balance, Mental Clarity, and Spiritual Awakening,* co-authored with Ken Wilber, Adam Leonard, and Marco Morelli, and his most recent groundbreaking magnum opus, *A New Republic of the Heart: An Ethos for Revolutionaries.*

There's got to be space for a radical teaching style in a controlled context. It's very important, and it can't be eliminated. But I also think it's really tricky to create adequate controls. Any attempt to create the right context is going to be challenged, and therefore the first efforts will probably not perfectly stand the test. We're going to have to evolve it, but we can't let go of it. We have to find a way.

Adi Da's Dharma contains some really important insights about radical spirituality, such as the difference between the way of grace and the way of effort. The way of grace is more radical. The way of effort is ultimately a way of seeking, and it isn't radical. Adi Da would often speak about the world of Buddhism as mainly a way of effort and therefore ego-based. Except in some cases around great lamas who also functioned as gurus, it is not really lit by that radical flame of living enlightenment on the other side of our egos. The presence of divinity itself is the beating heart of existence, and it is the divinity in me that recognizes that divinity in the guru. Guru Yoga isn't merely cultic and mythic, even though it is often treated that way. It is actually a radical principle of divinity itself, awakeness itself, spreading like a wildfire. There is no method of ego to find its way to non-ego. It just doesn't work. Those two lines never cross—they run parallel. But even though seeking will never get us there, that which is beyond seeking doesn't go away, just because most of the time we are in a divided mind, tending to seek. God bats last. God will not be suppressed.

After I left Adi Da, I had to submit myself to the way of effort and discover how much it gave and how, paradoxically, there was something still missing. The radicality of the living divine, which is beyond anything anybody can see, and which blows you away because it *is* you, isn't adequately accounted for in any of the ways of effort. In the presence of that nuclear fusion of radical direct grace you are transfigured, transcended, and released.

So on the one hand, the guru principle is radically necessary.

Adi Da used to say, "You may as well argue with the Earth orbiting the Sun as to argue with the guru principle." There has never been a transmission of realization that did not start with a realizer. You need a flame to light a fire. But on the other hand, the guru inevitably becomes a target. And in a sense, the reaction to the guru becomes a sideshow that derails the thing itself. Therefore, the inherency of our divinity and the irrepressibility of evolution as it expresses itself among people of varying degrees of awakeness is what we have to trust, even more than particular embodiments. Perhaps in this day and age the tactical way forward is the monastery strategy. Maybe the guru has to go underground for a while, and just like in the Dark Ages, keep all the learning alive in the monasteries.[8]

Most of my dialogue partners shared my view that radical spirituality serves an important developmental niche at the edges of human evolution. It keeps the fire of awakening burning in ways that the more conventional technique-based forms of spirituality can't. And so it is vital to preserve it and establish well-defined spaces with the right conditions to optimize the white-hot intensity of spiritual transmission, so that it can freely and uninhibitedly work its transformational miracles.

The next challenge then becomes one of minimizing the risks of unfavorable impact when the transformational heat becomes too much. After the collapse of our sangha, I spoke with Ken Wilber about this thorny issue on several occasions, and he offered some hands-on practical advice to address it based on his Integral wisdom:

There will always be room for the radical approach with its cutting-through industrial-strength transmission—always. But because we have all these different dimensions of ourselves that we have to take into account for a genuinely comprehensive and effective post-postmodern spirituality, the question of reducing the risks of this kind of spiritual practice is going to be an experimental one: is this radical transmission going to be adequately part of all these areas?

At a certain point in your own work you started to feel that you could gather together individuals of a similar degree of realization and let them cooperate in their own holonic group, and you found that that was just working better. In general, that's a very good idea. But in addition to that you can also ask, "What if we group individuals at different stages of Growing Up and individuals with similar kinds of neurotic damage?" Because both of these factors will determine just how much radical transmission they can take before they break. This will be different for different people. And so we are always running a pragmatic balancing act here. We don't want to get extreme and go overboard, so that every single person has to be met with their own uniquely different approach. We just want to group together people of similar kinds of spiritual realization, similar stages of development, and similar degrees of Cleaning Up. And then given those, how much radical transmission works with individuals at those different stages? How can I adjust that a little bit? Or how much power do I actually turn on? These are important questions because all these factors have a strong role to play in just how well the transmission will actually take.

One of the big mysteries now is that if you are just sort of blasting your radical transmission through a hundred people and give them all a similar degree, a third of them get better, a third of them don't change, and a third of them get worse. Why do we get those differences while you were doing the same thing? We know enough now about what's causing some of those differences. So we really want to focus on finding out just what factors are most conducive to people being able to actually receive a transmission in a way that helps open them up, and not just break them down. Everybody in those different groups might want realization. They may all be really sincere seekers, but they have very different makeups, and very differently structured psyches that react to radical transmission in very, very different ways. One of the things we know in terms of factoring in Growing Up and Cleaning Up is that there are relatively few numbers of ways that we can group people that will take into account a large number of those differences. And so we really can, without having to go too crazy, start working with all these dimensions. If we look at almost any teaching situation, like education itself, we recognize that we have to have first grade, second grade, third grade, fourth grade, fifth grade, sixth grade. You can't skip grades and go from first grade to sixth grade. This is true for Growing Up and for various phases of Cleaning Up. And it's even true for Waking Up in general. And so because we now have information about the whole trajectory in all these areas, we can start to create a much more sophisticated curriculum.

But behind it all: the better that radical transmission, the more ultimate juice is going to drive the whole endeavor. This is the bottom line at the heart of *real* Guru Yoga—of which there aren't many around. Genuine radical transmission is one of the things that makes Guru Yoga, particularly when it's done with these other understandings around it, an absolutely crucial form of spiritual development, and losing that would be a catastrophe for human beings.[9]

This more integrally nuanced way of exposing people to the transformational power of radical transmission based on their maturity in the different dimensions of their being is a viable principle that will help prevent unnecessary hardship, while optimizing the actual transformational results.

Ultimately, however, how human development actually works in all its particulars is still largely a closed book. Nobody knows the final answers about best practices or how to create the most catalytic environment for transformation. What many have testified to is that being in relationship with a living transmitting realizer supercharges the transformational process like nothing else.

The way, for example, Terry Patten writes about his paradoxical experience with Adi Da speaks to the mysterious, multilayered complexity that seems to be an inherent part of real transformation. His words are thought-provoking and, given our postmodern sensibilities, also intriguingly unconventional:

> I received transformative blessings not just from the aspects of Adi Da that people would regard as legitimate and praiseworthy. I got tremendous value from aspects of my experience others would regard as preposterous, "abusive," and unreasonable. Some of my most profound learnings came after I left; they were printed, as it were, "in the inside of the label" (and visible only upon tearing it apart). I don't endorse or excuse all his behaviors. Again, I've been a fierce critic (and, viewed conventionally, also a victim, or survivor, of "abuse" who suffered real injuries and processed a great deal of rage over them), but grew tremendously in the process. And now I hold all of it with gratitude, even though I remain not only devotional but also critical.[10]

Terry's experience evokes the larger question: what does it really take to enduringly transform? It is clear that in this field of inquiry we are still dabbling in experimental territory. And thus so far our most profound questions about the subtle workings of human development remain open-ended as well as deeply challenging—but at the same time utterly thrilling. How do we actually embody more of the self-radiant brightness of radical awakening and canalize it into this imperfect relative world so that it really *transforms* it? How do we do this in a way that is genuinely evolutionary? And how do we live this awakening relationally, which we always envisioned as the ultimate fulfillment of the utopian dream we were pursuing together?

Even the very first step of escaping the gravitational pull of the ego and cultivating radical self-realization has always been known by the wisdom traditions to be a gargantuan task, only accomplished by a few in any generation. And so the advanced ideal of an awakened sangha of people living together and relating to one another based on a shared state of intersubjective nonduality still only lives in the lofty future visions of some of our luminaries. We haven't yet fully cracked the code of such a utopian future. In our spiritual laboratory at EnlightenNext we experienced an early taste of what an awakened Higher We, lit up by the creative vibrancy of the evolutionary impulse, could be, and we all felt its enormous potential to become a force of real change in the world.

As a result, I have come to feel that for us as the human species it is paramount to keep the vision of living together beyond ego alive. We cannot leave even a single stone unturned to find our way to its fruition. Let us therefore not cynically dismiss the pioneering efforts of a more radical spirituality merely because it flies in the face of our postmodern sensibilities. Let us suspend our final judgment and sincerely grapple with the nuance and complexity of the questions that are still unanswered. "Let's make room for the whole elephant," as Terry writes, "not just the contours we have been able to grasp so far in a process that is still young, not yet entirely illuminated in all its nooks and crannies, and, thank God, dynamically alive."[11]

12

Why EnlightenNext
Collapsed and
the Narrative Reversed

After having explored some of the successful achievements as well as some of the dysfunctional dynamics of our work and the way I enacted my guru role, I will now share what I have come to understand was actually happening in my students' minds and hearts during the course of their often longtime devotional engagement in our sangha. How did *their* experience evolve as the years went by, and how did this evolution eventually lead to the collapse of our community?

Let us revisit, for a moment, then, the atmosphere during the final years of EnlightenNext . . .

Throughout this defining phase of our communal history, frustration over the rigidity of our hierarchical system grew, especially among my senior students. As a result of their many years of intense spiritual training they had by now evolved into an exemplary level of spiritual maturity. Still, I kept holding them on a leash, exercising control over their lives. My mythic guru persona couldn't fully contain the truth that they had outgrown this type of rigid, hierarchical guru-disciple relationship, and that the time was ripe for them to differentiate from me. They had reached the point where they needed to self-actualize and grow into their own unique expression. I had always spoken about higher individuation as the purpose of the teaching, and consistent with that, many of my senior students were given the opportunity to be community leaders in their own right, often presiding over their own centers in their countries of origin. After all, in my mythic way of thinking back then, this higher individuation was to occur *within* our work or in connection to it, not outside of it. I was convinced that my relationships with my closest students were eternal and unbreakable, and that their submission to me as the master meant that we were all in it together till the end. But this was not the truth of their world. Many of them felt ready to venture out, assume a greater measure of responsibility and leadership, put the skills and talents they had come to master in service of the larger evolutionary process, and engage in cultural transformation in new ways. Yet I remained oblivious to their legitimate developmental needs. In my mind there were still worlds to evolve into together.

And so they began to feel increasingly locked into a rigid hierarchical system that could no longer support their further evolution. They began to see how the very same hierarchy that had heretofore served as a developmental vortex—having drawn them up and effectively given birth to the higher goal they had all aspired to—now began to interfere with the emergence of that higher goal.

During a two-year period before the crash of EnlightenNext, the tension between my mythic guru role and my senior students' desire for autonomy and freedom gradually intensified. They began to get a sense that I didn't really have a clear vision about how to move forward and adapt the sangha structure to better accommodate those who felt constrained by it. And they were right. Near the end, I didn't really know where to steer the ship. Still, I wasn't ready to let go of the rudder either. So they began to feel that the way I enacted my role as the guru at the top of the pyramid began to become an obstacle for them, a glass ceiling they would never be able to break through. And thus it became increasingly clear to them that the rigid hierarchical structure of our community had become an impediment to expressing the higher individuation they had now matured into.

◀ ▪ ▶

Meanwhile, a problem of a more worldly nature began to coincide with my senior students' growing need to individuate: our organization was failing financially. The proper management solution for our precarious situation would have been to scale back on some of our biggest, least cost-effective projects. But in my evolutionary zeal I only wanted to expand even further and declined to make the right decisions for the financial health of our organization.

My position as both the guru at the top of the power hierarchy *and* the head of EnlightenNext created a double-bind for my students on the board. Any business-savvy solutions they came up with to try to save our organization had to be approved by me as, in our mythic guru context, final authority over everything—even organizational matters, about which I really wasn't an expert—rested with me. As long as I wasn't prepared to give my team of board members the degree of authority they needed to run EnlightenNext properly, their hands were tied. And so despite the urgency of the situation, nobody was able to make any sensible moves to address our financial crisis effectively. This was a source of great concern among my students, especially those who were employed by EnlightenNext and depended on its success for their own financial survival.

In my refusal to let go of my organizational authority, I disregarded one of the most basic lessons of modernity: the separation of powers. I was the spiritual head of the movement, and so I shouldn't have been its chairman as well. I didn't possess the right skill set to lead an organization and was unaware of my limitations in that regard.

And so the collapse of our community was set in motion, not so much by my harsh teaching style and intense use of evolutionary pressure, as the public narrative often has it, but first and foremost by the tension between my senior students' need to individuate and my mythic guru persona's resistance to allow them to do so, to which were added the increasing stresses of our organizational troubles. As these two forces joined, EnlightenNext erupted into its final crisis, which sealed the fate of our community. The moment I signed away my power as the spiritual head at the top of the hierarchy, the entire hierarchical structure of our community began to collapse in on itself, level by level. My leadership position was the linchpin holding everything together. The senior students who wanted it all to stop left right away. The few who wanted to continue could only watch how the dramatic implosion was destroying their cherished community. There was a painful irony to this tragedy: my worst fear had always been that if I gave up my power, everything we had so carefully built up would completely collapse—and sure enough, it did. Yet paradoxically, the very reason that everything fell apart was exactly because I didn't give up my power and allow my students more autonomy. By trying to avoid my worst nightmare, I in fact turned it into a reality.

After the senior students had thrown in the towel, the forces of disintegration quickly spread to the resolute core group.

Like the senior students, many in the resolute core, because of their high-intensity training, had also experienced major breakthroughs into Higher We states, and several of their holons were able to sustain these states with a degree of relative stability. Their longtime commitment to the practice had transformed them into an extraordinary group of spiritually awake, beautifully radiant and vibrant human beings—exemplary embodiments of the teachings of Evolutionary Enlightenment. Most of them had moved through the all-important milestone in our practice trajectory, where the power balance within the self shifts, the ego takes a backseat, and the authentic self awakens to such a degree that it crosses the threshold from 50 to 51 percent.

When this pivotal tipping point occurs, the authentic self becomes the dominant part of our identity and a fresh energy dynamic begins to animate our being. We are no longer primarily motivated by the personal fears, attachments, and desires of the ego, the force in us resisting change. Instead, our evolution is now mainly fueled by that formidable mystery of unstoppable evolutionary energy—pulsating with ecstasy and urgency—which is as alive in every fiber of the kosmos as it is in the depths of our own spirit. This makes all the difference, because we have literally entered into partnership with the very same energy and intelligence that created the universe and that continues to drive it. A fearless, passionate idealism begins to surge through us. We awaken to what I call kosmic conscience—the recognition that the evolution of the interior of the kosmos actually depends on *us,* and we feel inspired by a powerful sense of moral obligation to dedicate our lives to serving this grand evolutionary unfolding.

Most of my resolute core students had awakened to their authentic self in this profound way and were living happy, creative, and inspired lives.

Still, despite the fact that the greater part of their inner experience had now become one of beauty, generosity, and expanded awareness, in the holons they continued to relentlessly scrutinize the smaller parts of their interior that were still egoically driven—exactly as they had practiced for years. Whenever ego would reveal itself in the clear mirror of the egoless We-field that was generated in their group gatherings, they kept calling one another to task in the same old strict ways. And so some of them began to feel that this strong emphasis on ego, appropriate as it once had been, was no longer completely in sync with the uncontracted transparency of their actual inner experience, in which the authentic self had now taken the lead. They began to grow more and more uncomfortable with the amber-mythic residue in our system, especially with the rigidity of the pyramid hierarchy, in which you always had somebody above you to answer to, and with the obligation to adhere to strict rules. They began to feel that the way in which these aspects had, over the years, remained an organizing principle in our sangha needed to change.

And so, even as they lived in a visible state of vibrant evolutionary awakeness, an undercurrent of frustration began to build.

This bright, awake evolutionary zeal, along with this slumbering sense of dissatisfaction, were both present in the spiritual-emotional atmosphere among my resolute core students in the period before the crash of EnlightenNext. When they then heard the bombshell announcement that the senior students had pulled the plug on our organization, the resolute core reacted with shock and disbelief. When

I then furthermore admitted that I had reacted to the growing crisis in our sangha with stubbornness and pride—motives in myself that I hadn't seen—they were utterly dumbfounded. For all these years they had committed their lives to being embodied exemplars of the teachings, which at their level of involvement was extremely demanding. They had endured thousands of hours of strict, disciplined practice; they had fought inner Dharma wars to the point of almost giving up; and they had rigorously scrutinized every unwholesome ego-based motive they could find. And now they were told that even their guru was affected by unconscious motives. If even he couldn't live his own teachings, then who was he to set the bar so high for them?

They felt outraged, even duped, and took my confession as a justification to relax their constant striving. They had been living in too-muchness for too long, trying to be at their best all the time. Now they were experiencing a liberating existential relief.

In no time, the once so coherent group of people governed by a spirit of love, respect, and the ecstatic urgency of the authentic self descended into chaos and began to disperse. They left the premises within a mere few months. Their departure marked the definitive end of the resolute core, our exemplary group of warrior monks who had lived their lives lit up by the truth and beauty of Spirit.

After the abrupt collapse of the defining core of senior students as well as the resolute core, the committed core began to disintegrate as well. This happened more slowly and somewhat discontinuously because the committed core students were not in direct relationship with me as the guru. They were all guided by the senior students, and so their focus was on them. Consequently, their views on the painful situation were heavily influenced by the messages they heard from their senior leaders. As long as the senior students supported my sabbatical, the committed core continued to back me up. But the moment the senior students gave up on me, their groups turned as well.

When I relinquished my power as the leader of EnlightenNext, it wasn't yet clear to me that my agreement to step back would initiate the sudden, irreversible implosion of our entire community. I trusted the initial agreement and explicit understanding between myself and my senior students that we would gather together again after my six-month sabbatical, assess my progress, and reevaluate the situation. But by the time those six months had passed, EnlightenNext had completely fallen apart. There was nothing left for me to come back to. In the absence of my leadership, those in charge had deliberately dismantled the entire organization.

Some of the senior students *did* seem to think in terms of some sort of continuation, as they still assisted me with my personal inquiry via Skype and were waiting for me to "break through." But as EnlightenNext had already been torn down, their actual intentions regarding the future of our work weren't clear.

For a long time I couldn't help but ask myself over and over again: why did my senior students not honor their commitment to uphold the organization during my sabbatical? Even now, this question still at times comes back to haunt me. They were the passionate co-creators of our precious vessel for intersubjective awakening. They had invested many years and all their life energy, intelligence, and spiritual depth patiently building up our highly coherent sangha. For many, it was as much their life work as it was mine. Why, in the end, did they find it not worth saving?

After I relinquished my leadership role, there was a critical window of opportunity for the senior students and the board to save the organization. The double bind caused by the mythic absolutism I had adopted in my guru role had disappeared; those in charge could have steered the ship in any direction they envisioned. They could have softened the rigidity of the hierarchy and prepared our community structure for a bright new future. But despite their pledge to look after the organization in my absence, they shut down EnlightenNext.

Some of them, it must be said, were clearly heartbroken to see the forces of destruction tear our sangha apart, and a few of them tried to save our international organization. But their laudable efforts ran aground because they had lost the support of the community to make such an endeavor work.

Still, there was no obvious reason why *everything* had to collapse. It was absolutely within the realm of the possible that EnlightenNext could have gone through an internal change process. If I had been able to gradually let go of my absolute authority and mythic identity and make more room for my students' blossoming autonomy, our sangha might not have collapsed. Instead, it might have opened up like a lotus flower and become self-generating and less centralized. A significant part of my vision had already been realized. We had achieved a degree of relative stability of collective awakening in the holons, and it was time to come together as peers, co-create the future vision of our sangha, and move into the next phase.

In the end it remains somewhat perplexing why we, as a collective of talented, devoted, intelligent, creative, and spiritually mature people, weren't able to deal with this crisis. As Diane Musho Hamilton Roshi once said to me, "Andrew, I thought if any community could handle a crisis like this, it would've been yours."

Ultimately, I take full responsibility for my own part in the collapse of our community. My investment in the mythic guru persona had compromised my ability to acknowledge the now-so-obvious truth: that my maturing students were ready to self-actualize and grow into their own unique expression, and that the time had come for the mythic-traditional values in our sangha culture to change, so that our practice approach could evolve in lockstep with my students' maturity.

In one of our dialogues, Diane Musho Hamilton Roshi offered a sensible suggestion for how this might work: "We have to start working with a developmental stage model of practice. The training trajectory we offer should somehow mimic development. The early stages of practice are often going to look like a mythic meme structure, because the aspirants need to cultivate surrender and become aware how intensely they organize around their own preferences. At later stages of practice, more differentiation needs to be included." Then she added, somewhat pensively, "The critical question, of course, is: how long does the first phase of the practice need to last?"[1]

And this, indeed, is where I dropped the ball. For a good decade and a half, our approach to practice, with its binary divisions between ego and non-ego and our distinctly hierarchical sangha structure, provided a powerful training ground to break the spell of compulsive mental-emotional patterns and create the spiritual breakthroughs we all aspired to. But even as this high-intensity training began to translate into real spiritual maturity, my mythic guru persona didn't allow me to pick up on my students' cues that the end of this "first phase" was imminent, and that it was time for me to relinquish the old ways.

"As teachers, we have to allow our students to leave to differentiate as they grow up," Diane continued. "We have to give them the space to stand on their own two feet, and then reintegrate in their own way—much like the way you do it in a family—rather than seeing their differentiation as a betrayal, as one would do from a mythic meme structure. It would have changed the entire discourse in your case." Her words rang strikingly true to me. I felt betrayed when those closest to me began to come into their own, and I couldn't see their individuation as a natural sign of the upward pull of stage development. She then aptly pinpointed the foundational tension brewing in our community: "The traditional discourse and the developmental discourse create trouble with each other."

When I discussed this issue with Sally Kempton, she too pointed out that "higher individuation is the one thing that invariably needs to happen with a maturing community. The students outgrow the traditional relationship, and the teacher has to let them go. I wouldn't say we're over the traditional guru-disciple relationship, because obviously it's useful in certain stages of sadhana. But the teachers have to have done enough soul-searching to understand their own limits and know that there comes a point when in a certain way no one can take a student to the next stage. It's got to be the guidance of your own self, your own soul." She then identified what is needed to facilitate such a higher individuation: "We have to find a new language that allows senior students to leave without breaking the relationship."[2]

This indeed is the challenge. The amber-traditional mindset, out of which the mythic guru model arose, rarely supports such a smooth transition. Because of its emphasis on eternal devotion and its in-group/ out-group dynamics, the traditional guru often tends to feel more effective the longer he can hold on to you, whereas ideally he should consider himself more effective the quicker he can declare you a successful graduate of his school.

The future of the Triple Gem needs to include new ways to support the transition into higher individuation, so that when the time naturally comes, the guru-disciple relationship can enter into a more mature phase—or, if it's appropriate, dissolve its current form. Only if we succeed in building this understanding into the teacher-student model can we avoid the unnecessary psychological backlash that comes with the denial of the incontrovertible reality that every developmental trajectory sooner or later hits the point where the student needs to differentiate in order to self-actualize. As much as I had been oblivious to that fact before, it is all the more obvious to me now.

What is harder to understand, though, in all its psychological, spiritual, and social complexity, is the perplexing way that to so many of my former students the narrative suddenly switched following the crash of EnlightenNext. Almost overnight, their story about me and life in our sangha completely flipped to its polar opposite. Many former students went from believing that their guru was one of the great spiritual innovators of our time, and that together we were pushing the leading edge of the evolution of consciousness, to being convinced that I was a fraud and they had been trapped in a cult.

This latter story gained traction in the mainstream and has now become the loudest voice, and to this day it continues to drown out the objections of gentler and more appreciative voices that still hold dear the profound love of Spirit that kept us all so closely connected for so long. Many of my former students are now joined together in a spirit of collective denial—denouncing everything that was good, sacred, and beautiful about our work. The why question has a multi-layered answer, and we will explore it in depth in the following pages.

A major contributing factor to the tenacity of this denial that I want to point to at the outset of our inquiry involves the power of the internet and social media to control the narrative.

With the sudden loss of their physical community, many of my former students' conversations about the crash of EnlightenNext moved to cyberspace, where their now inverted narrative began to lead a life of its own. In several online forums people tried to process their emotional shock and come to terms with the magnitude of everything that had transpired, venting their outrage about how they had all been victimized. Some of my former students told me that they had to disengage from these online forums because the groupthink was so one-sided, emotionally charged, and impenetrable that it was hard to voice a different opinion. The atmosphere in these forums, they said, was so claustrophobic that they began to feel like mini-cults themselves—obstructing free, deep, and independent inquiry, whereas these students felt the need to dive within and find their own authentic voice without it being tainted by others' prejudices.

Unfortunately, the narrative circulating on these sites has now come to define our legacy in the public eye, while the depth and sanctity of our project continues to be denied in these online echo chambers.

How are we to understand the psychospiritual reasons for the sudden and extreme switch in the narrative? Why is it that when students leave their guru, they often go through a complete rewriting of their history? What causes such an abrupt reversal in someone's meaning-making? And why is it so difficult to keep a balanced perspective, in which both the baby and the bathwater are acknowledged?

After the collapse of our community, I had several long, illuminating conversations with Ken Wilber about my fall from grace, the disintegration of our sangha, and the puzzling conundrum of the sudden switch in the narrative. Ken offered his take on why the collapse of EnlightenNext had occurred and described what he believed were the psychodynamics behind the sudden switch of narrative:

Andrew: Very often when a scandal breaks and a teacher falls from grace, he loses half of his community, while the other half sticks around. Those who stay often do so because they still feel in touch with the goodness, truth, and beauty of what the Buddha, the Dharma, and the Sangha bring to their lives, even if the teacher's transgressions might have been reprehensible. But in my case the fall was extreme. I literally lost my entire community, and many of my former students have even opposed my returning to teaching. I have grappled with why the responses have been so extreme. I knew most of these people intimately. A lot of them were my friends for ten, twenty, even thirty years. What forces cause such extremity?

Ken: A vast number of people who are now involved in spiritual concerns, including a large number of your students, are at what we would recognize as the green [postmodern] altitude. Many of the problems that developed in your community were green-generated problems. As much as you attacked those and pointed them out, it was hard for people to get over them.

Somebody once said that you can't reason a person out of a belief unless they were reasoned into it first. People don't adopt the stages of Growing Up because they reason their way into them, and so you can't reason them out of their stage of development either. Logic and evidence don't help here. They have to go through a growth process in which they really work on seeing their green structure and trying everything at that level. Then slowly they will start to see it as an object. The more they do so, the more they will be able to let go of it and transcend into the next-higher stage. The process of Growing Up requires a specific kind of practice. Meditation and spiritual transmission alone are not enough to catalyze stage growth. But you weren't working with specifically focused practices to help your students transform out of green into teal . . . [so] they didn't have specific ways to work on Growing Up. Still, you were attacking their Growing Up issues. And whenever you, as the guru, made a remark to them, they would start by trying to agree with you and nod their heads. But in the background they still had this fundamental green belief system that was making the real judgment. And so they would go along with you. But deep inside, this resentment kind of starts building and building, and you keep hacking away at it. Then all of a sudden, the student realizes, *God, I can't do it!* And then that flip occurs, where people change their opinion, often 100 percent. They go from "Andrew can do no wrong and I love him" to "Andrew can do no right and I loathe him. He has destroyed my life, and everything that's gone wrong is because of him." Suddenly you hear the whole photographic negative of everything they had been saying about you before when they were still convinced that their involvement with you was the best thing that ever happened to them. And they were saying true things at the beginning! They were getting insights and transmissions that were just blowing them away. They were truly Waking Up. Yet they weren't advancing in Growing Up. So they remained at the green level and became more resentful, because Growing Up was not getting addressed, even though the Waking Up was extraordinary. They're off here [*gestures high*], and they're getting into groups where they're sharing a We consciousness that is becoming transcendental. But what's going on down here [*gestures low*]? Green, green, green.

Andrew: But what's confusing is that for the last eighteen years or so, especially since we became friends and I started learning more about Integral philosophy, the stage distinctions became so familiar that we started using them as part of our everyday language.

Ken: Right. Well, there are two types of knowledge: knowledge by description and knowledge by acquaintance. When you read a textbook on spiral dynamics and you have to take a test on it, you can memorize the definitions of all of the stages. When you are at orange, you have knowledge by acquaintance of that stage [because] you are there! And if someone asks you, "What does orange say about this?" you just have to look inside, and you are going to give a very straightforward, knowledgeable response. But then they ask you, "How does this look from green?" or "How does it look from teal?" or "How does it look from turquoise?" If you've memorized all the descriptions, you can just sort of repeat what it looks like, but you're not *there*. That's just knowledge by description, not acquaintance.

And so, no matter how much people were able to speak about these higher stages, if they weren't really doing practices that helped them shift, they weren't getting knowledge by acquaintance. They were just getting knowledge by description. And so talking about all these distinctions in a description fashion wasn't necessarily changing people's acquaintance, their actual identity, the actual stage they were at.

Andrew: The evidence would demonstrate that what you're saying has to be true.

Ken: Oh, I think so. And that's why green remained there. And then when the whole thing exploded, what you saw in almost every area was just green everywhere! An angry, frustrated, bitter green. As big a green explosion as you could get.

Andrew: Wow! And, how would you explain someone like me, who's a child of postmodernism? Where did this grasp of the vertical context—my inclination toward verticality—come from?

Ken: Well, in your case it came from your own genuine and deep enlightenment. The primary overriding drive that you were always manifesting to students was Waking Up and getting people into—however it was conceived—wider and wider and truer and truer, more authentic states. You were helping them become more awakened, more realized, more enlightened. And that was central to you. When you transition from being an egoic separate self, an isolated individual, to discovering the Ground of All Being and a radical, infinite release into ultimate reality, it is the biggest transformative change a human being can go through. When something like that happens, it profoundly impacts your being in a way that just changes it forever. And that was always the fire you had—and you were authentically, honestly, genuinely working to have other people have those realizations as well.

But then the questions are: Where were you at in Growing Up? How much shadow material have you been Cleaning Up? To what extent were you really Showing Up?* Were you really including the Triple Gem? And when things aren't going right in some of those areas, then resentment can start to build.

As we discussed, although Growing Up was talked about, it wasn't really being engaged in with specific practices. In addition, you yourself were developing a mythic absolutist approach that you would start getting caught in, and so you pushed your students and your project harder and harder. That then got combined with whatever shadow material you had, which you started to increasingly display. And those were the forms that your transmission was often moving through . . .

As all these elements came together, the green resentment intensified. And so things just started to become a little worse and a little worse, and even though there were still breakthroughs, there was also increasing backlash. And as long as you had an attitude of "I'm doing it right, I'm gonna keep going forward," then that's not the best response to have when you've got mythic absolutism, shadow material, and a mountain of green resentment building up all around you. The straight "I still got it!" is not gonna be a really good way to handle all of those turmoils. And so eventually the green resentment reached this sharp tipping point, because nobody likes being treated like that.

What turned up the flame even further in your case was the original power of the transmission. One of the things that makes Guru

---

*Whereas Waking Up, Growing Up, and Cleaning Up refer to the inner work we do within our own consciousness, Showing Up is about using the fruits of our inner work to benefit the exterior world and to engage in its many dimensions and challenges in a much more meaningful and impactful way. To Show Up is to move into full functioning and enact real change.

Yoga so essential is that some individuals awaken to a really profound, industrial-strength capacity for transmission of some of the very highest states. People can *feel* that, and of course it's attractive, and they are drawn to that. Particularly before green resentment had built up really big, people were very open and having awakenings just being in your presence. It was astonishing. That's why so many people came to you at the beginning. It was authentic and genuine, and people knew it. That was what was so historic about it, and why your fame as a spiritual teacher, if you will, began to spread quite rapidly. You were doing that authentic transmission, and just being in the presence of that energy was bringing about real transformation in people. This upped the level across the board, and because it was all lifted up so high, it was also ready to crash in an even more heavy way.

I believe that what was mistaken about many of the most extreme responses after the fall of your community was the looking back and not acknowledging the aspects that were true at the time . . . When you look at the earlier phases of your work, there was this almost unanimous outpouring of love, admiration, and dedication. What that meant was that there were some components that were working authentically, accurately, and correctly. Those weren't just lies. Everybody who was devoted to you wasn't just caught up in complete self-delusion. Nobody is capable of that degree of self-deception. Your students were expressing authentic feelings in many, many ways. But when they then later said that everything you were doing was wrong, they're really just condemning their own capacity for any sort of authentic judgment. It would mean that when they thought you were real, they were completely screwed up and wrong from the beginning—which I don't believe. There were genuinely important and good things happening in your work, in many ways, and that really needs to be remembered.

I think it's very, very important to keep in mind that these kinds of situations contain an unprecedented amount of crucial lessons for us to learn. And that includes the very positive things as well as some of these negative things. Some of the negative issues were due to culture at large, some were due to the community, some were due to you. They're all lessons and they're very valuable.[3]

Ken's green resentment hypothesis is illuminating. It offers an explanation for the perplexing switch in the narrative. But it also clarifies why it proved to be so challenging for most of my students to actually move their center of identity gravity firmly and stably into the higher *stages of Growing Up*, even while they were able to enter into extraordinary spiritual *states of Waking Up*.

But the goal of the teachings of Evolutionary Enlightenment was not only about cultivating higher states of consciousness. In my years as a teacher I had all too often seen how these higher states, for all their undeniable profundity and transcendental beauty, are usually temporary. They do not guarantee lasting transformation. And so what I was most passionate about was to catalyze the emergence of a new and higher *stage* of development as a stable structure, a permanent acquisition—not just in individuals, but in a collective of people who are able to hold this higher awareness and facilitate its further development. Still, what we actually pushed into was a series of collective *states* of enlightened awareness, and so I started to work from there.

As these states began to erupt with increasing frequency among different groups of my students, I began to devote all my time and energy to trying to find ways to stabilize them. My understanding was that if enough of us were able to hold the higher *perspective* that was revealed in these transcendent We states, it could perhaps provide the foundation for a higher *stage* of development to emerge. And so I began to instruct my students to practice looking at their state experiences as an object and ground themselves in the higher view that is inherent within them, rather than simply being swept up in their extraordinary feeling qualities like ecstasy, bliss, and lightheartedness. In this way I was trying to catalyze a radical transformation in the very structure of the self—a turnaround so profound that it would establish the kosmocentric perspective of the authentic self as the primary locus of my student's identity. This thoroughly transformed self would then be strong enough to stably carry such a higher stage.

In the end, even though we at times reached into our goal, we didn't actually achieve it fully. For most people the results just didn't stick. Ken once alluded to one of the possible reasons for why this was the case. He pointed out that even the teal or turquoise stages are still not sufficient to accommodate such a profound change in the self's orientation.[4] Embodying the authentic self and its kosmocentric consciousness most fully is a lofty aspiration that requires third-tier stage development (see figures 3.1 and 3.2 or plates 1 and 2), which is still an extremely rare accomplishment that is mostly only alive in the visions of our greatest sages.*

What we *did* achieve over the years, however, was that the Higher We states we were able to access were no longer just peak experiences. As a result of our intense spiritual practice, the Higher We state had reached a certain continuity. It had taken on its own more or less stable pattern, and had turned into an extended plateau state. As Ken put it, "What it sounds like to me is that you're creating a stable plateau state or plateau experience, which means that it's a state that could be extended pretty much indefinitely, and that you have more or less permanent access to, and some individuals are experiencing it permanently."[5] He further suggested that this stable pattern could be understood as a morphic field,† a concept developed by biologist Rupert Sheldrake, referring

---

*See also figure 10.1 or plate 7, the Wilber-Combs lattice, for a visual representation of the relationship between states and stages.

†Ken made this suggestion based on the nonlocal impact this egoless field appears to have. In many cases it was not only limited to local practice groups. As described in chapter 4, whenever groups of us came together in cities across the globe, during a time when the superholon at Foxhollow was also gathering in this egoless field, all groups would have a very powerful experience almost effortlessly, whereas when groups would meet at different times and hence operate without that nonlocal support, they would have to work much harder to achieve the same results. During our final years the field had become so strong it would emerge during global conference calls, drawing large numbers of participants into it.

to a nonlocal subtle energy pattern of habit or memory that supports and shapes the structure and development of all phenomena, whether physical, biological, emotional, mental, cultural, social, or spiritual.* Because of our repeated access to this new spiritual phenomenon of an awakened Higher We, it was now no longer just a temporary state in our own individual interiors; it had also manifested as an actual subtle energy pattern in the kosmos, a concrete energetic support structure with a long sought after stabilizing quality.

And so, through repeated practice, what we achieved was an awakened Higher We state that, for many, had turned into an extended plateau state—and that was supported by a morphic field. But we hadn't yet been able to stably move many students into higher stages of Growing Up.

In our conversation, Ken pointed out that this was due to the fact that I wasn't working with specifically focused practices to help my students transform out of their current stage of Growing Up and into the next one. Perhaps one of our most direct ways to address Growing Up was our practice of the fourth and fifth tenets of Evolutionary Enlightenment, both of which call on people to live from a kosmocentric perspective, which is the perspective that naturally emerges in the higher stages of Growing Up (see figure 3.1 or plate 1).

The challenge with stage development is that the practices that catalyze it aren't yet widely understood. In contrast with the long-established, time-tested knowledge of spiritual states training, the discovery of psychological stages of development is still relatively young, having only come to the forefront in the last hundred years. Any effort to catalyze stage growth is therefore at best experimental, and no doubt imperfect. And so it was for us. Our spiritual experiment was a wild and at times messy attempt to fire on all cylinders of the human development potential. While doing so, we tried to figure out what worked and what didn't. We were engaged in a serious effort

---

*To get acquainted with Sheldrake's theory on morphogenetic fields, consult his 1981 book *A New Science of Life*.

to enact a multidimensional yet nonsystematized evolutionary practice, and the transformational results we managed to achieve mirrored these qualities.

When I inquired of Ken where he thought our Higher We breakthroughs would fit on the Integral map, he responded by reflecting on the pioneering nature of our endeavor and its results, from his characteristic fifty-thousand-foot view:

Andrew: How would you interpret the Higher We practices as we pioneered them at EnlightenNext? Some people used to believe we downloaded Aurobindo's supermind; others would say we went into a state of collective enlightenment, in which we were sharing one consciousness. I sometimes think of them as a newly emerging third-tier emergent stage, a state trying to become a stage, or a state and a stage trying to cohere, even though it was obviously not yet stable because the individuals in our holons weren't strong enough to support it in a lasting way. How do you see this phenomenon?

Ken: All of those to some degree were happening, and this is not just a throwaway answer. We really are genuinely pioneering all this right now. For the first time in all of history we're looking at a large number of new dimensions that we just didn't know were there, and we're trying to figure out how we can include all of them. That means all quadrants, all levels, all lines, all states, all types. And the initial attempts at that are going to be marked by trial and error. So I think all of those elements were kind of falling all over each other, and each of them represented a very genuine aspect of a reality that you were touching into. And my own thought is that as this continues, as it gets more and more pragmatic and we acquire more wisdom about how to include all these dimensions, we will start to have increasingly systematized ways to do it. And fifty or a hundred years from now we may come to a point where they say, "Here's a manual. Here are the exercises that can help with Growing Up; here's how we do Cleaning Up; here's the transmission you can have and the degrees of Waking Up that go along with that; and all of it sticks together like this."[6]

What we were doing at EnlightenNext was an early empirical effort to catalyze stage development—with mixed results.

In our conversation, Ken argued that our lack of working with specific practices for stage growth was one of the factors that contributed to the collapse of our community, because even though Growing Up wasn't adequately addressed, I still called my students out on their Growing Up issues. I tried to force breakthroughs, at times using immense pressure and even punitive strategies, which are usually not the most effective means to facilitate stage growth in a lasting and sustainable way. Many of my students were serious and sincere and wanted to live up to our lofty aspirations, but increasingly they felt they were unable to do so. They were up the creek without a paddle, if you will, and as a result, resentment began to build.

As this was happening, the complex psychodynamics that were at play in our work exacerbated the situation even further. My mythic absolutism, my shadow material, and my blunt style of hacking away at people's issues were colliding more and more with my students' green-postmodern sensibilities. They were especially disgruntled with the obligation to adhere to strict rules; with our binary thinking and its all-too-clear division between ego and nonego; and with the rigidity of the hierarchy, in which students were always accountable to other students of a higher rank. As these forces continued to tussle with one another, their green resentment intensified all the way to the point where it finally exploded. As soon as it did, their previously surrendered egos suddenly leapt back into the driver's seat. They turned around and began to express anger and outrage, believing they had been duped. At that pivotal point they started rebelling against the obligations inherent in our hierarchical system, and their once so appreciative narrative switched to its polar opposite: an eruption of "angry, frustrated, bitter green."

What I believe happened on a metaphysical level as our community collapsed and green resentment flared up all around us was nothing short of a spiritual tragedy. Most of my students lost touch with the vibrant, upward-pulling source that had nourished the deepest part of their souls for so long. They dropped out of the morphic field of awakened awareness that had worked like a support structure for them, a scaffolding that held them up at a level of awakeness that was significantly above their center of identity gravity. Most of them appeared unable to sustain their higher orientation independently and slid back into their *actual* center of gravity.

As long as they remained connected to the exhilarating spiritual field of our community, their narrative remained positive, a seamless expression of the spiritual brightness of this higher reality. But as soon as they disconnected from this sacred context, the bright, awake quality of their inner experience dissipated, and their narrative changed accordingly.

One of the most puzzling aspects of the sudden shift of narrative was the intensely reactive emotional charge that accompanied it. This suggests that a part of the explanation for this phenomenon could be found in the subterranean world of our shadows, where our insight becomes murky, and where deep unconscious forces govern.

Because this is not my domain of expertise, I spoke with Integral Zen master Doshin Roshi, who has built his work around integrating traditional Zen and shadow work, and who, somewhat facetiously, likes to refer to himself as "the shadow roshi." He shed further light on some of the classic shadow dynamics he felt were involved:

Have you heard about transference and countertransference? It's a psychological mechanism that applies to both individual relationships and cultures, the collective shadows, and it is in fact just another way of talking about shadow projections. Let's take romantic relationships as an example. When two people fall in love, they don't fall in love with each other, they fall in love with each other's projections, with the underlying archetypal image that always has something to do with what they need to feel whole. Then the honeymoon follows. Life is wonderful and full of bliss, until they get to know each other. Then they begin to realize that what they've fallen in love with isn't who they're currently in relationship with. So the bubble bursts, and the projection is withdrawn. You suddenly see the person as they are, unadorned by your projection. The deeper truth that has been repressed comes to the surface, and a crisis breaks out. When this happens, the relationship often doesn't survive, and divorce follows. And the bigger the projection, the bigger the divorce.

It's the same with the teacher-student relationship. What students transfer onto the guru is their own Buddha nature, which is unrealized and undeveloped. When we so desperately want to believe in something like a guru, who is greater than ourselves, we tend to ignore things. We pretend that they are not there. But everything we ignore we tend to build up resentment toward. And when the projection is withdrawn, that whole reservoir of resentment explodes in a story like a volcano. So what happens to this previously wonderful story when the projection is withdrawn and the shadow forces that have been building up under the surface get so intense that they just explode? The narrative turns to the complete opposite! We exchange the story of the positive projections for the story of withdrawing the positive projections, and that becomes the truth that we now conceive. Our mind is clouded by our own projections.

Now wherever there's transference, there's countertransference, and that's what the teacher is projecting onto the student. This could be an expectation of having the perfect student, and students behave like perfect students because they recognize you as the perfect teacher. It creates a symbiosis. An autonomous zone is created in the relationship, where the teacher's intentions are very pure because he is dealing with the perfect student. The teacher is doing all the right things, and he is doing them with great devotion and great caring, and together, teacher and student are creating a vortex that can lead to awakening.

In a traditional guru-disciple relationship, the teacher uses transference and countertransference to help inspire students to develop the discipline and devotion that they don't ordinarily have in order to Wake Up. And you were doing that. It is part of the power of the mythical guru. The reason that people will do everything the guru tells them is because they're projecting their own Buddha nature onto their guru. And even though this is a powerful teaching tool in an amber culture, it doesn't work in a modern or postmodern or Integral culture. This is what has to be replaced.

So, because we are so unaware of these psychological mechanisms on which we all operate, we have to do shadow work. The path of awakening in an Integral culture involves doing shadow work—individual and collective shadow work. There's no other way. The leading edge of what needs to happen in this twenty-first century, with teachers and students and their relationships, is that we really come to understand the mechanisms of transference and collective transference. We must withdraw our projections onto each other. And we must get real![7]

These unconscious projection dynamics are part and parcel of the guru-disciple relationship and need to be seen for what they are. The figure of the guru tends to become a receptacle of projections of some of the most basic human archetypes we know, like "the Perfect Parent" or "the Savior." These primordial archetypes have been alive in the human psyche for as long as humans exist. They hide out in the deepest pre-rational layers of our being, where they constitute the roots of the self prior to the development of the ego. These archetypal projections are therefore often hard to spot. And so they are more common than most of us imagine. They may occur in even highly sophisticated and mature seekers and can manifest in sometimes very subtle ways.

To some extent, I believe these factors were also involved in the collapse of EnlighenNext. It is a classic psychological scheme that the Savior is first adored and then betrayed and crucified; and the Perfect Parent has to be killed by the child so that it can gain its autonomy. In our case, these projections were withdrawn the moment the guru fell from grace, and promptly thereafter the archetypal roles reversed: my senior students assumed the role of the wise ones, set up a holon to address my problems, and began to instruct and mentor me, treating their guru like a lost soul in need of salvation or a child in need of guidance.

The intriguing reality of archetypal projection dynamics is that they can be both deeply problematic *and* extraordinarily catalytic.

When the projection process happens consciously and wisely and involves *transpersonal* higher potentials, it can actually generate positive transformational results. In our sangha we would consistently see how positive transference would empower and encourage aspirants to stay on course. Whenever they went through challenging times and their spiritual process stalled, it was their love of and trust in their guru that allowed many to pull through and carry on, again and again. When students project their own highest unrealized potentials onto the guru, all their energy and attention becomes riveted on the guru, and with that, on their own highest truth. This creates a real and coherent buddhafield with a strong updraft of awakened awareness and evolutionary power, a most potent environment in which to catalyze growth and awakening.

But when the projection process occurs unconsciously and involves *pre-personal* and unprocessed shadow material, like the unresolved need for the Perfect Parent or the Savior, then transference becomes disempowering. It causes a person to abdicate responsibility for their own growth and avoid the real developmental work they need to do.

Evidently, the truth and awakening power of the guru-disciple relationship cannot be reduced to transference and countertransference only. As we have explored in the previous chapters, the real power at the heart of this sacred relationship does not originate from *psychological transference*, but from *direct spiritual transmission* of enlightened awareness from teacher to student.

Still, as these projection dynamics are hard to entirely get around, being aware of them is important when entering into a guru-disciple relationship. The critical question in such a context is this: How can we create a real buddhafield, preserve it, and give ourselves over to it with intensity, so that we will receive its benefits while avoiding the trap of unconscious transference?

In light of the overwhelming intensity of the emotions that were unleashed when EnlightenNext collapsed, the abrupt reversal of my students' attitude toward me and our project feels a lot less surprising. The amalgam of powerful emotions, both conscious and unconscious, made it almost impossible to maintain a balanced perspective and not be caught up in extremes.

When I spoke with Terry Patten, he reflected on his own ordeal of leaving his guru, Adi Da. He described how he too had to struggle mightily to integrate the immense spiritual gifts he had received from the controversial great sage with his individual sovereignty as a human being. What makes Terry's perspective particularly compelling is what he learned from his ordeal: the ability to embrace the totality of his experience as a paradox in which both unrepentant devotion *and* critical skepticism are legitimate perspectives and can thus coexist:

> When people go through the profoundly disorienting process of leaving the guru and their sangha, they have to fight almost a life-or-death struggle to recover some of their personal power and autonomy. I think it's a really rare person who can give themselves over so fully, have a transformative experience, and then, when they leave, not make the guru or the community the devil. I had to really hate Adi Da for a while to get through what I had to get through, but I ultimately ended up integrating all of it. I think the cultural narrative around spiritual communities is so binary these days. Either the teaching is clean and it never violates anybody's boundaries, or it's an oppressive cult and should

not be allowed. That's why the guru is guilty until proven innocent, and the cult is evil until proven passively benign.

When I left Adi Da, I had this enormous body of experience
that was among the most important in my life, which I could only
access in the mood of utter love, devotion, and surrender to
him. This whole dimension of all I had been given was available
only in this state-specific condition. But then there was another
huge body of very important experience that had come from my
individuating—my standing up, my saying no, and my willingness
to give him the finger on a certain level. And the *no* was not soft;
it was deep. And in that I got in touch with other aspects of my
life and power.

What that meant was that each perspective was both true
and partial, and there was no way to hold all of reality from a
particular place. It cracked open my head. I knew that whatever I was looking at, I was looking at a piece of reality, and I
knew I had to be in touch with and in conversation with multiple truths. I had to learn to be open enough and paradoxical enough to hold contradictory realities simultaneously. And
that is not easy. Psychoemotionally and cognitively it has been
very challenging. It's a big deal. But that is how I have made my
way through that contradiction. So I am an unrepentant, ragged
bhakta *and* a skeptical critic. I have both dimensions available to
me because they each locate truths that are important, and if I
divorce from either of those truths I'm diminished in a way that
is a problem.

Now, how do we design that for everybody? That's the
million-dollar question. I can only say that I would never have
gone here if I had not been forced by the utterly irresistible
attractiveness of the guru originally, and by the impossibility of
staying in the claustrophobia of his container; and then by the
violence of the antiguru skepticism that enveloped me in the
world I emerged into. All those things forced me to hold different levels of complexity.[8]

Many of my former students haven't yet been able to work through these formidable cognitive, spiritual, and emotional challenges in order to integrate these paradoxical, state-specific worlds into a larger embrace. Their heads haven't cracked open yet, even as a few seem to have made some progress toward a more integral appreciation of our endeavor and have begun to come to terms with it in their lives.

During a deep and intimate conversational moment, I confided in Doshin Roshi, "I have no idea how to resolve or heal this incredible wound that exists in the soul of my former community. A lot of people say they have moved on, and I don't know if that's really possible at the level of the soul. I know it's not possible for *me* at that deep level. So why is it that this enormous chasm seems almost impossible to heal at the moment?" He responded in his typical Zen-like but compassionate way, elucidating what he saw as the psychological responsibilities of both my students and myself in this situation:

> Well, I suspect because it's almost impossible to heal at the moment! Let's just notice what is, and our limited capacity to answer the *why?* question. I can't answer the *why?* question. I can say some things that just show how complex it is, and how our understanding isn't adequate for the task of resolving it.
>
> There is so much to learn from what happened in your sangha and what's continuing to happen as you return to teaching. It's not something that I want to take sides on, but I want to support your sincerity and your students' sincerity. They are sincere as well. But what's more important than supporting individuals is supporting this larger process of growing into a better understanding of what needs to happen with the student-teacher relationship in the twenty-first century, because there is so much at stake. It's what some people would call a wicked problem. It is so complex that it exceeds our ability to answer it fully. To come to more advanced answers, our whole belief system, our whole map of reality, has to expand and evolve. The fact that there are no satisfactory answers yet creates such a moral dilemma for

someone who's caught in it—and you're caught in it, and so are your students, ironically.

As for your students' part of the responsibility, it's really easy to make you the bad guy, blame you, and avoid the moral dilemma of growing and expanding consciousness, rather than clarify it to the point where you can actually see what's really happening. You're such an easy scapegoat here.

From the guru's side, an effort needs to be made to compensate for the process of ego inflation that naturally occurs. It needs to be balanced with an equal dose of humility. When I talk to you personally, I feel humility coming from you, and I notice that your prior students don't. And I don't know whether they've had enough contact with you after you've done all the work, or if their minds were already made up that there is none there. I don't know exactly why, but something tells me this has something to do with the degree of the total expansion and the total collapse. The all-or-nothing way in which you led your sangha created the all-or-nothing way in which it collapsed.

There's a balancing that has to happen that's part of nature and that doesn't happen easily in our culture. In the postmodern-green, pluralistic, egalitarian culture, there's no humility. There's no forgiveness possible. The green belief system is deeply unforgiving. It wants to rescue all the victims, and it can't forgive perpetrators. There, it's one strike and you're out! You're not only banished, but banished forever. This is the cultural collective shadow of postmodernity. The postmodern mindset tends to persecute and blame anyone who has the *cojones* to really step up and try to do something new—all the pioneers—and it does so with the best of intentions. But it tends to forget that when you make omelets, you're going to break some eggs.[9]

Even as it is clear that the situation that arose at EnlightenNext is one still in need of healing, in the culture at large there are hopeful indications that we are maturing in the way we relate to our spiritual teachers.

It was spiritual practitioner-turned-meditation teacher, author, public speaker, and ordained interfaith minister Philip Goldberg who pointed this out to me. Ever since he featured our work at EnlightenNext in his book *American Veda: From Emerson and the Beatles to Yoga and Meditation and How Indian Spirituality Changed the West,* an engagingly written and well-researched account about the evolving spiritual landscape in America, I have developed a warm friendship with him. In our refreshing conversation, Philip drew my attention to the signs of cultural evolution that are emerging as a promising silver lining around the dark cloud of recent controversies involving gurus, and the paralyzing crisis of trust that has ensued:

> There's a certain amount of spiritual wisdom—just maturity—in being able to balance spiritual independence and humility. We need to be humble enough to take on a teacher, and yet retain a certain amount of discernment and personal responsibility. Not everybody can handle that.
>
> I hope that people can start to see gurus in a different way. They're all strong personalities, often with great gifts and great flaws, which makes them prone to falling prey to these controversies. One of the things I've observed around the spiritual scene, sort of from the 1960s onward, is that a certain level of individual maturity has developed that allows people to go through these spiritual upheavals. They discover the guru's humanness; they come to terms with the fact that the path is not what they expected it to be; and they do so with a certain amount of grace and in a spirit of ongoing learning. The assumption of perfection on the part of the guru seems to have been relaxed, and the younger generation of seekers may have a healthier attitude than some of the baby boomers did. At least they seem to have learned from some of the mistakes of projection and wishful thinking that we made around gurus.
>
> I'm wondering how many of the people who were with you could now have dinner with you and say, "Boy, we went through

a lot, and I learned this, and you learned that, and now I'm where I am, and I'm really grateful for what you taught me. You made mistakes, and this is what I think they are. But I truly appreciate that you're making a sincere effort to come to terms with all this." I hope that some of your people who are now teaching on their own recognize that they're in that position partly because of what they learned from you. I don't know to what extent they need to hold on to the anger, but at a certain point even understandable anger doesn't serve.[10]

I share his hope that we have all learned from the hard lessons of the past; that we have indeed moved into a deeper level of sanity and maturity; and that we are ready to prepare the ground for advancing the Triple Gem into a bright new future.

13

Triple Gem Integral

In the previous chapters we have laid out a vision of a more integral Buddha and Dharma. In this final chapter we will explore the evolution of the third of the Three Jewels of enlightenment—the Sangha, the communal We-space, as it matures into its integral expressions. We will then complete our journey by probing into the promising potential of a truly integral Triple Gem, in which the Three Jewels are sparkling together, shining their light into the world. But we will start by clarifying why the project of working toward an integral We-space of individuals adept in the art of human relatedness and enlightened communication is a lot more consequential—even downright urgent—than we might imagine. The import of such an endeavor far surpasses the particulars of our work and leads us straight into the most alarming predicament we face today: the critical emergency of our world in crisis.

We are living in a pivotal moment in history. A series of interlocking crises in multiple domains of life have coalesced into one massive metacrisis: environmental degradation, the threat of economic collapse, escalating geopolitical tensions, a worldwide public health crisis, a refugee crisis, the imminent danger of global terrorism and nuclear destruction, the depletion of our natural resources, species extinction, the collapse of biodiversity, overpopulation, starvation, political polarization, the crumbling of the world's democracies, the resurgence of forms of tribalism—the list goes on and on. Holding an even incomplete enumeration of these flash points in our awareness is more than most of us who feel overwhelmed and powerless can bear. Together, they have produced an unprecedented global emergency that impacts not just limited groups of us locally—like our earlier civilizational breakdowns used to do—but of us, everywhere. As these crises continue to unravel, it begins to dawn on an increasing number of us that our comfortable middle-class way of life may no longer be sustainable, and there is growing, and legitimate, concern that even civilization itself is no longer guaranteed. Many of our old systems, we have come to see, are inherently self-terminating, like a cancer, killing the host. We are rapidly careening toward the edge of the cliff, and many of us have come to the chilling conclusion that self-destruction has become an actual possibility.

If we, as a species, are to survive this metacrisis, if we are to leave a planet in which future generations can thrive, we need to learn how to get along with one another, start working together, and formulate a comprehensive global response to our dire predicament. Yet what we actually see in the real world seems diametrically opposed to what we now so desperately and urgently need. Public discourse is increasingly polarized. We are continuously fighting bitter culture wars between the apparently irreconcilable worldviews of amber traditionalism, orange modernism, and green postmodernism, and it isn't clear at all how we can effectively communicate with one another across these value spheres so that we can begin to co-create new and practicable solutions to our most tenacious world problems.

What *is* clear is that alongside all the external crises we face, our cultural space has become fractured by an interior crisis of meaning-making, a crisis that has been brought to a feverish pitch by the excesses of postmodernity—extreme relativism, narcissism, nihilism, and the deconstruction of all grand narratives. We lost our North Star and ended up in a cynical post-truth world, overwhelmed by a raging storm of information and disinformation—a world in which whoever controls the narrative holds the power. This situation has severely compromised our ability to truly come together based on a set of sane shared values, so we can design intelligent, workable solutions and take decisive action to course-correct the multiple crises that are now upon us. We are living through a cultural watershed in which we are clearly running up against the limitations of the postmodern worldview.

In his provocative book *Trump and a Post-Truth World,* Ken Wilber boldly argues that the failure of the postmodern leading edge to effectively lead has caused an impasse at the very edge of evolution itself:

> The green postmodern leading-edge of evolution itself has, for several decades, degenerated into its extreme, pathological, and dysfunctional forms. As such, it is literally incapable of effectively acting as a real leading-edge. Its fundamental belief—"there is no truth"—and its basic essential attitude—"aperspectival madness"—cannot in any fashion actually lead, actually choose a course of action that is positive, healthy, effective, and truly evolutionary. With all growth hierarchies denied and deconstructed, evolution has no real way to grow, has no way forward at all, and thus nothing but dominator hierarchies are seen everywhere, effectively reducing any individual you want to a victim. The leading-edge has collapsed; it is now a few-billion-persons (or so) massive car crash, a huge traffic jam at the very edge of evolution itself, sabotaging virtually every move that evolution seeks to take. Evolution itself finds its own headlights shining beams of nihilism, which can actually see nothing, or narcissism, which can see only itself. Under this often malicious leadership (the mean-green meme), the earlier levels and stages of development have themselves begun to hemorrhage, sliding into their own forms of pathological dysfunction. And this isn't just happening in one or two countries, it is happening around the world. . . . Evolution, in a decided move of self-correction, has paused and is in the process of backing up a few paces, regrouping, and reconstituting itself for a healthier, more unified, more functional continuation. What virtually all of these regroupings have as a primary driver is a profound anti-green dynamic acting as a morphic field radiating from the broken leading-edge itself.[1]

This dark evolutionary cloud, fortunately, has begun to show a silver lining. In response to it, a space for emerging Integral conversations is opening up in our culture, as philosophers, thought leaders, cultural creatives, visionaries, and an ever greater number of concerned citizens with an open view feel ready to move beyond the old ways and are entering into a serious exploration of a viable path forward. Examples are manifold, but include informal networks like the Intellectual Dark Web,* a group of loosely affiliated public intellectuals including clinical psychologist and cultural critic Jordan Peterson; mathematical physicist Eric Weinstein and his brother, the evolutionary biologist Bret Weinstein; neuroscientist and philosopher Sam Harris;† alternative media personality Joe Rogan; and other bold thinkers from both the Left and the Right of the political spectrum. Sense-making media platforms like Rebel Wisdom and Future Thinkers, along with many more courageous souls who dare to think way outside the box, are also part of this growing stream of Integral thinking and teal conscious-

---

*The name Intellectual Dark Web was coined by Eric Weinstein and popularized in 2018 by opinion writer Bari Weiss in her *New York Times* article "Meet the Renegades of the Intellectual Dark Web," May 8, 2018.

†On September 9, 2019, Sam Harris interviewed me about the collapse of EnlightenNext on his podcast *Waking Up App*. He was open enough to want to explore our case in a public forum, declining to go along with the cynicism around spiritual communities that is so prevalent in our culture, which testifies to the admirable spirit of intellectual curiosity and authentic inquisitiveness upheld by some of the Intellectual Dark Web thinkers. The interview was critical but was also conducted from a place of sincere interest in how something that seemed to have a lot of spiritual promise could have gone so wrong. He presented our story as "a cautionary tale" from which something could be learned, emphasizing that "this is a very mixed story" and "[I] was not merely a fraud." As Harris explained, "I know enough about Andrew's experience—about the kinds of practices he did, and who he studied with, and the effect he had on others—to be reasonably convinced that he had a legitimate awakening, and that he had direct experience of many of the things I teach in this course—and that he was producing such experiences in others." He also expressed some appreciation for my efforts to come to terms with my mistakes and take responsibility for them: "Here is the rare case of a fallen guru who appears to have taken some responsibility for his fall"; and "What makes you so unusual is that you appear to have taken some responsibility for this and have apologized for much of the chaos you caused. And as to whether or not your former students accept your apologies, that's another matter."

ness. And it is in this cultural space that the creative juice of post-postmodern evolution is now most alive.

Such emerging Integral conversations are exactly what we would expect to see as evolution attempts to remove the impediments to its own further unfolding so it can course-correct. As my longtime friend and Integral philosopher Steve McIntosh* astutely remarked during my conversation with him, "In order for a new stage to emerge, the previous stage has to become successful enough to manifest its own pathologies. Postmodernism has now become successful enough to provide a plat-form for its own transcendence, both in what it succeeds in doing and in the now increasingly obvious manifestations of its pathologies. The pathologies of green [postmodernism] provide the points of departure for our move into Integral."[2]

Many of these emerging Integral conversations—notably the ones of the Intellectual Dark Web—explicitly expose the pathologies of extreme postmodernism such as woke ideology, cancel culture, radi-calized forms of feminism, identity politics, and over-the-top political correctness, to name a few. The Intellectual Dark Web thinkers are willing to have these difficult conversations irrespective of the social cost. They see the process of inquiry and good faith dialogue as more valuable than defending their own personal and philosophical posi-tions or winning the debate, and they're open to changing their minds if their conversation partners make a better point. With this attitude, they intend to model ways to have more truthful dialogues and move beyond the toxic polarization of our public discourse. Their conversa-tions are honest attempts to reorient our post-truth world toward a higher synthesis of the competing worldviews of our culture wars, and they aspire to evolve our shared cultural We-space by restoring the

---

*Steve McIntosh is a social entrepreneur and cofounder of the Institute for Cultural Evolution. He is the author of the 2020 book *Developmental Politics: How America Can Grow Into a Better Version of Itself,* and coauthor, with John Mackey and Carter Phipps, of the 2020 book *Conscious Leadership: Elevating Humanity Through Business.* His ear-lier works on Integral philosophy include *The Presence of the Infinite, Evolution's Purpose,* and *Integral Consciousness and the Future of Evolution.*

meaning of truth and rebuilding our capacity for real sense-making.

Some of the Intellectual Dark Web thinkers, like psychologist, YouTube personality, and author Jordan Peterson, when they are at their best, seem to take their listeners on a real-time journey of inquiry, at times reaching right beyond the horizon of their own thinking, and in doing so they often leave their audience with a thrilling sense of novelty. This quality of generative dialogue, in which we remain mindful of what wants to emerge in a conversation, is a trait we were cultivating in our intersubjective We-work as well. Yet many of the Intellectual Dark Web conversations, as thought-provoking as they are, mostly remain at the level of separate egos exploring rational thoughts with openness, humility, and a desire to build on one another's insights.

Amid the emerging Integral conversations, there is, however, another intriguing stream of thought that at least in some of its expressions strives to master the art of dialogue in a deeper way. It too originated in response to our metacrisis, and it did so as a bold attempt to design a new "Game B" vision for humanity.

In 2013, businessman and entrepreneur Jim Rutt, past chairman of the Santa Fe Institute, a science and technology think tank, gathered a group of courageous creative thinkers in Stanton, Virginia, for a series of meetings to discuss their deep concern that civilization is on a dangerous path, possibly even heading toward its own destruction. They observed how our age-old rivalrous, game-theoretic ways of cooperating, which they call "Game A," have produced structures that are now in the process of breaking down, often at an alarmingly rapid pace. Their objective was to figure out ways to create an alternative operating system for society based on antirivalrous dynamics, which they call "Game B." This new game would be more sustainable and consistent with human nature and the limits of our ecosystem. Whereas Game A is finite, Game B would have to be an infinite game, designed in such a way that all of us can continue playing it. Transitioning into this new model of cooperation would entail a lot more than simply reorganizing the deck chairs on our sinking Titanic. It would be based on nothing less than a radical whole-systems change, including new systems of government, economics, politics, education, and health care.*

In 2014, the Stanton group split into two camps: those who were convinced that real change has to start with institutional reform, versus those who believed that personal and spiritual transformation are a prerequisite for social change and thus the foundation on which a genuinely new Game B needs to be built.† Some of the essential future aspirations for humanity of the latter group sound close to my own original vision of collective evolutionary emergence and are well worth exploring further—especially the ideas expressed by inspirational thinkers like Jamie Wheal, one of the world's leading experts on peak performance and leadership; Jordan Hall, techno-wizard turned philosopher; and Daniel Schmachtenberger, social philosopher and futurist.

In just a few words, Schmachtenberger summarizes the urgency to implement a new Game B, and why it requires a psychospiritual approach: "Rivalrous dynamics multiplied by exponential tech is self-terminating. Exponential tech is inexorable. We cannot put it away. So we either figure out antirivalry or we go extinct. The human experiment comes to a completion. That's the core thing. Figuring out antirivalry is a psychospiritual process, inside of ourselves."[3]

Along with their recognition that some measure of psychospiritual development is required to move beyond rivalrous dynamics, these Game B philosophers also insist that this radical systems-change needs to be informed by the wisdom of our collective intelligence. The

---

*Among the original Game B thinkers were those who would later be associated with the Intellectual Dark Web, like the Weinstein brothers, Eric and Bret. There are connections and overlap between these two movements, as several Game B thinkers are in dialogue with several of the Intellectual Dark Web figures. In many ways, the Intellectual Dark Web can be interpreted as an emerging Game B phenomenon.

†As the group dispersed, its ideas went into what Jim Rutt calls "spore mode." The Game B idea itself, however, lived on and was developed further, independent of the formal group, by those who felt inspired by it. In December 2017, biologist Bret Weinstein reintroduced the Game B notion into the public sphere to a larger audience on *The Joe Rogan Experience,* and recently the idea has begun to take root again and is gaining traction.

multidimensional complexity of our challenging world problems, they assert, is more than a single brain can process or even grasp. "We are probably not gonna solve the complex, wicked, existential problems we face with individual horsepower, playing rivalrous games. We are probably gonna need to get together and be able to create a higher form of collective intelligence and sense-making," as Jamie Wheal remarked.[4] Whenever we collaborate and harness our collective intelligence, creative novelty is more likely to emerge. And thus now more than ever, our cooperation is more pressing than our competition.

To cultivate greater coherence between us, unleash the creative power of our collective intelligence, and increase our capacity for shared sense-making, Wheal, Schmachtenberger, and Hall suggest a practice injunction for better communication, which they call "Rule Omega."

The practice goes like this: Listen to the messages of your conversation partner(s) from a space of nonreactive openness. Even if what you hear strikes you as completely distorted or even flat-out wrong, do not close down. Remain mindful and discerning enough to hear the "signal within the noise." Every perspective contains a partial truth and is as such worth the benefit of the doubt. So stay humble and assume that it might be uttered for reasons you do not grasp. Be curious and ask more questions until you catch the signal in the noise. Then, when you respond, strengthen that signal and reduce the noise. Refine what you heard; express it back to the speaker in such a way that what you say is closer to what he or she meant to express. If you can build on what others say and allow your own thoughts to be evolved by other people's responses to you, you increase the truth level of the conversation.

Turning Rule Omega into an actual skill and achieving a level of communication in which our collective intelligence breaks through and catalyzes a deeper quality of creativity and shared sense-making requires deep transformational work in both the psychological and the spiritual dimensions.

We need to cultivate the spiritual skill to "move into that level of self that is deeper than belief systems,"[5] as Schmachtenberger instructs us, and then from there, witness our own and other people's perspectives.

On the psychological level, practicing Rule Omega takes advanced abilities of listening, discernment, and expressing our thoughts. But perhaps most importantly it calls on us to develop what Game B thinkers call "sovereignty." Cultivating this noble quality requires us to develop the capacity to stay connected to our authentic self and respond to the world without being hijacked by our ego and its reactivity—our personal traumas, defensive patterns, shadow material, or ideological certainties—and take responsibility for our own inner state. Jordan Hall defines sovereignty as "the ability to be present to the world and to respond to the world—rather than to be overwhelmed or merely reactive. Sovereignty is to be a conscious agent."[6] And so becoming a sovereign soul means learning to see the world around us with clarity, relate to it without closing down, make sense of it intelligently, and act in it wisely from our authentic center. True sovereignty is a mature achievement. It only emerges after we have gone through an unusual degree of catharsis, have gained a solid understanding of the patterns of our own psyche, and are able to sustain a more or less stable quality of presence. It is always a work in progress.

Communicating in the collaborative spirit of Rule Omega creates a container of safety, deep intimacy, and mutual trust, in which everybody can allow themselves to be vulnerable and share information truthfully. We don't need to withhold anything because we can be confident that we will not use one another's sharings in rivalrous game-theoretic ways.

And so it is fair to say that some of the Game B philosophers take the notion of co-creative dialogue farther than what most of the Intellectual Dark Web thinkers aspire to achieve. Rule Omega dialogues are, in their tenor and flavor, more oriented toward moving beyond our typical ego dynamics to achieve a deep intersubjective coherence in which our collective intelligence can flourish and generate surprising new insights. Much like our work at EnlightenNext, these dialogues aspire to create a Higher We and catalyze cultural emergence.

Yet several Game B thinkers are acutely aware that so far they haven't reached their high aspirations, and some, like Jamie Wheal, are very vocal about that:

How do we enter this postconventional communitas, coherence, whatever it would be, without the moment? . . . The peak of it wears off, reverting back to Game A power structures and game theory. Because that's what I keep seeing. I see people glimpsing it; people being lit up, recognizing it as something new, important, magical, profound, healing—fill in the blank; [people] starting to even agree to organize around it: "We are a new family." "We are a tribe." "We are the frothy edge of evolution"—and whatever it would be. And then the wheels come off Monday morning when the checks have to be stroked, or when the project plans are late.[7]

And Wheal doesn't hide his frustration about what he observes: "It's breaking my heart/freaking me out/concerning me that our efforts to create group coherence seem to be going so badly so far." Jordan Hall echoes these concerns: "Coherence as it currently is able to manifest . . . is extremely fragile and quite difficult to hold together, even in just ordinary conditions, much less in quite challenging conditions."[8]

Time and again these thinkers have noticed that the moment ego reasserts itself, rivalrous Game A dynamics once again take over, and the Higher We collapses. And so they unequivocally recognize the daunting nature of the task at hand: if collective intelligence is to be liberated among and between many more of us, and if it is to effectively contribute to the creation of a better world, we need to figure out how to break out of the centrifugal force of the ego and the games it plays. Yet in many cases they haven't come up with a compelling answer for how to move into this transegoic space with any sort of stability.

In one of his dialogues, Jamie Wheal observes that the kinds of groups that have so far actually succeeded in dropping into what he (after anthropologist Victor Turner) calls *communitas,* or "high-performing true group flow," are almost always ruthlessly meritocratic organizations, like the special operations forces of the military, sports teams, and jazz bands. These groups, he argues, are "tightly controlled, highly focused, and quite exceptional." They "massively overtrain" and new members are "brutally selected" based on their ability to contribute to the goal.[9] The end result? Small, exclusive groups of highly skilled people, able to enter into coherence beyond personal egoic concerns and uphold an unusual level of depth and intensity. Yet these types of groups, with their often top-down, overly hierarchical structures, do not match up well with our postmodern values of inclusion. But perhaps even more importantly, their small-scale elite character is antithetical to our aspirations and sense of urgency to scale up our now much-needed collective intelligence.

And thus the kinds of groups we would all want to see flourish in today's world are the more egalitarian, inclusive communities of We-space practice, where everyone has a voice, and the greatest possible diversity of collective sense-making can be given free rein to work its co-creative miracles. Yet it is exactly in settings like these that coherence is often hard to reach, and when it does arise, it all too easily breaks down. In his at times colorful language, Wheal accurately sums up the reasons for this phenomenon—reasons that to my ear seem to correspond with the by now well-established pathologies of green postmodernism:

> Any singular voice can hijack the thread. . . . Things take an awfully long time, quite often, to get to consensus. Consensus is fragile and can be firebombed by anybody playing the SJW [social justice warrior] card or any other kind of agitator, victim, drama-triangle kind of dynamics. And because we value inclusivity, we are obligated to stop the presses when anyone says, "Help, help, I'm being oppressed." Right? And so the ability to weaponize cultic sensitivity, nonviolent communication, and all those things is abundant. And when you have narcissists or sociopaths or just, you know, chatty Cathys and needy Neds infiltrate these scenes, and they often do, it never gets off the ground.[10]

And so as we transition to the more evolved values of inclusivity and wider embrace, the chances that We-spaces collapse seem to increase. And as Wheal points out, when the whole house of cards comes tumbling down, it's often not a pretty sight. Participants lose trust, and their perception of one another dramatically switches from "seeing each other's light from each other's light," to "seeing each other's shadow from each other's shadow," as he poetically recites[11]—a phenomenon reminiscent of the atmosphere during the collapse of EnlightenNext, when the bright We-field of our community literally turned into its polar opposite: a shadow-infested field of dark release.

So even as these more inclusive groups are much closer to what we actually need in these times of crisis, not many of the We-space initiatives that are currently out there can present compelling and demonstrable success in accomplishing their goals. "Most of them," Wheal underscores, "are all about just fucking talking better with each other, which I don't find super compelling. I think that's pretty weak sauce when it comes to overriding all of evolutionary biology, the prison house of language, and game theory dynamics. I don't think they are really adequate. They are aspirational."[12]

Meanwhile, our alarming predicament keeps impressing on us that now more than ever we need to learn how to master the skill of communicating with one another beyond ego and bring to life the mysterious collective intelligence that lives between and among us, but is not specific to any one of us. Skills like these are indispensable for communicating across the value spheres; they bring sanity back into our polarized public discourse and heal the unbridgeable cultural divides in our broken society. We need to create a new culture in which we can have difficult, open conversations that really make a difference, and have the power to open a portal into the next stage of our evolution. How to optimize the art of human relatedness is the all-important koan for our times.

And so, if our We-space experiments really are to live up to their promising potential, we must resolve the tenacious dilemma of how to steer between inclusivity and excellence. We want to reach for as much inclusivity as we can to still create coherence across the group. So how do we embrace both span and depth, and design vibrating, generative We-spaces that integrate the best of both worlds? This, indeed, is a Gordian knot.

Some of my colleague teachers' work is pushing the boundaries of intersubjective emergence, like Saniel Bonder's "Waking Down in Mutuality";* Terry Patten's "Integral Trans-Rhetorical Praxis";† my former students Thomas Steininger and Elizabeth Debold's "emergent dialogue" process;‡ and Patricia Albere's "Mutual Awakening Practice."§ These teachers are keenly aware that achieving a stable Higher We depends on mastering the spiritual capacity for authentic ego transcendence. Their work is distinguished from some of the other We-space initiatives out there, such as those that focus on nonviolent communication, Bohm dialogue, or some forms of circling, because it is explicitly rooted in a context of spiritual practice. All of them seem to have discovered a dimension of awakened awareness that transcends the limits of subjective interiority and emerges in relationship with other people. They are entering new territory, exploring the deepest levels of human relatedness.

When I discussed this thrilling subject with my friend, spiritual teacher Patricia Albere,** founder of the Evolutionary Collective, she spoke passionately about the promising possibilities of shared awakening, which, she asserts, reach far beyond the potential of individual awakening as espoused by the traditional enlightenment schools:

> For the whole Axial period, when Buddha came up with the Three Gems, it was a very big deal to have individual awakening, individual development, individual transformation. We spent the last three thousand years developing ourselves to attain solo enlightenment, personal salvation. But I think there's a new Axial period now in which the science of the day is that

*See www.sanielandlinda.com.
†See www.terrypatten.com, including the 2013 paper "Enacting an Integral Revolution: How Can We Have Truly Radical Conversations in a Time of Global Crisis?"
‡See www.oneworldindialogue.com as well as chapter 13 of *Cohering the Integral We Space*, edited by Olen Gunnlaugson and Michael Brabant.
§See www.evolutionarycollective.com.
**Patricia Albere is the author of two books: *Evolutionary Relationships: Unleashing the Power of Mutual Awakening* and *Mutual Awakening: Opening to a New Paradigm of Human Relatedness.*

all there is, is things relating. Relatedness is the substance of existence. And that which we will be awakening into will come from creative union. The practice of the future is no longer what it was for the last three thousand years: contemplative prayer with eyes closed, not moving, not speaking, and in absolute silence. It's no longer all about my subjective experience of awakening, end of story. If we have our eyes open and enter into deeper and deeper real connections and awaken there, we are matching something that is wanting to happen. From that deeper fabric—the place where I do love you—the love goes back and forth easily, because our personalities and our nonsense are not in the way. If we root there, we can deal with differences. . . . The potentials of the universe do not come into fruition when *individuals* reach some level of freedom. We need people together in a certain way in order for the new world to come into being. . . . The nature of the consciousness, in my experience, is that it literally empowers people uniquely and individually to do what they're here to do. So I do feel that the consciousness that is now coming in has more to do with the 7.5 or so billion of us. It has to do with finding your particular role in the whole by serving something larger together with others. And so we are here to create a matrix with other human beings—a sacred connection—that is allowing the universe to embody something new.

As her scintillating aliveness to the wonders of mutual awakening, or "shared unity," as she often calls it, was obvious, I asked her, "How do you feel about Thich Nhat Hanh's statement that the next Buddha will be the sangha?"

"I think it's true," she responded without hesitation. "And I think there's another way of seeing it, too. The kind of sangha we're working on is not a community, it's a being, a collective body. And that, I feel, is the next emergent structure. I think there will be collective beings who are truly connected and living and breathing and feeling one another and having a whole different realm of possibility in life because of their level of connection."[13]

Such a deeply felt experience of awakened relatedness opens up exhilarating new possibilities for our future, and as we experienced in our work at EnlightenNext, the luminous, ecstatic consciousness that often goes along with it is extraordinarily appealing. The potentials unleashed after a group of over thirty of my students broke through into intersubjective nonduality on July 30, 2001, felt so rich and complete that I assumed for a while that my role as guru would eventually become superfluous. The enlightened buddhamind, I felt, had now been liberated into the collectivity of the sangha. Enlightened awareness was no longer confined to the I-space, but had awakened among and between these people. But when I shared with Ken Wilber my sense that my guru role would eventually no longer be necessary and asked him what he thought about Thich Nhat Hanh's famous prediction, his response took me by surprise: "That's a green meme view! There will always be people ahead of their time, and they will be the gurus and teachers."[14]

It's clear that the Vietnamese monk's much-quoted adage points to an essential evolutionary understanding that no single individual will be the leader around whom a more integrally mature way of life unfolds; and no one person, no matter how enlightened or proficient, can be wise enough to solve the complex problems of our times. But it is also true that this statement is often co-opted by the green zeitgeist to flatten out authority, hierarchy, verticality, and deeper attainment, and as a way to downscale the function of the guru as a catalyst of such greater depth. Therefore, whenever it's being used in this way, we need to be aware that reducing the Buddha to the sangha risks invalidating the guru function, which represents the mystery of enlightened awareness itself. And so even as I consider our collective breakthrough into intersubjective nonduality to be the most significant realization of our work together, I still feel the guru has an indispensable role to play in the spiritual ecosystem. The transmitting presence of an authentic master turns the practice structure of the Triple Gem into a powerful developmental vortex of evolutionary energy, able to catalyze breakthroughs into higher states and stages. Without the guru, the transformational change the community of practitioners would be able to accomplish would be more modest. The reason is that the ceiling to which any collective is capable of rising to on its own depends on the developmental level of the majority of the individuals in the group. As Wilber writes in *The Religion of Tomorrow*:

> The psychograph of each individual in a particular group will be a determining factor in the depth or height that the group itself can achieve. . . . It is a prerequisite that individuals must be at the Integral level for "Integral We" practices to be successful, although anybody can be invited to those practices; but realize that an "Integral" depth of the "We" will not be achieved in any group where the majority of those individuals are not themselves at Integral.[15]

It is therefore essential that we associate with teachers who are aware of the stages of Growing Up and can help facilitate our growth through them.

But the most immediate effect of the guru function is still its unmatched ability to move us into higher states of waking up. States, by their very nature, are more fluid than stages. They can be peak experiences, unlike stage development, which follows a slow process in which the whole of each stage transcends and includes the whole of the previous stage. And so because states can be more readily felt, they are more easily transmitted by the guru.

And thus the principle of the guru as the vehicle of enlightened mind must not be sidelined. Since ancient times, taking refuge in the Buddha, the Dharma, and the Sangha has been considered the optimum way of disseminating enlightened awareness into the world. This is one of the many precious insights we inherited from the spiritual treasure trove of the premodern era, and it needs to be salvaged as we upgrade our practice structures to include the evolutionary gains of modernity, postmodernity, and the emerging Integral consciousness. Our sages already knew that the Buddha, the Dharma, and the Sangha represent three irreducible dimensions of the same underlying reality.

They are simply different expressions of Spirit—equally real and equally indispensable. When joined together in an Integral spiritual practice context, they intensify one another, saturating the Triple Gem with a sacred updraft of exhilarating transformational energy that awakens us to a unique spiritual depth and quickens our developmental growth.

And so the spiritual practice structure of the future cannot be a collective or a sangha only. It needs to include all three jewels of the Triple Gem. "The new Buddha," Ken Wilber elegantly summarizes, holding Thich Nhat Hanh's adage in mind, "is not going to be the Sangha, but the unification of the Buddha, Sangha, and Dharma in a single ongoing nondual Awareness and Awakening."[16]

◆ ◆ ◆

As we have established the merit of an integrated Triple Gem practice context, the time has now come to explore how this context, and our own development within it, matures as it takes the journey from its currently prevailing green postmodern forms into its Integral expressions at the teal and turquoise levels.

If we look at the developmental spectrum as a whole, what stands out right away is that its consecutive levels tend to alternate between a more communal and a more individualistic orientation—an observation that both Integral Theory and Spiral Dynamics* frequently point to. In my conversation with him, Integral philosopher Steve McIntosh summarized this intriguing phenomenon: "In the context of history, traditionalism is very communitarian. Modernity moves dialectically toward an individualistic frame. And then, postmodernism moves back—the pendulum swings in the other direction—toward an emphasis on community. And then the move toward Integral, of which you and I are part, moves back toward an individualistic level." He then elucidated how our attitude toward the Sangha aspect of the Triple Gem profoundly changes as we evolve from green to teal, and our orientation oscillates from communal to individualistic:

*Spiral Dynamics is a popular developmental model pioneered by Don Beck and Christopher Cowan, and based on the work of Clare W. Graves. It describes eight levels through which both individuals and collectives move, based on the value systems they hold.

The whole notion of community is essentially green. Green culture and green consciousness naturally translates the hunger for spiritual growth into a longing for community. Green craves community and wants to create community. But as soon as people in a green community graduate into Integral, it sort of naturally destroys the community, just like the chick hatching out of the egg destroys the egg. This is because Integralists aren't very interested in pluralistic inclusive communities. Once you become Integral, the last thing you want to do is hang out with a bunch of green, beady narcissists. You don't want any part of a green community because it's like nails on the chalkboard. Integral people want to be in a community with others who have achieved Integral consciousness. When modernism emerged, modernists were not interested in creating an inclusive community. They wanted to create an elite society, like the Royal Society of Science in England, where you were surrounded by accomplished peers who were carefully selected. It's the opposite of green, which wants to include everybody, especially those who were wounded, those who were victimized. Those are the people who green really wants to reach out to, parent, and love.

When you have Integral consciousness, you certainly want a form of communion, but you want communion only with other Integralists. Even though it might be selfish and elitist, you find your community with your Integral peers. And because so few people, at least in our lifetime, are going to be authentically Integral, it's necessarily an elite group. And most of those people naturally have a kind of allergy to green spiritual communities.[17]

Steve's point is clear enough: while green craves community, teal once again moves to a more individualistic orientation and develops an aversion for green's all-inclusive communitarianism.

The move from green to teal—the first stage of the Integral stages—is a significant developmental progression. Our inner world now opens up even further, as our worldcentric consciousness begins to widen into kosmocentric consciousness, able to embrace all of manifest reality. People at this stage become aware of the whole spectrum of development. They recognize that every single one of the previous stages has a unique and valuable role to play in the evolution of the whole. They perceive the patterns that connect in the structure of the kosmos and begin to reembrace hierarchy, at least in its healthy forms. But there is another emerging quality that defines the character of this stage. Developmental theorists such as Jane Loevinger and Suzanne Cook-Greuter have referred to it as "autonomous" or "self-actualizing," or as psychologist Abraham Maslow puts it, "self-actualization" (see figure 3.1 or plate 1). Self-actualization points to the desire to realize our deepest potentials, bring out our innate talents and creativity, and achieve the self-fulfillment that goes along with maturing into our own authentic self. In teal consciousness, this deep urge to become the most we can be is one of the primary drives in our awareness. We want to grow into the positive power of our own unique self and stand free from the personal and social conditioning that makes us inauthentic. Self-actualization is the second-highest level in Maslow's hierarchy of needs (with self-transcendence being the highest). For Maslow, self-actualization is no longer a deficiency need born out of lack, like the needs that characterize the earlier stages of his model, but a growth need that stems from the desire to follow our budding aspiration and evolve as a person. In other words, as we move into the self-actualization stage, the very nature of our motivation changes dramatically, and this alters the quality of everything we do.

This irrepressible desire for higher individuation is the drive that was awakened in my students during the later years of our work together—and that eventually led to the crash of EnlightenNext. As a teacher I hadn't fully come to terms with the positive nature of this natural and inevitable developmental shift, even though I had always spoken about it. I felt threatened in my guru role when my students began to blossom into their own uniqueness and express their aspirations to put their gifts in service of a larger goal.

In all of its promising positivity, however, the teal stage also brings along its own unique challenges. Teal's dislike of community, combined with its fierce individualism, can become an obstacle to creating Higher We coherence, and it can prevent us from appreciating the guru function and the Sangha aspect of the Triple Gem. Teal people often choose to stand alone, rooted in their own awakening sovereignty, and tend to dislodge themselves from the nurturing environment of community. But the very powerful desire to become a sovereign soul can be hijacked by the ego, unconsciously and unknowingly, especially in this climate of culturally mandated independence. This is where the guru can fulfill an important role. A real master will intuit where the student is stuck and when she may not be responding or acting from her own awakened sovereignty. The nature of ego is such that there will always be pockets of egoic resistance in ourselves that we don't want to see and tend to avoid at all cost. These are exactly the places where our self-contraction is most dense, where we are most stuck, and therefore, where our real work is located. As Carl Jung so poignantly put it, "That which we need the most will be found where we least want to look." Deep down we know that working through these knots will feel like painful surgery. And so without the relentless vertical pull of the guru's awakened mind, we would not so easily choose to face our deepest obstacles head-on. Instead, we are more likely to subtly and unconsciously—or perhaps even overtly—exempt ourselves from such a challenging ordeal. Without the transformational incentive provided by the guru function, most of us would be more inclined to avoid interventions that would really break the spell of our egoic self-contraction and change us most fundamentally. And so one of the functions of the guru is to help us distinguish clearly between our egoic separateness and our awakened sovereignty.

Real sovereignty is a rare quality that cannot be easily assumed or taken for granted. It arises only after we have gone through a soul-level struggle with life's biggest questions, have reckoned with our egoic tendencies and conditioning, and have come out on the other side truly transformed.

◄ ■ ►

As we evolve out of teal and move into turquoise, the mature Integral stage, our sensibilities oscillate back toward a more communal orientation, and our positive appreciation of the Sangha aspect of the Triple Gem reasserts itself. In turquoise, kosmocentric consciousness begins to blossom, and we experience the wholeness of existence. Whereas teal saw wholes and paradigms, turquoise brings all these wholes and paradigms together. To the turquoise eye everything connects with everything else and the universe reveals itself to be one boundless, unbroken whole consisting of holons within holons within holons (wholes that are simultaneously part of larger wholes, and so on, ad infinitum). Reality is a grand, self-perpetuating kosmic process animated by Eros, the loving intelligence that is driving the evolution of all that is toward ever-greater complexity and inclusiveness, and we are all both an inseparable part and a distinctly individual expression of this kosmic unfolding.

The fourth and the fifth tenets of Evolutionary Enlightenment as described in chapter 3 are articulations of this turquoise consciousness. The fourth tenet, the process perspective, calls on us to see ourselves from a Gods-eye view and realize that we are not separate from this vast and awe-inspiring evolutionary process. Our body-mind is the instrument through which the universe becomes more conscious of itself. The fifth tenet, kosmic conscience, calls on us to awaken to the moral obligation to dedicate our lives to serving the further evolution of the interior of the kosmos.

In turquoise, the self-actualization process that began in teal deepens and matures. Self-actualization is now no longer purely about our personal growth, nor is it for our own sake. It is for the sake of the whole. It is no longer an individual right or a private choice, but a powerful moral imperative arising from our felt sense that we are here to serve the evolution of the whole. And so we feel driven to uncover our innermost personal essence at the level of the soul—our deepest soul purpose—to bring to fruition our unique gifts and develop the skills that correspond to them, so that we actually have the means to contribute to the evolution of the kosmic process. The sense of fulfillment and empowerment that comes along with that is felt to be of secondary importance; it is merely a byproduct of having found our authentic voice in this kosmic orchestra.

The vision EnlightenNext was working to achieve—and occasionally realized—was the marriage of this communal turquoise stage of Growing Up with the state of intersubjective nonduality in the Waking Up dimension. Whenever both would cohere, it felt like we were actually opening up a new dimension of evolution, an Integral awakened field of shared consciousness beyond ego, allowing all of us to effortlessly relate and communicate with one another from the mind of enlightened awareness itself. In such moments my students would experience a profound level of "autonomy and communion," as I had at times described the goal of our teachings—an experience, I had added, that would then be lived "in a context of natural hierarchy." To this day, these principles together are the essence of what I envision a genuinely Integral sangha to be.

So what would it be like if we could live and work together based on these fundamentals? To answer this question, let's dive a bit deeper into what each of these principles means.

The simultaneous experience of autonomy and communion seems at first glance to be a paradox. We tend to assume that we need to withdraw from communion and relatedness in order to fully grow into our autonomy and bring forth our uniqueness as human beings. Or we might be prone to believe that we need to sacrifice a degree of autonomy or independence if we want to experience harmony and communion with others. But what we found at EnlightenNext was that when this field of seamless coherence would emerge among the different groups of students, they would simply notice that their sovereignty was still fully present, and some would say even heightened in that state. That which had appeared so paradoxical and contradictory from their egoic consciousness had simply become perfectly compatible in this transegoic state. When nondual suchness becomes the basis of our relatedness with one another, a field of trust, oneness, and coherence emerges, in which our uniqueness miraculously blossoms and a more mature kind of autonomy, inherent in our own higher development, is released. In this egoless We-field, our unique creative potential unselfconsciously bursts forth because we are now liberated from the egoic limitations that otherwise obstruct the free flow of creativity and higher emergence. We are most radically ourselves and at the same time ecstatically part of a larger whole. The one and the many unite, yet remain delightfully distinct. The paradox between autonomy and communion, we discovered, is resolved in the direct experience of intersubjective nonduality.

The state of autonomy and communion we experienced at EnlightenNext, especially during the later years of our work, sounds strikingly close to the qualities of sovereignty and coherence that some of the Game B thinkers aspire to achieve. Like them, we were training in how to tap into the rich potential of collective intelligence by going beyond the rivalrous dynamics of the ego and the games it plays, and enter into the seamless collective coherence of a Higher We. For years our lived experience revealed to us that when the power of deep spiritual communion combines with the force of our self-actualized autonomy, collective intelligence thrives. When everybody's unique differences and perspectives are given free rein to arise from a basis of prior unity, the mysterious ascending drive of evolutionary Eros comes alive. Then the communication between people becomes a crucible of co-creation—a space in which surprising collaborative insights emerge that far exceed what anyone could have come up with individually, and in which original solutions to old problems are found. And so the skill of "enlightened communication" or "intersubjective nonduality," as I call our Higher We practice, is what we now urgently need if we want to create the vibrant evolutionary environment necessary to appropriately address the wicked problems we face today.

But this vision of autonomy and communion only fully takes place when we enact it in a context of natural hierarchy. Natural hierarchy refers to the organizing principle of the community. It is the relational order that spontaneously emerges between individuals when the paradoxical coexistence of autonomy and communion is a living reality for the majority of the group members.

Even though hierarchy is itself a most natural phenomenon, inherent in the structure of reality, there are as yet no examples of how to fully actualize natural hierarchy in a collective of people. After the unhealthy forms of dominator hierarchy characteristic of the early stages of human development, and the ruthless decimation of anything exuding even a whiff of hierarchy by the extreme postmodernism of the green altitude, we have yet to see healthy forms of hierarchy emerge in any kind of Integral context. EnlightenNext was no exception. Despite some of our leading-edge achievements, the hierarchy in my former sangha became too rigid, and we did not fully manifest that part of our vision.

So the question of how to create a thriving evolutionary sangha with a smoothly functioning, built-in natural hierarchy is still very much up in the air. How do we establish a truly Integral context in which developmental differences between people are honored? How do we create a situation in which those with greater potential are not held back in any way? And how do we establish a natural hierarchy in which those with more limited potential are included in a way that they can blossom and don't feel demeaned, but fully respected? What would happen if spiritually awake, developmentally mature, sensitive, intelligent people came together beyond ego and the games it plays, and everyone fully appreciated the developmental distinctions between one another, in all of the different domains of human potential?

Surely the kind of communal structure that would emerge would be entirely different from any sangha we have seen so far. I envision such a community to be more like a dynamic organism in which the relationships between individuals change according to what the group is focusing on or doing together. If everybody's unique qualities and perspectives can be freely expressed and their unique skills fully enacted, while the natural authority they create is completely honored and embraced, then the spontaneous flow of roles will no longer get clogged at every turn because of egoic power dynamics and rivalrous games. The natural hierarchy—which is latently present in every collective—will then be liberated so that it can truly function as the organizing principle of the sangha. In this free enactment of developmental differences, the evolutionary impulse will begin to vibrate between everybody, and new insights, awakenings, and evolutionary breakthroughs will burst forth. The sangha as a whole will actually begin to feel like a new being brimming with creative dynamism and evolutionary directionality. An extraordinary new form of relatedness will come into being, a Higher We in which unique individuals live together based on the recognition of their nondual oneness and each other's self-actualized sovereignty.

Such an Integral sangha, where autonomy and communion, or sovereignty and coherence, coexist in a context of natural hierarchy will be the crucible of a luminous field of awakened awareness in and through which evolutionary potentials that do not yet exist will be born, and from which a brighter future will find its way into the world.

At this point, however, a truly Integral Buddha, Dharma, and Sangha that is fully rooted in mature Integral turquoise consciousness is still mostly aspirational. Turquoise may be the very edge of evolution for a small but significant few of us, but it does not yet exist in any culturally significant way. As Steve McIntosh told me in no uncertain terms:

> Turquoise can only emerge in any meaningful way if it does so in both consciousness and culture. So if this post-Integral turquoise level that goes back to communitarianism is to emerge, it must wait upon the appearance, the sort of the coming-of-age, of this previous Integral level, the individualistic teal stage of Integral. And teal hasn't reached any kind of critical mass yet. The vast majority of people who identify as Integral are essentially center-of-gravity green and don't know it.[18]

Ultimately our Integral aspirations will need to be enacted in real life, with real people. If we are serious about creating a new Integral culture that supports the healing of our broken cultural space and fosters its further evolution, we need to create transformational community structures that have a pioneering mindset—communities that focus on moving groups of people into Integral awareness. The effect such transformational communities can generate may feel like a droplet on a hot skillet to some. Others, however, would argue that it might be more influential than at first glance we might imagine.

Ken Wilber has often called attention to the intriguing hypothesis that if around 10 percent of a society's population grows into a new stage of development, a tipping point is reached, and societal change is set in motion. The ideas and values of that new stage then begin to trickle down into the entire society and become crystallized in the form of new public rules and laws.* As the pathologies of green postmodernism are now becoming more and more obvious to an increasing number of us, the tipping point into Integral consciousness may indeed be right around the corner. Around 5 percent of the population has already reached Integral consciousness, and some developmentalists estimate that this number might increase to 10 percent within a decade or two. If this is true, a promising set of Integral values would become the new social operating system, one that would bring healing, stability, sanity, genuine care, and a lot more compassion into this polarized world. And so the creation of Integral practice structures, in which a small but significant number of us devote ourselves to our own inner growth, can be truly consequential in terms of increasing the critical mass toward such a tipping point.

Some people say that engaging in intensely focused practice communities is no longer the way forward in today's world. To them it feels like a regression back to the world-denying and dualistic seclusion of monastic life in the ancient world. They conclude that since the nondual traditions have clearly taught us that there is no place where Spirit is not, practice should be enacted in the midst of normal life. This view says that life itself is our best teacher, and our relationships offer us exactly

---

*See, for example, Wilber's *Trump and a Post-Truth World: An Evolutionary Self-Correction*, p. 72. Wilber often illustrates this principle by pointing out that the French and American revolutions occurred when 10 percent of the population had reached the orange altitude, and that the postmodern revolution of the sixties burst forth as 10 percent of the population reached the green altitude. In both cases their respective values quickly began to saturate the culture at large.

the lessons we need to transform us into better persons. The world is the monastery now.

But how successful is this strategy? For most of us, a dedicated practice environment seems indispensable, especially if we care about Waking Up into the self-radiant brightness of ever-present awareness. Until we can actually see the universe through awakened eyes and perceive the all-pervasive living presence of Spirit lighting up every fiber of reality, we need practice structures in which we surround ourselves with others who put Spirit first. As Terry Patten said in our interview, "Sometimes we have to have an incubator, a safe space in which radicality, uncompromised by relativity, is given a chance to own everything. We need to be able to create an environment in which the highest awakening has its opportunity to simply make its point in a powerful way. But then we also have an obligation to create the conditions in which that radical realization can find its expression in this relative world."[19]

This sense of obligation to express awakened awareness in the real world grows as we mature through the Integral stages and become more passionate about dedicating our lives to the evolution of the whole. Especially in the turquoise altitude, which is fully Integral and includes all of life's dimensions, inner and outer, direct societal engagement will by definition be embraced. This radically Integral orientation breaks open the boundaries of our practice communities and connects them to the larger world. The skills and talents we have acquired in these enclosed training environments will then be deployed to directly serve the evolution of society and culture. This is the point where the world truly turns into the monastery, and we will move through it as fully integrated, conscious, inspired human beings, always firmly rooted in our practice.

Steve McIntosh probably says it best, as he envisions the beneficial influence of this future turquoise altitude rippling out into the broader culture:

One of the ways that we can envision an Integral, communal structure is to think about how this elite society of Integralists can mature to the point where they have communal structures that can serve lower levels—that can serve the entire spiral of development. That's something that's in the future that we haven't achieved yet. There are not enough people with authentic Integral consciousness to form a culture of any real impact in the larger world, and therefore their ability to form organizations is strongly diminished. But we can speculate that in the future, when there's enough Integral consciousness and enough Integral culture, authentic Integral organizations could start to cohere and begin to tackle the turquoise task of creating a higher level of community.

Just like scientific medicine is perhaps the greatest fruit of modernity, the greatest fruit of this Integral stage of human history will be the technology of raising consciousness. Right now, we still don't know how to do this in a methodical and reliable way. But once we get those methods down, then that will give us the power to serve the entire spiral, seeing it as one big community by gently persuading people and fostering their evolution up the stages.[20]

If we care to see this promising future vision turn into reality, what we now need most are engaged Integral practice communities where the Three Jewels of enlightenment, the Buddha, the Dharma, and the Sangha, can shine together and work their transformational miracles—spaces where inspired souls are living an integral Dharma of Waking Up, Growing Up, and Cleaning Up; where an enlightened Buddha is the source of a spiritual wisdom and transmission that awakens the generative power of enlightened awareness among the community of practitioners; and where an Integral sangha dedicated to the evolution of consciousness and culture and to the ongoing emergence of a Higher We can thrive.

All these Triple Gem Integral hives combined, each with their own unique character and project, will catalyze a collective force of Integral wisdom ready to impact the wider world. Together they will serve the evolution of our human family across the developmental spectrum, and even the whole body of life, because all of it is now at stake. The integral awareness they will disseminate will help heal the pathologies of green postmodernism and it will carefully push through the obstacles that cause the current congestion at the leading-edge of evolution. Their uplifting influence will urge us all to cross the threshold into the brave new world we would all love to live in, and would be proud to leave to our children.

This, indeed, is what we are now aspiring to help foster with our online platform, called Manifest Nirvana, a living, evolutionary, intersubjective world space, or monastery of the future, where sovereign souls, radical spirits, and integral pioneers will find their home.

May the pursuit of conscious evolution we all share be a light upon the world!

Epilogue

It's June 2021. For almost two years now I've been living in South India with my beloved wife, Alka, and my closest student, Daniela Bomatter. On a teaching trip here in 2019 all my Indian friends independently but seemingly in concert insisted that we move our base to the Motherland. "India is calling you," many of them said. It truly appeared that the universe was sending a message, so we soon responded wholeheartedly and moved halfway around the world with our black German shepherd in tow. It all happened very quickly and felt like the forces of destiny were at work, commanding us at a soul level to be obedient. Then COVID hit. Public teachings came to a screeching halt, and ever since then, like the majority of human beings on planet Earth, we have been mainly housebound. Now being an active spiritual teacher means sharing the highest (and deepest metaphysical and philosophical) truths online, in the newly ordained and at times sacred platform called Zoom. It took some getting used to, but slowly I made the mind-blowing discovery that the indefinable and uncontainable mystery that consciousness is can actually be transmitted and shared in cyberspace. As spiritual luminaries and scientists have proclaimed, consciousness is indeed nonlocal.

Every day since the crash of EnlightenNext I have been in a perpetual state of reflection and contemplation about what happened, how it all happened, and why. And after all these years (and countless hours writing this book), I truly feel that I have explored every corner of this territory passionately and rigorously, gained a lot of clarity and insight, and worked through what needed to be worked through. And yet still this inquiry rarely leaves me alone. This is what it must be like for all those who can't seem to ever completely recover from the overwhelming grief of having lost a child, a parent, a lover, or a beloved teacher.

What saves me again and again and continues to illuminate my heart and liberate my mind is the unfathomable gift of enlightened awareness that my guru miraculously bestowed on me thirty-five years ago. That meeting opened a portal to the deepest dimensions of the infinite subjective interior of the universe. That portal continues to reveal the immanence of the Absolute, of that which is timeless and eternal, in ways that are always ever new. Indeed, every day it feels like I am being born again into that sublime and sacred mystery, no matter what may appear to be happening in the increasing chaos of the relative reality of time and space.

But most important is the radical discovery of the evolutionary impulse. In the mid-1990s, my students and I dramatically awakened to its ecstatic and insatiable creativity. This is what continues to inspire me more than anything else. The larger world of East meets West postmodern spirituality is still primarily focused on realizing the Buddha's Being Enlightenment. Most liberation seekers haven't yet fully come to terms with the fact that the whole universe is moving, whether we like it or not, toward an ever newly emerging future that we have an opportunity to consciously and intentionally co-create, if we so choose. The perennial promise of a spiritual freedom comprised mainly of unimaginable peace is no longer the be-all, end-all answer.

In that evolutionary context, continuing to cultivate the seemingly infinite potential of intersubjective nonduality, or the shared higher state of enlightened awareness, is forever the main focus of my life. It really does seem that if we can truly meet one another beyond the veil of separation and duality that the individual and collective ego so powerfully generates, then at least in theory there would be no problem that we couldn't solve together. This has always been and will be the unique yet unfulfilled promise that Evolutionary Enlightenment holds.

The fulfillment of that promise is what I am calling *Manifest Nirvana*. It's when the unmanifest nirvanic heavenly realm that the ancient realizers discovered, said to be beyond this world of time and space, can be located and attained directly in the here and now, in this world, as a shared, seemingly infinite, evolutionarily charged field of awakened consciousness. What I am describing has been described as Heaven on Earth, the land of Shambhala, or, simply, Paradise.

In our most profound moments and deepest periods of intense spiritual work, my former community and I reached those extraordinary heights of both vision and ecstasy. For my current students and myself, realizing those same profound awakened states and becoming stabilized in those higher stages of consciousness, and then giving their transformative gifts to the world, continues, in a more evolved form, to be our bold aspiration.

manifest nirvana

Manifest Nirvana is a monastery of the future, an evolutionary ashram, an integral temple, a church of verticality—a sacred intersubjective space that exists both as a nondual dimension beyond the world and as a trusted spiritual home within it.

Manifest Nirvana is a place where the call to awaken to higher stages of consciousness is alive and where enlightenment or awakened awareness is real.

Manifest Nirvana is an integral hub, a meeting place, and a developmental vortex to catalyze second- and third-tier capacities in consciousness.

Visit www.manifest-nirvana.com for more information.

Acknowledgments

There are many people I would like to full-heartedly thank, because they have had a significant impact in helping me to navigate the last years, which have been the most challenging in my life:

First and foremost, my guru H. W. L. Poonja, for giving me the ultimate gift that can be given; my beloved wife and life companion, Alka Arora, for her heroic loyalty, infinite compassion, and unfailing confidence in my heart; Hans Plasqui, for being such a talented and inspired scribe, good listener, and deep and beautiful soul, without whom this book would never be what it is today; Daniela Bomatter, my closest student and best friend, who has so courageously and consistently defended the uncompromising radical truth of the teachings; Susan Olshuf, whose kindness and big heart supported me when so many others turned away; Ken Wilber, whose unwavering friendship and boundless wisdom perpetually awakens direct access to the highest perspectives and life's deepest source of meaning; Silvia Polivoy, for her soul-level encouragement and her powerful declaration that "no one should ever give up their power"; Tim Mansfield, for never forgetting the truth of what we were aspiring to accomplish and for passionately bearing witness to the glory of it all; Michael Parfitt, for appearing out of nowhere and expressing such doubtless support and inspired conviction in the future potential of Evolutionary Enlightenment; Eric Allodi and Christine Guinebretiere, for their unwavering confidence and loyalty and for organizing my return to public teaching; Vincent Drouot and Annick Macher, my longtime students, for never losing touch with the liberating light of the Triple Gem; Jack Engler, for being so deeply kind and for always only supporting the very best part of myself; Robert Masters, for helping me understand that what we do is not always synonymous with who we are, and who so directly told me to reclaim the reins of my life; and Diane Musho Hamilton Roshi, who has been a true friend and in whose wise reflection I have always been able to see more clearly.

I thank my students past and present for giving so much of their hearts and souls to bring the Dharma so powerfully alive. My gratitude also goes to all those interviewed for this book, for so generously sharing their wisdom to help contribute to the multiple perspectives I wanted this book to convey.

APPENDIX

An Open Letter to My Former Students

An open letter to all my former students upon return from my sabbatical, posted on May 12, 2015:

Dear Ones,

It has been almost two years since the structures of our shared utopian experiment collapsed so violently and so completely. It's also been almost that long since I have dropped out of sight. As most of you already know, I was asked to step down, which I reluctantly agreed to. Ever since that moment, I have wanted to find out what happened. I have understandably been desperate to find out why this has all occurred. Why did this terrible destruction have to happen?

To be honest, for a long time I have simply not been able to take in the unbearable truth that I somehow actually caused this collapse to occur. How could this be the case? I have dedicated the last twenty-eight years of my life to the spiritual upliftment of humanity, to the evolution of consciousness and culture. For so many years I thought of little else. So with all of this in place, how could I have caused this collapse to occur? As I have let this in, I have had to embrace both the truth and beauty of where we all went together and my own participation in the downfall that occurred two years ago.

During those years, just the notion of higher development, the extraordinary possibility of emergence, would make my heart beat a little faster. It really was possible, and I could always feel the immanence of the miraculous always just around the corner. Over the years I took many risks so that great leaps forward could actually happen. I also wholeheartedly encouraged others, my students, to do the same. It was all so amazing because it was so tangible. My gift was my capacity to inspire others to believe that it was possible and to be willing to take great risks so that miracles could really happen. As the years went by I gradually began to define the meaning of the spiritual life lived in earnest in our postmodern era as the willingness to be someone who would care so passionately about what appeared to be humanity's next step at the leading edge that they would be willing to make any sacrifice and take any risk so that that future could emerge here and now in the present between us, as our very own selves. And it actually happened. More than once. These perceived and intuited potentials did reveal themselves again and again, and so many of my students saw and felt the power and potential of what we had all given so much for. It was so exciting and such a grand spiritual adventure, the likes of which most people never experience or even imagine.

At the same time, as all this was happening, slowly but surely cracks appeared in the shared fabric of our new world. Some people left. This had been happening from the very beginning, when it all started back in 1986. The existential challenge of what we were trying to do together was simply enormous. In some cases the challenge was just too much, and people also suffered, at times unnecessarily.

Over the previous fifteen years I had become an evolutionary through and through. I had experienced a profound awakening to a process perspective, and to be honest I now understand that in that light I have come to see my students as means to an end—hopefully a higher end—but not as ends in themselves. I gradually lost sight of people's humanity, including my own, and only saw all of us as the living, self-aware consciousness that in an evolutionary context was going somewhere. And that was all that I believed was important or really mat-

tered. I even stated this clearly and unequivocally at times when I was teaching. As I was losing touch with my own simple humanity and everyone else's, I also was simultaneously not paying attention to the gradual growing of my spiritual ambition, of my spiritual ego. I believe that my intense longing for the evolution of consciousness in my students was real, but I have begun to see more and more clearly how over time my pride and my desire for fame and recognition slowly but surely began to blur and corrupt my vision. The worst part of it is that I was oblivious to the many different ways some of my students were being pushed too hard and at times too relentlessly to make breakthroughs, and too often breaking down as a result. It's hard even now for me to grasp how I could not see this happening right in front of my eyes. The very human, frail, fallible, and vulnerable dimensions of myself that I was denying I was simultaneously denying in those who had come to me for liberation. I was blind and ambitious and yet sincere in my spiritual aspirations as a teacher and as a thought leader. The left hand didn't know what the right hand was doing much of the time. I became more and more a living paradox.

Most often when I would teach I would experience the grace of my guru, the gift of enlightened awareness, which would engulf my being in the most glorious way. The amazing part of it all is that in the midst of the growing problems I have been describing, I was simultaneously continuing to evolve and develop as a teacher and as a thinker. I was moving and was still often creative in finding ever-new ways to express the inexpressible. And I was still curious. Even after twenty-eight years of being a guide and a guru and a public thinker, I was still reaching and stretching to understand more and more about life, reality, and the meaning and purpose of it all. It was really because of this that I wrongly felt that I was okay and in good shape and on the right track. This fact of my still evolving and developing as a teacher made it that much easier for me to avoid and deny that slowly the world that I had given so much to give rise to over so many years was beginning to crumble from the inside. My closest and most devoted senior students were beginning to see through my façade, could see that I was out of control, and see that I didn't even know it. What made *matters much worse is that I ignored the evidence; I ignored their respectful pleas for me to slow down and listen to them. For over six months during this period I literally couldn't sleep, and night after night I convinced myself that I had no idea why this was the case. My self became more and more divided. I was still an inspired teacher and speaker, but I adamantly remained steadfastly and obstinately oblivious to the growing storm I was creating.*

It was only a matter of time before the entire edifice came tumbling down, and it has taken me the better part of these last two years to begin to come to terms with all that has happened and all that I have done. I realize that much harm has occurred, and that I am to blame. I justified my at times ruthless attacks on my students' egos as being akin to the revered Tibetan master Marpa's ruthless treatment of his famous disciple, Milarepa. And at times this indeed was the case. There were times when with individuals or groups of individuals my arrow of discriminating wisdom hit the bulls- eye, and magic happened—dramatic and meaningful liberating clarity and love beyond description emerged, and new potentials and miraculous pos- sibilities that had been previously unimaginable and unseen were collectively experienced. In those historic moments it all seemed worth it. But there were and have been too many moments where I simply have been wrong. Not only did my arrow miss the target, it caused unnecessary pain and suffering to too many people. For this I am deeply and terribly sorry. Too much suffering has resulted from my at times misguided efforts to create breakthroughs. I should have known better.

Slowly, over time, I have come to see the parts of myself that were broken, that I have been in such ferocious denial of. In that denial I became at times untrustworthy. I see that now. So many of you trusted me with your souls, and I proved myself at certain pivotal moments unworthy of that trust. Again, I am sorry.

What I feel dreadful about is that the very idealism that I inspired and released in so many of you I have wounded in the worst way possible. It's dif-

ficult to bear that this is the case, but it just is. I would do literally anything to turn back the clock, but I can't.

I am committed to finding a way to honor all that was real and true that we stood for, for so many years. There is nothing else for me to do. There is nothing else I want to do.

I still believe in the fundamental principles that I taught and stood for all these years. I feel the teachings are basically sound. Like someone said to me recently, the teachings of Evolutionary Enlightenment are self-consistent. That is one of the reasons why so many of you stayed for so long. And that is why we spent so many hours learning how to look at reality through the extraordinary multidimensional lens that the teachings provide. That being said, it has also become obvious that there have been important gaps in the teachings from the very beginning. Even though I always said the teachings were a work in progress, I certainly was not aware of the obvious and important holes that I had left in them. The most obvious and the most important has been the absence of Agape, or love, as a fundamental principle that stands in contrast to and in support of the emphasis on Eros that I gave so much importance to over the last ten to fifteen years. Eros is the vertical manifestation of the Absolute principle. Agape is the horizontal manifestation the Absolute principle. To say I neglected Agape is an understatement to be sure. Eros and Agape both are essential ingredients of a truly evolutionary Dharma. They balance each other. They hold each other in a dynamic embrace of loving, creative, and Integral tension. My overemphasis on Eros with little respect for Agape created the circumstance where a collapse was inevitable. And that's why it happened so fast, and for this I am to blame.

In order to open up to the deeply painful truth of my own central role in this great calamity, I have had to open my heart in ways I have denied myself for most of my life. That's what has made it possible for me to begin to truly let in the damage I have wrought and the harm I have caused to too many of you. I only wish I had been more awake to and in touch with my own flawed humanity from the very beginning. If I had been, so much of this would have never happened.

Over these two years I have struggled to awaken to my shadow, to those unconscious forces and drives within us that will, as long as they remain hidden, continue to wreak havoc with our lives. This will remain the case even if in many other ways we are unusually conscious and aware, and as hard to believe as it may be, even if we may be lucky enough to have access to enlightened awareness. I know this is hard to fathom, but it certainly has been true in my case, and has been true in many other cases where powerfully awakened teachers have acted out in either destructive or self-destructive ways, or both. It's been a significant part of the rocky legacy of Eastern enlightenment coming to the psychologically informed West. Ironically, I spent much of my early career speaking and writing about this very issue.

I often wonder how much of the outrageous evolutionary fire could have awakened and been shared between us in the way that it was without there being some kind of fallout, some measure of pain and suffering. And if that's possible, then how much would have been acceptable, and when would it all have become too much? At this point I really don't know.

I do know that without the ultimate challenge this enormous calamity has given to me personally on a soul level, my own ego would never have backed down. It's been extremely challenging on many levels to even begin to let in what has actually happened and why it has happened. And I know there is farther to go.

I am beginning to become simply human after so many years of hiding out in transcendence. It's like coming back to Earth after almost a quarter of a century of flying above the clouds. As much as I spoke about the need to "embrace Heaven and Earth," I was obviously still rejecting so much of what it means to be a fully human being.

In so many ways I thought I was awake when I was clearly not. In my rejection of Agape, I was also rejecting the feminine principle in myself and in others and most painfully in women as a whole. I am ashamed of how badly I blamed women for their evolutionary challenges. Instead of being truly encour-

aging, after some time I let my frustration with the enormity of the task at hand get the better of me. I blamed and condemned instead of encouraged and nurtured, which was, after all, my job as a mentor. Many people accuse me of hating women. This is not and has never been true. But I was in so many ways arrogant and insensitive and even cruel in my impatience at times. Uncovering deep (and outdated) developmental structures in our psyches takes time and long-term commitment. It takes a deep vision and love of ourselves. Not blaming and condemning and ridiculing. I apologize to the women who were affected and am so very sorry for being so lacking in the real heart that was desperately needed. I failed many of you in the worst way, and for this I really have no excuse. I became a caricature of the very behavior and attitudes in men that I was so sure I had transcended. And the painful and ironic truth in all of this is that I did have a real passion and commitment for a very radical expression of women's liberation. I had seen a truly miraculous potential and possibility. But in the end I proved to have neither the patience, nor the skill, nor the deep humility and care (Agape) to create the conditions that would have made a stable breakthrough actually possible.

In the middle years of my teaching career, at times I came up with and tried many outrageous stunts in order to once again catalyze big breakthroughs. Also, to be honest, I was many times actually in a state of desperation because I cared so much and was trying to get my students to care as much as I did about what was possible, the very promise we had all given our lives for. But as well-meaning as many of these attempts were on my part, some were certainly just too much—too outrageous and simply lacking in compassion and a deep appreciation of what is actually involved in change at the deepest level. More often than not what is needed is simply more love and encouragement, not more shocks, challenges, and confrontations with one's own division. There were times, of course, when strong challenges are called for, and many former students have reminded me of the many ways in which I did help them reach breakthroughs through harsh tactics, but there is no doubt this happened too often, and more often than not it caused more harm than good. I apologize for this. I should have known better, but I was misled by the conviction that with-out such big pushes, most people would simply compromise their own inherent potential to evolve and grow in the deepest and most profound way. I was a revolutionary, and publicly declared myself as such, and that's why many of you came to me. But that can no longer be an excuse for my own insensitivity and at times ruthless attempts to force deep changes to occur. Again, I deeply apologize to any of you who suffered unnecessarily because of this. Elisabet Sahtouris's famous statement that "no evolution occurs without stress" became a justification for those times when I inappropriately pushed people too hard to let go and face themselves.

Over these two years away, I have come to appreciate with growing regret that the hierarchies that I had used as a teaching tool gradually, over time, become ossified and rigid, becoming for some not too different to being held in a straightjacket or a prison. Originally this was intended to humble my students' culturally conditioned narcissism and often exaggerated sense of self-importance. And for many years it actually did help a lot of people learn how to become humble, learn how to keep their egos in check, learn how to put Spirit first. In our time this is no small feat. But instead of helping people grow spiritually, over time the hierarchies ended up putting people in boxes, actually inhibiting the very growth they were intended to nurture. I know some of my students who made very deep commitments to our work together have suffered very much as a result and, for good reason, are angry about this. I am very sorry that this happened, and in particular, I apologize to those previously known as the resolute core students. With all of my interest in Integral philosophy, I should have known better and seen the obvious error that I was making.

Finally, what has been hardest for me has been facing and coming to terms with the fact that I have let down so deeply and betrayed my former students whom I was closest to, those former senior students who had entrusted me with their lives and souls and who gave so much to make it possible for the promise of Evolutionary Enlightenment to come alive in the world. And largely because of their commitment, it actually did. So much that is good, true, and beautiful has come into being as a result of the precious commitment of those who dared to be leaders. I know they also have made mistakes and at times caused much suffering, some of which is yet to be atoned for, but it must be said that most really did give from the deepest parts of themselves and did have the courage to care more than most. I know that when push came to shove, when I, their teacher, seemed not to have the resources to live my own teachings, it was experienced as the ultimate betrayal. I who had demanded so much was, when my turn came, seemingly unable or unwilling to do the very thing I had asked of them. I am so ashamed about this, and my public apology was really meant for them.

Almost two years after my fall from grace and the collapse of EnlightenNext, I still care as much as I ever did about most of what I taught and a lot of what I stood for. I am committed to giving the rest of my life to trying to make good on it all. What that will mean, of course, remains to be seen. Through this process of coming to terms with all that has happened, so many important questions have understandably arisen. As I make progress in my inquiry, I will be writing more about it here.

I still love you all very much and hope from the bottom of my heart that you will find it in yourselves to believe that even gurus with big egos can find the courage and humility to change. I know that in Embracing Heaven and Earth, I boldly stated that once enlightenment has occurred, an individual gets frozen in their development—that from then on their evolution actually comes to a halt forever.

I am committing the rest of my life to proving myself wrong.

With deep love,
Andrew

Notes

CHAPTER 2.
A RADICAL HEART

1. Adi Da. *The Basket of Tolerance* (Clearlake, Calif.: Dawn Horse, 1989), 252–53.

CHAPTER 3.
THE ECSTATIC URGENCY
OF EVOLUTION

1. Versions of this basic scheme can be found in several of Ken Wilber's books, including *Integral Spirituality, The Religion of Tomorrow,* and *Integral Meditation.*

2. Andrew Cohen and Ken Wilber. "God's Playing a New Game: Integral Spirituality, Evolutionary Enlightenment, and the Future of Religion." *What Is Enlightenment?* 33, June-August 2006, 72–73.

3. Ken Wilber. *Integral Spirituality: A Startling New Role for Religion in the Modern and Postmodern World* (Boston: Integral Books, 2007), 248.

CHAPTER 4.
A HIGHER WE EMERGES

1. "Essential Elements of Evolutionary Enlightenment, Do We Still Need Gurus?" Part 5 of a no longer available multimedia interview with Andrew Cohen from the early 2000s.

2. Andrew Cohen. *Evolutionary Enlightenment: A New Path to Spiritual Awakening.* (New York: SelectBooks, 2011).

CHAPTER 7.
LET MY HEART BE BROKEN

1. Andrew Cohen. *In Defense of the Guru Principle* (Moksha Press, 1999), 18–19.

2. Cohen, *In Defense of the Guru Principle,* 1.

CHAPTER 8.
AWAKENING TO THE TRUTH
OF SUFFERING

1. Sister Joan Chittister. *Radical Spirit: 12 Ways to Live a Free and Authentic Life* (New York: Convergent Books, 2017), 18.

CHAPTER 9.
THE OWL OF MINERVA FLIES
ONLY AT DUSK

1. Charles Eisenstein. "Why the Age of the Guru is Over," July 2011. www .charleseisenstein.org.

2. Doshin Roshi, Conscious 2 TV, "How I Created a Cult: The Story of Andrew Cohen and EnlightenNext." A six-part documentary series, first episode October 16, 2016. This series was edited and re-released and is no longer available in its original form.

CHAPTER 10.
DEATH OF THE MYTHIC GURU

1. Ken Wilber. *One Taste: Daily Reflections on Integral Spirituality* (Boston: Shambhala, 2000), 209–10.

2. Deepak Chopra, personal communication with Andrew Cohen, Wednesday, November 29, 2017.

3. Jeffrey Kripal. Interview with Andrew Cohen, November 20, 2018.

4. Kripal. Written answer to Andrew Cohen's interview questions, February 24, 2019.

5. Ken Wilber. Afterword to Amir Freimann's *Spiritual Transmission: Paradoxes and Dilemmas on the Spiritual Path* (Rhinebeck, N.Y.: Monkfish Book Publishing, 2018), 53.

6. Wilber, *Spiritual Transmission,* 44–50.

7. Wilber, *Integral Spirituality,* 160.

CHAPTER 11.
WHEN SHADOW MEETS THE
BODHISATTVA IMPULSE

1. Andrew Cohen. *Enlightenment Is a Secret: Teachings of Liberation* (Enlightenment Media, 1995), 7.

2. Ken Wilber. *The Eye of Spirit: An Integral Vision for a World Gone Slightly Mad* (Boston: Shambhala, 1998), 298.

3. Philip Goldberg. *The Life of Yogananda: The Story of the Yogi Who Became the First Modern Guru* (Carlsbad, Calif.: Hay House, 2018).

4. Sri Mata Amritananda Mayi Devi. *Awaken, Children!* quoted in *What Is Enlightenment?,* Spring/Summer 2000, 37.

5. Andrew Cohen. "A Declaration of Integrity," October 18, 2006. www.americanguru.net.

6. Diane Musho Hamilton Roshi. Interview with Andrew Cohen, November 30, 2018.

7. Sally Kempton. Interview with Andrew Cohen, February 19, 2019.

8. Terry Patten. Interview with Andrew Cohen, November 15, 2018.

9. Ken Wilber. Interview with Andrew Cohen, August 22, 2018.

10. Terry Patten. "Integral Evolutionary Spirituality, Spiritual Teachers, Cultism, and Critics—My Response to the Integrales Forum Position Paper," June 6, 2010. https://www.terrypatten.com/integral-evolutionary -spirituality-spiritual-teachers-cultism-and-critics-my-response-to-the -integrales-forum-position-paper/

11. Patten, "Integral Evolutionary Spirituality, Spiritual Teachers, Cultism, and Critics."

CHAPTER 12.
WHY ENLIGHTENNEXT COLLAPSED AND
THE NARRATIVE REVERSED

1. Diane Musho Hamilton Roshi. Interview with Andrew Cohen, November 30, 2018.

2. Sally Kempton. Interview with Andrew Cohen, February 19, 2019.

3. Ken Wilber. Interview with Andrew Cohen, August 22, 2018.

4. Andrew Cohen and Ken Wilber. "A Living Experiment in Conscious Evolution." *What Is Enlightenment?* 35, January–March 2007, 54.

5. Cohen and Wilber, 50.

6. Ken Wilber. Interview with Andrew Cohen, August 22, 2018.

7. Doshin Roshi. Interview with Andrew Cohen, December 7, 2018 and August 29, 2018.

8. Terry Patten. Interview with Andrew Cohen, November 15, 2018.

9. Doshin Roshi. Interview with Andrew Cohen, December 7, 2018.

10. Philip Goldberg. Interview with Andrew Cohen, October 17, 2018.

CHAPTER 13.
TRIPLE GEM INTEGRAL

1. Ken Wilber. *Trump and a Post-Truth World* (Boulder, Co.: Shambhala, 2017), 73–74.

2. Steve McIntosh. Interview with Andrew Cohen, November 30, 2018.

3. Daniel Schmachtenberger. "Humanity's Phase Shift." Rebel Wisdom, November 7, 2018. YouTube.

4. Daniel Schmachtenberger, Jamie Wheal, Jordan Hall. "Making Sense of Sensemaking." Rebel Wisdom, September 4, 2019. YouTube.

5. Daniel Schmachtenberger. "The War on Sensemaking." Rebel Wisdom, August 19, 2019. YouTube.

6. Jordan Hall. "On Sovereignty," February 19, 2018. www.medium.com.

7. Jamie Wheal, "War on Sensemaking 3, the Infinite Game." Rebel Wisdom, January 24, 2020. YouTube.

8. Hall, "On Sovereignty."

9. Wheal, "War on Sensemaking."

10. Wheal, "War on Sensemaking."

11. Wheal, "War on Sensemaking."

12. Wheal, "War on Sensemaking."

13. Patricia Albere. Interview with Andrew Cohen, August 21, 2018.

14. Andrew Cohen. *Is the Next Buddha a Sangha?* June 24, 2017. www.andrewcohen.com.

15. Ken Wilber. *The Religion of Tomorrow: A Vision for the Future of the Great Traditions* (Boulder, Co.: Shambhala, 2017), 623.

16. Wilber, 625.

17. Steve McIntosh. Interview with Andrew Cohen, November 30, 2018.

18. Steve McIntosh. Interview with Andrew Cohen, November 30, 2018.

19. Terry Patten. Interview with Andrew Cohen, November 15, 2018.

20. Steve McIntosh. Interview with Andrew Cohen, November 30, 2018.